More
Connecticut Lore

Other Schiffer Books by the Author

Connecticut Lore: Strange, Off-Kilter, & Full of Surprises. ISBN: 978-0-7643-4315-5

Other Schiffer Books on Related Subjects

Gone But Not Forgotten: New England's Ghost Towns, Cemeteries, & Memorials. Summer Paradis and Cathy McManus. ISBN: 978-0-7643-4552-4

Connecticut's Seaside Ghosts. Donald Carter. ISBN: 978-0-7643-3000-1

Connecticut Ghosts: Spirits in the State of Steady Habits. Elaine M. Kuzmeskus. ISBN: 978-0-7643-2361-4

More Lost Loot: Ghostly New England Treasure Tales. Patricia Hughes. ISBN: 978-0-7643-3627-0

Copyright © 2016 by Zachary Lamothe

Oujia is a registered trademark.

Library of Congress Control Number: 2016940187

Published by Schiffer Publishing, Ltd.
4880 Lower Valley Road
Atglen, PA 19310
Phone: (610) 593-1777; Fax: (610) 593-2002
E-mail: Info@schifferbooks.com

Type set in DIN & Rockwell

ISBN: 978-0-7643-5144-0

Printed in the United States of America

"Schiffer," "Schiffer Publishing, Ltd.," and the "pen and inkwell" are registered trademarks of Schiffer Publishing, Ltd.

For our complete selection of fine books on this and related subjects, please visit our website at www.schifferbooks.com. You may also write for a free catalog.

Schiffer Publishing's titles are available at special discounts for bulk purchases for sales promotions or premiums. Special editions, including personalized covers, corporate imprints, and excerpts, can be created in large quantities for special needs. For more information, contact the publisher.

We are always looking for people to write books on new and related subjects. If you have an idea for a book, please contact us at proposals@schifferbooks.com.

More Connecticut Lore

Guidebook to 82 Strange Locations

Zachary Lamothe

Schiffer Publishing Ltd

4880 Lower Valley Road • Atglen, PA 19310

Dedication

This one is for Danny,
the littlest reader on the block,
as well as for Jackie, Mom, and Dad.

Contents

SECTION 1:

Abandoned and Forgotten 14

SECTION 2:

Ghosts and Other-Worldly Entities................................. 34

SECTION 3:

Unusual History 78

SECTION 4:

Out-of-the-Way Locales 118

Acknowledgments

First, a tremendous thank you to my wife, Jaclyn, and Mom and Dad, Linda and Ken, for helping in every capacity of the writing process, including accompanying me to research destinations in the middle of nowhere, traveling to far-reaching book talks, and listening to me process through ideas.

A big thank you to all the librarians and independent book sellers who have hosted me for readings and/or signings over the last few years. A heartfelt thanks to Wally Lamb for his continued support and his invitation for me to be part of the national launch of his latest novel. Thank you to Colin McEnroe at WNPR for having me as a panelist in a discussion of Connecticut folklore.

I am grateful to the following individuals who helped guide specific chapters of this book. Chuck Straub for his information on Liberty Hill; Joan Hill for her materials on Wells Woods; Marian O'Keefe, town historian of Seymour; and the Derby Historical Society for the chapter on Great Hill Cemetery; Thomas Sparkman for the information (and the directions) to Taft Tunnel and the bridge remnants in Lisbon. Jon Chase, town historian of Montville, for his input on"Having a Blast" chapter; Alain Munkittrick for the Elmcrest information; Chuck Pease for his invaluable information regarding the Weltes, as well Ed Wilczek and Pam Kinder; Jim Semmelrock, Kathy Cummings, the Siderewicz family, and Candice and Matt Brown for their stories about the spirits of Norwichtown; Suzanne Uzmanski for enlightening me as to who the Jobers were;

Pat Kmiecik for information on Day Pond and the ghost of Burr Hall; Jeanne Kurasz for her input in the UFO chapter. Thanks to Tom D'Agostino for the true identity of Maud.

A special thanks to Katie Burritt for her creative input and to Laurie Knitter for her literary expertise.

Thank you to the organizers of Last Green Valley for their wonderful Walktober series. Through this I was able to set foot in Bara-Hack, Woodstock Cemetery, and inside the Ponemah Mill, where Keith Fontaine led the group on a fascinating tour through Taftville's past.

Thank you to my editor, Dinah Roseberry; without her there would be no book!

Finally, a big thank you to all of those who have supported me in my first writing endeavor, *Connecticut Lore,* and to those who have come to the author events. Many of the places you suggested have found their way to these pages.

Preface

The question I hear the most is: "What gave you the inspiration for writing this book?" Simply said, I would visit the destinations in the book if I were writing about them or not. After years of exploration, especially on the back roads of Connecticut, I felt I had gained wisdom on the topic of, as I like to call it, off-beat regional travel, and that I could then share my views with others. As a writer looking for a topic for my first book, *Connecticut Lore: Strange, Off-Kilter and Full of Surprises*, I decided to follow the tried and true mantra of "write what you know." Since I was familiar with the lore of the state as well as travel to areas that are not highly publicized, I figured I would begin there.

My desire for adventure and travel was always present in my life, even from an early age. My mother, the English teacher, brought me to the birthplace, resting place, or museum dedicated to many heroes of American literature, including Emily Dickinson, John Steinbeck, and Edgar Allan Poe. As I became older and was able to choose my own destinations, trip ideas strayed off the beaten path. As a pre-teen, one year my parents asked where I would like to vacation. Popular spots would have included Cape Cod, New York City, or a theme park like Six Flags, but I chose Pittsburgh. In taking my own trips in my twenties and thirties, instead of all-inclusive resorts in the Dominican Republic, I chose to explore abandoned train stations in Detroit, seek out the best barbecue in Kansas City, and find life-size Charlie Brown statues in Minnesota. Adventure—and the research behind it—thrilled me.

It was not simply gaining access to the Michigan Central Depot in Detroit, but it was looking at photos and researching its history and redevelopment ideas before I visited. My undergraduate degree was in American studies, where I was lucky enough to be able to dig further into my love of folklore and exploration. One project I worked on was a survey of the Norwich State Hospital and adjacent lands.

Sometimes, though, especially when trying to find ways into abandoned and forgotten places, the adventure was in simply being able to gain access! On one trip to the Norwich State Hospital, I was told we had clearance from the governor. My group had to supply identification cards as well as Social Security numbers weeks prior to our visit. We were all set to meet our group leader at the commuter lot next to the property at 9:30 at night on the first of August 2002. My first red flag should have been when, to gain entry into one building, the instructed method was for me to be hoisted in through a window. I thought this was peculiar, but trusted that it was legitimate. After exploring one side of the property, we drove to the other. From earlier visits, I had seen many of the buildings, but had not been allowed into the Awl and Salmon buildings due to the state of disrepair. This night we were promised a trip in; I was especially psyched to visit the maximum security facility. We drove up to the door, again thinking we had clearance, since this was certainly not a discreet way in. To my surprise, our entry into the maximum security building was via bolt cutter snipping the lock off the barred door. After seeing the sights of the two previously off limits buildings, hospital security finally reached us. In the end, we never had authorization from the governor, but instead had met with a random former security guard who broke us into the abandoned state institution. Typically my research does not become as hair-raising or law-breaking as this, since I always gain needed access through legal measures. The field work is part of the adventure, though. This being said, please gain proper and legal access to any site mentioned.

Another difficult part of the research process is the idea of legend versus reality. In some cases, the true account is not nearly as interesting or fun as the folktale. This has led to heated moments at various times. At an author event, I was asked by two individuals about Dudleytown. To make a long story short, both of the men had had very different experiences in the ghost town. Each argued his point and could not comprehend the other's view. Being the mediator, I had to step in and say that we all can experience different occurrences even in the same location. I have also had individuals approach me regarding a variation of a tale or the historic account of a legend that I did not list or discuss. In these cases, their version was the "correct" account. The tale of Jemima Wilkinson, which is included in this collection, illustrates the idea that legends and folktales are certainly not always historically accurate. On a stop on my book tour for my first book, a few residents of the town of Ledyard mentioned her to me and wondered if I would include her story in the new book. Variations of Wilkinson's story exist, some placing her

in Ledyard; others never mention that she even spent significant time in the state. The most startling discovery was that the town did not even exist when Wilkinson was said to have been a resident there. No matter the truth, she has been ingrained in the essence of the town. When her name was mentioned at the library reading, many in the audience nodded in recognition.

Unfortunately for my wife, the final aspect of researching this collection has come at a price in my personal life. Take the fact, for example, that we spent a weekend in the Litchfield Hills following our wedding day. We had a simply wonderful time with great restaurants and perfect weather, staying at the incredible Hidden Valley Bed and Breakfast in Washington. Between sips of wine, apple picking, and taking in spectacular views, we attempted to explore Dudleytown, visited the shrine at the Lourdes of Litchfield, and searched for the Wildman of Winsted. Not your typical honeymoon trip. Heeding my own advice, the focus of my research trips tends to be the places in the "While You're There" sections with stop-offs at the unusual spots along the way. Luckily for me, my wife is more than a good sport and actually enjoys finding out-of-the-way locales herself!

Enjoy Volume Two!

How to Use This Book
Check the Visitor Information section on page 171 for specific visitor information on the places I visited.

Section 1:
Abandoned
and Forgotten

Having a Blast on the Trail of Connecticut's Industrial Heritage

North Canaan, Salisbury, Kent, East Granby, etc.

For all of you *Connecticut Lore* connoisseurs you may recall that Mine Hill in Roxbury was highlighted in the first collection of off-beat travel destinations. Mine Hill, accentuated by the large blast furnace rising through the leafy landscape, is just one brick in the mighty furnace that is Connecticut's industrial heritage.

Beckley Furnace Industrial Historic Site

Beckley Furnace standing proudly as a testament to the region's industrial past.

Although certain aspects of this chapter (New-Gate Prison and Copper Mine, Connecticut Antique Machinery Associ-

ation, and the Eric Sloane Museum) were already on my list of must-sees for this volume, the impetus for the chapter occurred by accident. On what has become an annual trip to the northwestern part of the state in autumn, I was driving on Route 44, and a sign read something to the effect of "Beckley Furnace Industrial Historic Site" and then pointed down the aptly named "Furnace Road" in the East Canaan section of North Canaan. (This road also led to the Land of Nod Winery that I was interested in visiting, but was unfortunately closed since it was early in the morning). One of the best aspects of road-tripping is the discovery of new and unexpected places. Although my for-pleasure western Connecticut jaunt was mostly just that, I managed to throw some research into the mix (and truthfully my research destinations do bring me pleasure), but the Beckley Iron Furnace was not on my itinerary for either reason.

Understandably, the focal point of the park is the immense stack of the iron furnace, although the picturesque Blackberry River rushing by came a close second. My wife and I were the only visitors to the furnace that crisp October morning, so we were able to explore it up close, covering a full 360-degree area around the structure. The waterfall on the grounds greeted us with a pretty sight. As an avid consumer of knowledge, I appreciate good signage. Generally speaking, the northwestern Connecticut region provides appropriate signage. This was no exception at Beckley Furnace. Not only did the signs give a history of the location, but they described in detail, thankfully in layman's terms, the process of using the blast furnace and creating pig iron. A sign also brought us to our next destination on Lower Road (the road that the furnace is on), which was the Canaan Furnace #3. Personally, I had no idea that Connecticut was the predecessor to Pittsburgh as the iron capital of America.

Today's Iron Furnace Number 3 is denoted by a sign near a bridge over the Blackberry River. The sign that calls #3 the "Furnace in the Fields" mentions that it is in a nearby field, but I was not able to see it. On a relatively small section of the river were three working furnaces (and a fourth that was never fully realized). The first was Forbes Company Iron Furnace, the second Beckley, and third, well the creatively named Number 3. Number 3 was the most modern of the East Canaan furnaces, which was fired up for the first time in 1873, whereas the Forbes furnace ceased production in 1885. All of them made iron that was used in the westward expansion of the United States for railroad and farming equipment. The materials used in the furnaces were derived from local sources as the charcoal was created in regional forests, the limestone was quarried close by, and the iron ore was mined in nearby Salisbury. Number 3 was the last furnace in the area to be lit as it stopped operating in 1923. Beckley's tenure lasted from 1847 to 1919 and, just like Number 3, was one of the final furnaces in the region to stop operating. Beckley's iron was often used for wheels of train cars since it was known to be extremely durable.

The focal point of today's visit to Beckley was the chimney, now standing solitary but around which many buildings had stood. The casting shed was directly in front of the chimney and was a brick building topped by a curved, metal roof. Also on the property was a bridge that crossed the road and went to the furnace. The bridge was used to take the materials needed from the storage area on top of the hill and dump them into the top of the furnace stack. Furnaces were often positioned on hillsides so that the top of the stack could be accessible. The furnace is the large stone tower and has a central chimney. It is separated into three sections: the upper or the stack, the middle or the bosh, and the bottom or the crucible.

Charcoal that was produced, as previously stated, in nearby forests was used as fuel. When the charcoal reached the necessary temperature, the iron ore and the limestone were added into the top of the stack. A water turbine caused air to flow directly into the furnace, which was used as a catalyst for the combustion of the charcoal. Air, preheated by an oven, caused the furnace to run more effectively. Excess gas was then turned into fuel that was an early take on recycling. The 800-degree hot air was blasted through tubes called tuyeres (Beckley eventually had five of them). The carbon dioxide in the fire caused the transformation of iron ore into iron. The molten iron then collected into the crucible. Once the crucible was full, it would be tapped so that the liquid could be collected and solidify in sand molds. The casting arch was where the molten iron poured into the sand molds, which resembled piglets nursing a mother pig, hence the term pig iron, also called ingots. This all happened in the casting shed in front of the furnace. Today, the foundation of the casting shed can still be seen near the front of the furnace stack. Slag, a waste product created by this process that is made from silicon and resembles glass, is collected on the top of the poured iron. Some slag was used in the creation of slag-based concrete as well as in the manufacture of some buildings and roads. The excess slag was taken across the river and dumped into what is known as a slag heap. Beckley's slag heap once covered 900,000 cubic yards! Today's forest has regrown itself around the former slag heap. The liquid iron was removed in what was called the furnace hearth. Beckley was owned by a powerhouse company of the day, the Barnum Richardson Company.

Although they may sound cute, salamanders (no, not the amphibian) could be a real problem with the blast furnace. These could be caused by a failure within the furnace or could happen when the furnace was shut down for a period due to maintenance. These salamanders were a congealed, hardened slab of iron that could clog a tuyere. Thirteen of these salamanders had been located at Beckley and one can even be seen on the grounds today. Another animal-related term happens when molten iron becomes wedged in the stack; this is called a furnace bear. Men would attempt to pry the bear out of the stack, but this was a trying and arduous process. When the molten iron hardened, this could be so detrimental that it shut down the furnace until it was removed. Supposedly, the bear resembled an actual bear climbing a tree and the salamander resembled an actual salamander.

Samuel Forbes led the iron industry in northwestern Connecticut. In 1759, Samuel and his brother, Elisha, built a forge that manufactured anchors. The iron from the northwest hills was known for its durability. Three years later, Samuel and others, including Ethan Allen (yes, that Ethan Allen), built the first blast furnace in the area in nearby Lakeville where cannons used in the Revolution were made. Forbes held the title of Iron Master creating the much needed cannon (hence the name of a nearby inn, the Inn at Iron Masters). A great supply of ore was found at what would eventually be known as Salisbury's "Ore Hill." Ethan Allen sold his share of the furnace to the Caldwell Brothers in 1765.

This is where the story veers a bit, but has the same ending with a naked Allen, intoxicated, beating George Caldwell. One variation tells of Allen and Caldwell in disagreement about the sale, which led to Allen stripping naked and giving Caldwell an old-fashioned whooping. The other variation tells of Allen and Caldwell imbibing one too many drinks after celebrating the sale of the furnace, which somehow led to a naked Allen beating the stuffing out of Caldwell. Later in the 1780s, Forbes made a slitting mill that manufactured iron knives, nails, and rods,

which helped America's war effort not only in the war for independence, but also the War of 1812. Also on the Blackberry River were a saw mill, a grist mill, and a cider mill. By the time Beckley furnace opened in 1847, iron production had been flourishing in the area for over 100 years. That year saw the northwest region equipped with fifteen furnaces with more added as the years rolled on. In 1946, the state's Department of Environmental Protection took control of the site. The group "Friends of Beckley Furnace" started in 1996 and has put great effort in recognizing and highlighting its importance in the region and the nation's history. Beckley was refurbished in the late 1990s when the lower part of the furnace as well as the casting arch were reconstructed.

Although Beckley, in the East Canaan section of North Canaan, was a major player in the scene of early Connecticut industry, the Salisbury/Lakeville region, just a quick trip up the road today, could be argued as even more important. Limonite was roughly considered the most desired of the ore found in the state. In 1734, it was discovered in Salisbury with an underground removal of the substance. Most ore was mined from open pits. The Lakeville section of Salisbury was actually nicknamed Furnace Village due to the first blast furnace started at that location in 1762. The extremely sturdy iron from Salisbury was used for iron products, including anchors, chains, and railroad car wheels. Initially, oxen-pulled carts were used to haul product at Salisbury, but eventually they were replaced by mine carts. Salisbury was such a key area for iron production that when faced with World War II, the United States government actually looked into the feasibility of reopening these sites. These areas are not alone though; many other villages and towns also had sites on the state's industrial heritage trail.

In Sharon, a mine produced fifty tons of iron ore that were utilized in furnaces in both Cornwall Bridge and West Cornwall. Magnetite was mined at Tuttle Mine, which is west of Winsted as well as in Norfolk and New Preston. In beach landscapes this chemical compound presents itself as a thin, grainy, black sand that can be found on the seashore from Rhode Island to the landscape around New Haven and also at Selden Neck, an island in the middle of the Connecticut River, which technically belongs to the town of Lyme and today is a state park that can only be reached via watercraft. Forges could also be found in other areas of the state, not only in the northwest corner but in such towns as Killingworth in central Connecticut and Voluntown toward the east. Other blast furnaces were at Bull's Bridge (Kent), Lime Rock (Salisbury), Huntsville (Canaan), Chapinsville (Salisbury), Mt. Riga (Salisbury), New Preston, and South Canaan. Mt. Riga's blast furnace was built in 1810, and its iron was used in the USS *Constitution* or *Old Ironsides*. Other sites, like Macedonia (Kent) and Joyceville (Salisbury), made iron for the Civil War. Forty-three furnaces were in the Salisbury Iron Region, including twelve furnaces and numerous mines owned by the prestigious Barnum and Richardson Company. Salisbury was the center of iron making in the country. Iron was nicknamed "the metal of heaven."

Lime Rock, today known for its famed Lime Rock Racetrack (also featured in *Connecticut Lore* Volume One), was an important iron district. The iron mined here was used in the Greek struggle for independence against the Turks. All traces of an active iron industry had disappeared by the late 1920s, and the area was developed as an art colony.

Siderite, which is another kind of iron ore, was mined at Long Hill Mine in Trumbull; today the Old Mine Park denotes its location. This iron material could also be found in Bristol, at Ore Hill in Salisbury, and at Mine Hill in Roxbury, which was the largest outcropping of this ore in the country! Bog ore, which was extracted from a body of water, hence the name, could also be found throughout the state. It was found in North Haven close to Governor John Winthrop Jr.'s fourth blast furnace (and the first in Connecticut) near the present-day East Haven/North Branford. The Phelps Blast Furnace in Stafford Hollow (also known as Furnace Hollow, located in Stafford) was known for its manufacture of cannons and cannonballs, kettles, and pots, all used by the Continental Army. Also part of Stafford, in Hydeville, the Lafayette Furnace's iron was used in stove manufacturing. Bog iron was also mined in Hebron.

In 1639, the state saw the first sandstone quarry open in Hartford. Millstone Point in Waterford (the current location of the nuclear power plant) was home to a granite quarry. Barite was mined in Cheshire. Other minerals, such as bismuth, tungsten, cobalt, and nickel were mined in state. Connecticut was nicknamed the "arsenal of the American Revolution."

As previously mentioned, North America's first iron maker, future governor of Connecticut John Winthrop Jr., introduced the world of mining and iron manufacture to Connecticut. His first endeavor was in Braintree, Massachusetts (now an area that is part of Quincy); he later started the famed Saugus Iron Works in Massachusetts. By 1651, Governor Winthrop moved to Connecticut and built the state's initial iron furnace on the banks of Lake Saltonstall in today's East Haven/North Branford area that stayed in operation until 1680. In the same decade, Winthrop tried his hand at creating an iron furnace in New London (in the present day, the Uncasville section of Montville) along what was once called the Saw Mill Brook but is currently known as Oxoboxo Brook. This furnace utilized bog iron from nearby wetlands. Jon Chase, Montville town historian, mentioned that even today residents who live near the former mine site complain of iron content in their wells, making them utilize city water instead. Eventually, the iron industry left the Connecticut, Massachusetts, and New York region as the mines went dry and moved on to larger industrial cities, like Pittsburgh and Birmingham, Alabama.

Kent Iron Furnace

If you enjoyed visiting the state's iron heritage at Beckley Furnace, make sure to also stop at the Kent Iron Furnace. Located on the grounds of Eric Sloane's Sloane-Stanley Museum, this intriguing piece of Americana would be a must-see even without the adjacent iron furnace. Eric Sloane was an author and illustrator of over thirty books. Known for his titles, such as *The Diary of an Early American Boy: Noah Blake 1805, An Age of Barns,* and *The Cracker Barrel,* many of his works feature colonial New England life, with a great fondness for the rural American experience. Not only an accomplished writer but a skillful painter with a focus on landscapes, Sloane was noted for painting from memory. The museum is located on 31 Kent-Cornwall Road (Route 7) and holds a myriad of interesting objects. From the south, the museum is on the left side of the road.

Sloane-Stanley Museum and Connecticut Antique Machinery Association

Cross the railroad tracks and be greeted by the Connecticut Antique Machinery Association's Argent Company Locomotive #4 sitting on the tracks. The "Stanley" in the museum's name refers to the Stanley Tool Company of New Britain, whose CEO in 1969 presented Sloane with the idea of building a museum to house his collection of Americana, including paintings, tools, and other artifacts. Sloane was an avid collector of handmade colonial era tools and objects, which he displayed as works of art. His collection, numbering in the thousands, showcases handmade tools, such as shovels, yokes, baskets,

scythes, rakes, axes, and hammers housed in a barn-like building.

On the property is a re-creation of Noah Blake's log cabin from his book *Diary of an Early American Boy.* His studio is re-created inside the museum as well. Sloane was aware of his surroundings and the visitor is encouraged to do the same, to take appreciation in everyday objects, the simple life, natural beauty and environs. Sloane studied meteorology at MIT, and his understanding of weather patterns can be seen in his depictions of cloudscapes, which are truly breathtaking. Also on the grounds is the Kent Iron Furnace, which preserves another outpost of the state's iron industry. The museum was able to be built on the property near the town dump if it led to historic preservation. When the furnace was spotted, the builders saw this as the opportunity they needed. Thankfully the furnace was nearby, so the museum could be built and the furnace could be guaranteed safekeeping. The furnace produced iron from 1825 to 1892 and is roughly thirty feet tall. Like Beckley, only the furnace itself remains from the once active Kent Iron Works. Look closely and see if you can spot the salamander and the remnants of the water wheel and dam!

Next to the Sloane-Stanley Museum is the Connecticut Antique Machinery Association, which displays many artifacts of the state's industrial heritage, including gas engines, a blacksmith shop, antique farm tractors, steam rollers, and locomotives. On site is the Connecticut Museum of Mining and Mineral Science that includes a blasting exhibit, a display of fluorescent minerals and a miniature version of Mine Hill in Roxbury. Also on the property is the Cream Hill Agricultural School, which since 1994 has been situated here. Originally in Cornwall, it was disassembled and put back together in Kent. It was one of the first schools dedicated to agricultural science in the nation. Take a ride on the three foot narrow gauge railway pulled by the Hawaii Railway Company #5, 1925 Baldwin stream locomotive, which was used in the sugarcane fields of the Pineapple State.

Copper, Coin, and Prison

Simsbury, in 1728, was the site of the first steel mill in America, run by Samuel Higley. Steel is made from iron. Dr. Samuel Higley also had a copper mine in the Turkey Hill section of Simsbury, which comprised two shafts and shipped tons of copper to England. Dr. Higley is most notorious for minting his own copper coins, although this was not officially allowed by the English monarchy. Higley enjoyed a strong ale that typically cost three pence at a nearby tavern. Being the procurer of a copper industry, Higley cast his own three-pence piece, inscribed on the coin with "value of 3 pence," so he could trade in these coins for a tasty libation. Eventually, the coins' inscription changed to say "value as you please." Also pressed into the coins were "I Am Good Copper." The coins were roughly the size of today's half dollar, were made of pure copper, and can be seen today at places like the Simsbury Historical Society, the Connecticut State Library, and the Connecticut Historical Society. The images embedded into the coins included a buck with a full set of antlers, a broad ax, and a sledge hammer. Sadly, Higley died en route to England in 1737 transporting his copper to sell. A stamped coin with the year "1739" has been found bringing to light the idea that his brother, John, could have taken up the family tradition after Samuel's demise.

The most infamous copper mine in the state was also in Simsbury, whose original moniker was Massaco, a section that would become Granby and is now present-day East Granby. This is the Old New-Gate Prison and Copper Mine. Copper fever struck in 1705 when the area took on a greenish hue in this section of Simsbury. Two years later, a mine was created at this location, present-day Newgate Road in East Granby. After iron, copper was historically Connecticut's most precious metal. This copper mine never came to fruition as hoped and was shut down in 1745. It opened in 1773 as a prison and, during the Revolutionary War years, between 1776 and 1782, the site was used as a prison for British prisoners of war and colonist soldiers loyal to the Crown. The year 1790 marked the start of its thirty-seven-year run as a state prison. Not exactly well thought out, a job deemed for the prisoners was to mine for the copper. Unfortunately, those same mining tools led to many escapes or jailbreak attempts. The reputation grew as three riots broke out here. The first melee, which occurred in 1806, involved thirty men and began in the blacksmith and nail shop. One of the jobs for the prisoners was the manufacture of nails. In 1823, a larger riot happened involving 100 prisoners, ending with guards shooting two of the prisoners involved in the insurrection. The underground mines were the location of prison cells. Incredibly enough, the winding mines were turned into the prison; these mine cells were nicknamed "hell." The prison itself was named after the infamous Newgate Prison in London. John Hinson was the first prisoner held here in 1773 and escaped a year later. Many of the above ground buildings, built during its time as a state prison, are today in ruins. For individuals only in for a short sentence, the prison used treadmills that the prisoners would walk on for ten-minute intervals that would then provide energy to run machines or grind corn. Eventually, its use was discontinued with the advent of the new "modern" state prison in Wethersfield. In 1830, the mines were bought by the Phoenix Mining Company, but its mining endeavor did not pan out. The Connecticut Copper Company tried again in 1855, but only lasted two years. The former prison and copper mine became a tourist attraction as early as the nineteenth century.

A few years ago, the site was "closed for renovation" and unfortunately at the time of writing, there is no timetable for a return. I was able to drive by the site, but not go in, which is too bad because just like the Victorian tourists, whose good time included exploring the mines and prison cells capped off with a night of dancing at a nearby tavern, I too would have liked to rummage my way through the abandoned mine and prison.

Of course, with its notorious history, the place is said to be haunted. Any place that has seen anguish and insurrection tends to bring with it haunted tales. Couple that with a legacy of brutality, which some report occurred behind the walls of New-Gate, and ghost stories abound. Presences and unnaturally cold spots have been witnessed and felt.

Close to the prison/copper mine and located on the Metacomet Trail is the aptly named Copper Mountain (more commonly referred to as Peak Mountain). A hike up Copper Mountain affords the visitor fabulous views of the Hueblein Tower (also highlighted in *Connecticut Lore* Volume 1), Bradley International Airport, and the Southwick Jog, which is the small rectangular parcel of land owned by Massachusetts that juts into Connecticut, creating the dip in the would-be straight border between the two states.

The Cheshire Copper Mine, the Golden Parlour Mine in Wallingford, the Tallman Mine in Cheshire, the Stevenson Mine in Oxford, and Wylly's Copper Mine in the Manchester region were some of the state's other copper mines.

Make sure to visit this region's stops on the industrial trail; take it from me, it's a blast! *Ore*, if you need to iron out the details of your trip, please visit their websites for more information.

While You're There!

Well, since this chapter name checks almost every area of the state, picking just one entry for this section is hard. One of my favorite stop-offs when I am in the region is the House of Books in Kent. Located in picture-postcard-perfect and quintessentially New England downtown Kent and close to attractions like the Sloane-Stanley Museum and the Connecticut Antique Machinery Association, this local bookstore is the perfect place to browse for a new title to purchase. It has a superb section devoted to local interest and outdoors books. Look for their frequent in-store author book signings.

Hop on Down to Hop River

Coventry and Columbia

The Hop River today is a mecca for outdoor enthusiasts paddling on the river and cycling on the Hop River State Park Trail along the route of the former railroad that passed through this section of Tolland County. Once upon a time, this pristine body of water supplied the energy for a whole region. The name of the river, which looks like "hop" but is actually pronounced "hope" (sorry you beer drinkers), meanders its way fifteen miles through the villages of Tolland, Vernon, Bolton, Andover, Coventry, and Columbia, and finally terminates at its confluence with the Willimantic River. The river creates the border between Coventry and Columbia and is the location of the once-thriving Hop River Village. Along the river in the 1700s were mills powered by water,

The Hop River winds its way through the Connecticut landscape.

providing grist, cider, and sorghum to traders in the village, such as blacksmiths, basket makers, and tanners. As the years traveled onward, Eastern European and Irish immigrants flocked this way working nearby at the Hop River Warp Company textile mill. The warp was used for weaving. As you paddle down the tranquil river or pedal power your way down the path, think of the industry that once dotted the landscape. Also traversing the area is the Air Line Trail, which provides a rec path that covers much of this part of the state. The hope (or should I say "hop"?) is that this trail will connect to the nearby Charter Oak Greenway on one end and the Airline Trail on the other. Today, the name "Hop River" is also synonymous with a yearly chamber music concert at Andover's First Congregational Church.

Hop River Village

Researching the precise location of Hop River Village was not an easy task, since its location is not found on any modern maps. Through some investigation (thanks to my wife), my journey began on the aptly named Hop River Road that travels from Columbia to Coventry. Taking Hop River Road from Route 6, I first passed a handful of what looked like factory rowhouse homes and then parked at the lot just over the Hop River on the left. This lot is used as an access point for the rail trail. I took the trail from the lot, which is on the right (Coventry) side of the river. In exploring the area, I did not find many direct remnants of the village. Down the path, the most striking pieces of a bygone era were the electricity poles up alongside the former railroad bed. The trail crisscrosses the river through bridges like the one a short way down the path. On the river side of the path, the land slopes steeply down toward the water, and on the opposite side, it rises steeply up on the wooded side.

Center for Manufacturing

The wilderness overtakes a pole alongside the Airline Trail.

Heading back towards Hop River Road, at the bridge is a small waterfall and a wall on the Columbia side of the river. I could also see a former bridge, overgrown with ivy flanking the waterfall. At the base of the waterfall, a side run-off of water can be seen that could have been used as a sluiceway. I found no foundations or any other direct evidence of the once-present village at Hop River, although across from the dam nestled in the woods are foundations. The Dodd Center at UCONN has photos of the dam. Most of the village's houses are gone. It is truly amazing what is lost in the woods!

Columbia also had another center of manufacture closer to the confluence of the Hop and Willimantic Rivers, close to the present roads of Johnson and Cards Mill. I parked the car near a bridge that was erected in 2002. On closer inspection, I saw that an old bridge was present. Driving around the area, I took nearby Cook Hill Road by Scovill Cemetery, which dates from 1733.

William Beaumont House

On my drive through Columbia, a motorist inquired if I was lost (since the area probably does not get many tourists). After I told of my intention, he informed me about the William Beaumont House, just up the road in Lebanon. I followed him to the spot. Beaumont was a surgeon in the Civil War and wrote books that are still used today on gastrointestinal maladies. The land where his home was located is now "Beaumont Park" and consists of the home's foundation and two primitively made stone benches. The house was moved behind the Trumbull Law Office on the Lebanon town green and, at the time of my visit, was being moved across the green. I felt very fortunate to have the passerby show me another piece of history that I was unfamiliar with.

These areas of Connecticut do not have as much tangible evidence of the past as other historical parcels of the state, but still have a story to tell.

The Park River

Hartford

Once upon a time, not even that long ago, bodies of water were not the focal point for recreation and beauty in urban environments as they are today. The Charles River in Boston even earned a popular song based on its reputation, The Standells' "Dirty Water." Cleveland's Cuyahoga River was so polluted that it actually caught fire. Cities like Providence, whose downtown proudly revolves around its rivers today, had to literally uncover the waterways they once buried. For the twenty-first century visitor to Providence, it is hard to imagine the downtown without its lifeblood, the rivers that flow through it.

Although Hartford is associated with the mighty Connecticut River, its Park

River once ran directly through the center of town. Where other municipalities found ways to beautify and rectify the pollution problem of their precious rivers, Hartford covered theirs up. Not completely, however. The North Branch of the Park River meanders its way through the center of the campus of the University of Hartford flowing south towards the city's UCONN branch, going underground just north of the Mark Twain House, which was actually built on the banks of the river. The southern branch surfaces near Pope Park with its headwaters forming the branch in the Elmwood section of West Hartford. Other than a small, revealed bend of the river in Frog Hollow, the Park stays submerged through its journey downtown, eventually emptying via a small tunnel into the Connecticut close to the Connecticut Convention Center.

The idea of Hartford disassociating itself from what could have provided an oasis in the midst of an urban area seems to fit Hartford's present tired and run-down ambiance, despite the recent semi-yuppification of downtown. The capping of the river was done as a preventative measure for both sanitary and environmental reasons. Heck, historically the nickname of the waterway is the "Hog River," a name given not only for the nearby pigs whose defecations were dumped directly into it, but the overall state of its water quality, as it also became a refuse deposit for the mills and factories dotting the riverside depositing God knows what into the water source. These mills earned the river the early nickname "Mill River" (it had also been called "Little River" as well).

Another major reason for the coverup of the river was the potential danger of flooding and the havoc that would be wreaked onto Hartford's streets. Floods in 1936 and 1938 caused figurative antennas of politicians to go up, leading to the eventual coverup. In addition, flooding of the Connecticut caused backup into the park, whose downtown location could submerge prime Hartford neighborhoods. The project, performed by Army Corps of Engineers, started in the 1940s and lasted for decades. Picturesque landmarks, such as Bushnell Park and the Soldiers and Sailors Monument, were once accentuated by the river. Old postcards can be seen depicting these Hartford stalwarts accompanied by the park. The Bushnell waterway was rerouted into a tunnel.

Today's Park River can be explored given its perfect amount of water. Urban adventure kayakers can brave the park by launching in Pope Park or another surface spot. John Kulick of Huck Finn Adventures used to lead paddlers underneath the city, but, at the time of this writing, no longer does. He does offer a variety of paddling trips on the Farmington River, though. The "Goldilocks" water depth has to be when level is not too high, but not too low. As of yet, I have not paddled my way under the depths of the city, but those who *have* gone report it as not a trip for the faint of heart, as the tunnels emanate a stench in places, the water is still worthy of its "hog" nickname, and the walls are adorned with various graffiti designs, while the river itself is littered with all types of garbage, including a nearly submerged car! The underground passage does provide the perfect echo chamber. A kayak ride on the underground Park is reminiscent of a Walt Disney World ride, somewhat like "Maelstrom" at Epcot or "Pirates of the Caribbean" at the Magic Kingdom, only any large rats seen are certainly not animatronic. If you are interested in taking this trip, research best water levels ahead of time, plan the route, and travel with a number of fellow paddlers. The next time you are visiting the Bushnell Park Carousel, stop to think about what is going on close by underneath your feet. Most visitors and residents alike are not even aware that a river once ran through the downtown.

While You're There!

Back on the street level, one of Hartford's architectural gems is the Richardsonian-Romanesque-styled Union Station. Today an outpost for its Amtrak line, its design is noted for its façade of brownstone with rounded windows, sloped roof, and high ceilings.

Ponemah Mills

Taftville (Norwich)

Of all of the mills that dot the eastern Connecticut waterways, Ponemah Mill is the most impressive; it is the Big Kahuna, El Gigante. Ponemah, which means "our future hope," is named for a line in Henry Wadsworth Longfellow's "Song of Hiawatha." Built in the French Second Empire style with Italianate detailing, the mill has been unexpectedly compared to chateaux in the Loire Valley of France. Driving south on Route 97 from Occum, after a bend in the road, Ponemah Mill rises seemingly out of nowhere. The complex is massive: four main mill buildings, with two that can be easily seen from the road. The first, erected in 1871, is a looming five-story brick structure highlighted by two magnificent towers. The second, still an impressive facility, albeit not as tall but also punctuated by towers, stands only two stories and was finished thirteen years later in 1884. Ponemah was said to be the largest cotton factory in the world at one time. Other sources call it the largest building producing a single textile product in the country. Whatever the reality, it is nevertheless a hulking series of textile manufacturing structures.

The village of Taftville, named for the mill owners, sprang up around the mill complex. Its bell dictated the ebb and flow of its residents. After the initial wave of Irish immigrants, Taftville became a haven for French Canadian immigrants arriving directly from Quebec. Taftville, which prior to modern transportation was isolated from the rest of Norwich, became a microcosm of French Canada. Families shared tenements, 206 of them in all, with members working long hours at the mill. Although seemingly cramped by today's standards, this was in actuality a better life than the one left behind in the Great White North. The village included a corner store, a Catholic church whose mass was spoken in French, and a school. At its peak, Ponemah employed around 600 workers and had its own train tracks from which product was imported and exported.

Ponemah locomotive 1306 is owned and displayed at the Connecticut Trolley Museum in East Windsor. While the factory was being built, bricks were hauled from Dayville via the railway. The complex was originally powered by waterwheel and eventually switched over to electricity via the hydropower dam on site. The dam is 418 feet long and 24 feet tall. The waterfall is still there and generates electricity for Connecticut Light and Power. Mill building number one measures 750 feet long and 75 feet wide and rose (as previously stated) five stories high. The second mill building is 500 feet long and 100 feet wide.

The textile mill transformed raw cotton into usable cloth. Twenty million yards of cloth were manufactured yearly at its height. Legend says that one pound of cotton could be turned into one string of yarn measuring 100 miles in length. The factory used fine materials, including Egyptian cotton. After the textile company closed its doors in 1972, one of the last in the area to do so, the building was used for various purposes. Helikon, a high-end furniture maker, was located here for years. Norwich historian Dale Plummer tried to revive the textile industry in town by opening the Quinnehticut Woolen

The majesty of Ponemah Mills in Taftville.

Company in the early 1990s. Today there are plans to turn the former mill into loft-style apartments. The property has been purchased and work is slowly being done on it. Given the historic nature of the building, the historical commission has to approve every minute detail. At a time when former industrial structures are turning into mixed-use apartment and retail facilities, Ponemah would triumph in this capacity. Its stunning waterfront views of the Shetucket, which would be afforded to roughly half of the complex's population, combined with the industrial features, would make this prime real estate. With all of these encouraging aspects, it would still need to draw individuals to Taftville to reside. Unfortunately, the area surrounding the factory today does not have many attractions or businesses to lure potential mill-dwellers.

The story of Taftville, its French Canadians, and Ponemah Mills has been the subject of an annual walk in the Last

Green Valley's "Walktober" program for as long as I can remember. I recall as a child going on a walk led by Taftville historian Rene Dugas recollecting the history of the area. In October, 2013, I went on the walk again, especially intrigued at the prospect of being allowed *inside* Ponemah! The walk was led by Keith Fontaine, vice president of Hartford Health Care, who grew up in Taftville and the current fire chief of the village, Captain Tim Jencks. Keith and Tim's talk brought great personalization to the walk since they both have strong ties and affinity for the village. The tour led us all over the mill complex. From the administrative offices of the current developers to the fish ladder near the dam to the former workspaces, it was a comprehensive look into the former mill. I was impressed at the structural integrity of the building. So many now abandoned or once-abandoned facilities have fallen by the wayside due to vandalism, time, or both. The walls and floors are solid. Each floor

The Shetucket River runs through Ponemah.

of the factory was one large open space, which at one time would have been humming and chugging with the sound of textile manufacture. Although many of the floors were empty, signs of its manufacturing past were on display as relics of its former use. The protruding towers hold the staircases and the bell still rings! We learned that the most prestigious of fabrics were spun on the fifth floor. Since it was October, the view overlooking the Shetucket was breathtaking, certainly a positive for a prospective buyer. At the time of my visit, some of the windows were replaced, but the windows on the front still have many smashed panes. I was also impressed on how much farther back the complex goes than can be seen from the road.

I hope Ponemah's future is in good hands. It is a building that should not be lost to fire or urban renewal. Not only is its history an integral part of the region, but the building's design is truly spectacular.

While You're There!

Check out a baseball game at Dodd Stadium home of the Single A, New York-Penn League affiliate of the Detroit Tigers, the Connecticut Tigers. The stadium opened for its inaugural season in 1995 as the home of the Norwich Navigators, the Double A affiliate of the New York Yankees. After the Navigators left, the Connecticut Defenders took the field, the Double A minor league team for the San Francisco Giants. It is a pleasing ballpark, without a bad seat in the house, craft beer on tap, and cheesesteaks provided by Norwich's cheesesteak king, Philly's. For the fraction of the cost of a major league game, Dodd Stadium is a great place to catch a game that can be entertainment for a whole family. Former Dodd Stadium alums include Alfonso Soriano, Matt Cain, Brian Wilson, and Mike Lowell. From the "base burnin' ball bashin' fan pleasing" Navigators to the present day Tigers, who will make you "hear the roar," Dodd Stadium continues to be a quality and friendly place to take in a baseball game. The kids will be excited to get up close and personal with mascots Tater and C.T.

Elmcrest Psychiatric Hospital

Portland

When I travel across the state, I pick one of three major routes. The first is Interstate 95, the second is Routes 2 and 84, and the last, Routes 16 to 66, the final option being the most scenic as it winds through the towns of Colchester, East Hampton, and Portland on the way to Middletown. Where Routes 66 and 17A come together in close proximity to the Arrigoni Bridge, which crosses the Connecticut River into Middletown, there is a forlorn-looking establishment. On the left side of the road when traveling west on Route 66, this institution always gave me the impression of being psychiatric in nature, although the presence of Connecticut Valley State Hospital in close proximity made me conjecture otherwise. In researching the former use of the abandoned property, my first guess was correct: it was the former Elmcrest Psychiatric Hospital. The property's history dives further back than solely its use as a mental hospital; the three main buildings served as mansions for some of the area's notable residents.

The hospital is laid out in the cottage plan, meaning a campus of separate buildings as opposed to the Kirkbride style, which resembles a fortress. The property opened as Elmcrest Manor in

1938 and has been the subject of controversy, much of it rooted in the last ten years of its existence as a hospital. It was opened by Dr. Carl Wagner and his wife, Magdalena, who treated mostly wealthy patients suffering from alcoholism. When the Hartford Institute of Living was too full, those who could not detox there were sent to Elmcrest. The three original buildings on the property were used to house and care for the patients, although the experience was more like a retreat than a hospital stay, a far cry from the experience of those less fortunate at Connecticut Valley. After World War II the clientele of Elmcrest changed, and the institution began to take on more of the persona of a psychiatric hospital. Although Elmcrest was a private hospital, it began to take in more "charity cases," rather than the wealthy patients of its past.

In the 1990s, the hospital grounds housed 26 buildings, 129 beds, and 290 patients, both inpatient and out with 60% of its population being children. Although at a time when many institutions were closing, Elmcrest was chugging along. This was also a time period that scarred the institution with two publicized accounts of death on site. One eleven-year-old patient died of traumatic asphyxia while in a restraint in 1998, and two years later, a thirty-year-old expired due to a drug overdose on the premises. Through the late 1990s into the 2000s, the number of patients drastically decreased as buildings that were no longer needed became empty. This time period also saw a change of hands for the hospital, as it was bought by St. Francis Hospital in 1997, only to be acquired by Hartford Hospital under their Rushford Center banner in 2003. It closed three years later as the once bustling 14.9 acre campus shut its doors for the final time. No longer were the original mansions, cottages, or dormitories active with patients and staff.

The problem with any institutional building that has lost its function is what becomes of it. Similar to many others in the state that have idly sat by while nature and vandals do their part, Elmcrest's future remains in limbo. One proposition that almost bloomed to fruition was the transformation of the property into a shopping center, which would fit into the commercial surroundings of Route 66. The proposition was a plaza called Townplace and would have included a Walgreens Drugstore. CVS at one time also inquired about the land. Due to the economy's downturn, this plan, at least at the time of this writing, has not seen the light of day. Groups like Elmcrest Campus Advisory Committee want to save the beautifully designed mansions to find an appropriate re-use of the buildings. In 2014, a grant was given for the main three buildings from the Connecticut Trust for Historic Preservation. In Portland, the issue between demolishing and preserving is a hot topic. Many voices call for securing the mansions for adaptive re-use while others feel that they have deteriorated too far. Psychiatric hospitals can be more difficult than other properties, former factories for instance, to be reinvigorated given the actual and perceived connotations that accompany them. Those former patients who were treated harshly at the facility, no matter the architectural beauty of the buildings, would like to see them torn down. From purely a historic viewpoint, it would be wonderful to see these stately homes rehabilitated, like the patients they once housed, and once again fill the town of Portland with the pride and history that would occur with the refurbishment.

▶ Please visit www.elmcrestportlandct. com with updates on the status of the property.

Three Mansions

The three mansions on the property represent fine examples of three types of architecture: Greek revival, Italianate, and Queen Anne styles. The Hart-Jarvis House, which was built in 1829 in the Greek revival style, is noted for its four large iconic columns, which provide stability, with an ornate portico. The mansion is painted white with quoins outlining its corners. It has a gable roof and its flanking sections have dormers. The four chimneys are white brick. This was the girlhood home of Elizabeth Jarvis Colt, future wife of Samuel Colt, founder of the gun manufacturer that bears his name (see the chapter on the Colt Armory in this collection).

Another stately white mansion on the Elmcrest property is the Erastus Brainerd Jr. House and Carriage House. This home was built with Portland Brownstone constructed in the style of an Italian villa. Its designer was famed New Haven architect Henry Austin. The Brainerd House was built circa 1852. Erastus was the superintendent of the Portland Brownstone Quarry, which was the backbone of the town's economy. Its architectural features are marked by a front porch with fluted columns resting on urns. Its upstairs windows are accompanied by small iron porches. Erastus's father built this house next to the Hart-Jarvis House since his father purchased that property.

The final mansion of the three that were included in the grant for historic preservation is the John H. Sage House. This property was constructed in 1884 in the Queen Anne style. This two-and-a-half-story impressive home was built for Sage, who was an ancestor to a first settler of nearby Middletown, on the land where his father, Charles H. Sage, had his house. This complements the other two homes as it is also painted white. It was not built with symmetry as its entrance veers to the left of the center. The property is equipped with a greenhouse on site and sits behind an iron fence and a tangle of trees. The Sage House was the site of the infirmary during its years included in the Elmcrest Hospital.

Elmcrest surely represents buildings that we wish could talk. They have borne witness to use as mansions for the area's elite as well as safe havens for those facing addiction and psychiatric obstacles. The three mansions that sit blemished only by years of disuse and the illegal shelter for the homeless hopefully will be saved from the shadow of the wrecking ball. They provide beautiful examples of three different architectural styles that all have a unique history as private homes to the area's well-to-do and as part of a larger institution. Time will only tell what is in store for Elmcrest.

Bara-Hack

Pomfret

Pomfret's lost village of Bara-Hack is one of the most sought after legendary places in Connecticut. The place's notoriety stems from an investigation in the early '70s in which sounds were heard, although civilization had not been present for many a decade. Nicknamed the Village of Voices, Bara-Hack is mostly associated with eerie auditory happenings, but specters have been known to haunt this forgotten community as well.

Growing up in Eastern Connecticut, I was especially interested in Bara-Hack. It was "my side" of the state's answer to the notorious Dudleytown of the Litchfield Hills. After many a time scouring the wooded paths near Abington Four Corners in Pomfret, I had almost lost hope in ever actually finding the "lost" village. Like many of the more intriguing off-kilter places in the state, Bara-Hack is off limits to the public, and its land is strewn with "No Trespassing" signs. In the fall of 2012,

my luck in finding Bara-Hack changed for the better. The Last Green Valley is the name given to the region whose boundaries run from Norwich in the eastern part of the state north into Massachusetts to its nearby border towns. As mentioned earlier, the Last Green Valley Incorporated runs an annual collection of walks in the month of October every year, nicknamed "Walktober." The walks tend to be rooted in history, whether of a certain place, a time period, or an individual. They range from slow ambles through cemeteries and town greens to vigorous hikes in the less-trodden woods. When opening up the flyer for Walktober 2012 in late summer, I was elated to see a trip to the "Village of Voices." I realized the chances of seeing, hearing, or feeling anything unusual decreased drastically by being a part of a loud onslaught of visitors, but I could not resist checking out the infamous landscape for myself.

From the get-go, the guide let us know that this was not a ghost-hunting expedition, but instead a trip to the historical past of what was once a small working village. Although she was privy to the weird tales attributed to the place, she did not pay them any mind. A Harvard professor named Odell Shepard visited Bara-Hack in the 1920s and our guide attributed the legends surrounding the place as originating with him. As the tour began, we were informed of the history of the land. The area we were about to venture into was originally bought by Brit Obadiah Higginbotham, from wealthy Rhode Islander John Randall in 1780. The Higginbotham family was to be brought up during the walk numerous times.

In departing from the 4-H Camp parking lot, on the left following the road was School House Brook, named after the Moravian School House that once stood nearby. Deep down a path off Taft Pond Road, the entrance to the Higginbotham's village was delineated with two large boulders on either side. Bara-Hack's

A former sluiceway on the site of Bara-Hack.

The remnants of a foundation and chimney at Bara -Hack.

reputation as notoriously haunted has led thrill seekers illegally to this spot, which has led to historical items being moved from their original positions in the village.

The walking path was presumably the main thoroughfare of the village. Structures were seen on both sides of the path and were marked by signs telling the visitor what each was used for. Only stone walls and foundations remain, including that of a sheep fold, a barn, and Obadiah Higginbotham's second house. Reported apparitions in trees by the cemetery appeared to slaves, which marked one of the first ghostly encounters in the area. A testament to the presence of slaves was the chimney in Obadiah's house. The chimney was narrower at the bottom and widened out as it got taller. According to our guide, this feature was a clue that it was built by slaves. Another remaining structure was the corn crib with stones sticking up in the middle. Today, a corn crib sounds outrageous in this rocky outcropping of New England. One has to remember, though, that during colonial days, farming was a primary profession. Deforestation was commonplace to make room for fields for growing crops. It is easy to lose sight of the fact that the dense woodlands are deceptively young. All along the property, stone walls ran every which way. Hitching posts for horses were seen as well. With only primitive technology, people had to use stones to sharpen their tools. Evidence exists here of this, too. What looked like an ordinary gap in one of the stone walls was actually used as a sheep counter. To keep track of the number of sheep, farmers would scurry their sheep through this hole to determine the number of their flock. The Higginbothams were known for their spinning wheel manufacture; one of their wares can even be seen at Olde Sturbridge Village.

Down the hill from the main section of the village is Nightingale Brook, which is a tributary to Mashamoquet Brook. The brook was dammed to create a millpond. The Hurricane of 1938, which ravaged much of New England, destroyed the dam, but its remnants can be seen strewn wildly downstream. A sluiceway can also be seen. The brook separates the first Higginbotham house from the others. Up the steep hill is the remaining foundation equipped with another inverted chimney.

Unfortunately I did not encounter any ghostly apparitions of bearded faces and babies, nor did I hear the sounds of a working village, which legends say are some of the village's more notorious haunts. The most treacherous encounter I endured was climbing up the steep face of the hill near Higginbotham's first house. My hands, being full of note-taking devices, made my climb hairier than necessary. I did hear a flock of wildly chirping black birds overhead that seemed to circle back and forth, around and around the area where I was. I also did not find the much sought after cemetery, the sight of many of the haunting stories. Even though on the main path, I followed both sides of the fork in the road, I must not have followed the correct fork long enough.

Was Bara-Hack worth the wait that I had endured in seeking it? Well, maybe it did not send the chills down my spine that I had often read about, but it did give me a glimpse into the history of a prominent family whose history lies nearly untold in a back lot off a back road in rural Northeastern Connecticut. Overall the village was serene, not unlike a number of protected lands that nature is allowed to reclaim. Do the "No Trespassing" signs add to its mystique? If Bara-Hack were a protected nature preserve or park, would it hold such notoriety? These are worthy questions. The land is owned by the town, but has a claim with distant relatives of the owners, although no one has lived in the "village of voices" for about 120 years.

▶ Bara-Hack is located off of Taft Pond Road in Pomfret.

Section 2:
Ghosts and
Other-Worldly
Entities

Alexander's Lake

Killingly

The shimmering waters of the expansive Alexander's Lake in Killingly is a premier example of fact and legend intertwined to create a fascinating history to this body of water. The story of Alexander's Lake is deeply rooted in Native American tradition, but whose water remains sacred to those visitors from more recent times.

The lake was originally called Lake Mashapaug and was the first legally owned property in the town in 1702. It is a mile long, half-a-mile wide, and its waters are fueled by twenty-four nearby springs. Area residents know the lake mostly for its recreational use. This popular spot was home to Wildwood Park, a multi-purpose entertainment complex.

The history of the lake is muddled, in stark contrast to its clear appearance. Sources say that it is named after Nell Ellick Saunders, later to be called Nell Alexander, a Scotsman who settled in the area around 1720. The young European boarded a ship to set sail for Boston. Just before leaving the boat, Alexander found a gold ring onboard. In Boston, he sold the ring for other wares to trade. Through trading, Alexander was to amass a small fortune. He was even able to get back his original gold ring. With the bartering he had done, he was able to purchase $3,500 worth of acreage in Killingly. The ring, which brought him much success, he was to pass on to his son, Nell Alexander, who in turn gave it to his son, Nell Alexander, with successive generations of prosperous Nell Alexanders keeping the lucky ring. There is some truth that the wealthy Alexander family did own a fine home on the lake. Some have suggested that the lake was originally named Saunder's Pond after Nell's original last name.

A common legend associated with Alexander's Lake is that the tops of pine trees can be seen just beneath the surface of the water. The origin of this legend stems from the local native people who inhabited the area. After a successful harvest, they celebrated with a festive powwow with activities that included dancing, smoking, eating, and drinking. The feast lasted four days until the Great Spirit became fed up with the reveling mortals. The powwow was in an area known as Sandy Hill that was covered with towering pine trees. The Great Spirit toppled Sandy Hill, and the land and its inhabitants were submerged. One wise squaw survived, as she perched above the rest in a tall tree. This location remained above the water and became known as Loon Island. The story goes that for many a year afterward, the tops of the pine trees could still be seen close to the surface of the water.

Although much of Alexander's Lake's back story is either fully or partially rooted in legend, what is not exaggerated is the important role the lake has played in many individuals' lives. The Alexander family did own a gorgeous home on the banks of the lake. Wildwood Park, on the eastern shore of the lake, was a popular resort destination for local and vacationing families during the late nineteenth and twentieth centuries. It was accessible by street car to the villages of Killingly. The resort area of the lake consisted of various attractions, including a roller skating rink, bandstand, and stables. Monkeys were even an attraction at one point. The irony was that swimming in the pristine waters was not even legal until 1938. Much later, fire destroyed many of the buildings that once encompassed the Alexander's Lake resort area.

Alexander's Lake has been a vital part of the lives of local inhabitants in what is now known as Killingly since the days it was populated by native peoples. Legend has long been associated with the spot, from the story of tall trees close to the lake's surface, to its convoluted past and even includes a speculated sunken ship!

Although the Wildwood Resort is a thing of the past, the natural beauty of the lake remains. Couple the immaculate waters and unfettered splendor of the natural surroundings with eerie legends and it makes Alexander's Lake a must see destination!

———

Camp Columbia State Historic Park

Morris

The common trait of parks and protected land is that they are used for the enjoyment of the public, although their histories and features may vary greatly. Whether for hiking, swimming, bike riding, or simply enjoying natural surroundings, parks provide a pleasing oasis from the claustrophobic concrete superhighways and the monotony of cookie cutter developments. Although we may find these places as a literal and figurative "breath of fresh air," typically we do not stop to think why they are there. Sure, in some cases like Gillette Castle State Park in East Haddam the history confronts the visitor from the outset with questions surrounding why there is an actual castle in rural Connecticut. The back story of the park and castle accompany a visit to the park. Usually, Gillette Castle is not unknowingly stumbled upon. In most cases, the histories of state and local parks are not put out there as immodestly as in Gillette's case. The land could be left to the local or state government for a variety of reasons. Similarly to Gillette Castle, the land could be left by an individual who wanted preservation of his or her property. In other cases, it could have been land once used for a certain purpose that has long since passed—Gay City State Park in Hebron and Machimoodus State Park

in East Haddam come to mind, one being a former village and the other consisting partially of a former resort. Yet other towns in their development put aside land for public use and enjoyment from the outset. Whatever the reason, they all serve a common purpose: the enjoyment and recreation of the public.

Camp Columbia State Park in Morris is a relatively new acquisition by the State of Connecticut to its park system. The state park opened in 2004. The park consists of just about 600 acres and is actually designated in two parts: State Historic Park and State Forest. Although the park encourages visitors to enjoy its wooded hiking trails, the history of the park is the most alluring feature.

The name "Camp Columbia" derives from its use as just that, a summer camp for Columbia University's engineering program. Columbia University bought the land in 1903, although they had been operating a summer program in the area for twelve years. To escape the dreadful heat of New York City summers, the school decided to utilize this area in northwestern Connecticut. In conjunction with the engineering facility, the area had many different uses. They included as a pre-season football practice field, an earthquake monitoring site, and the location of a college training program for high school students. During World War I, the land was used for combat training for war-bound university students. Ralph Williams, a decorated Canadian war veteran, was in command of the program. Hundreds of yards of trenches were dug to create a realistic rendition of Europe's western front and trench warfare. The "practice" battles at times included live gunfire and explosives! The eventual President Eisenhower was president of the university and a proponent of its football program; under his tenure the football field was created. Legend states that, once upon a time, the New York Giants football team practiced here! In 1966, the camp ended

37

its use as the engineering program's summer residence, but was still occupied in one way or another until 1983.

Structures on the campus included a dining hall, residences, and a boathouse, since the land provided a small access to Bantam Lake. The most prominent feature, which still stands today, is the stone tower that rises above the state park. This stone structure was used as a water tower and was dedicated in 1942 as a gift from the graduating class of 1906. Although the tower prominently stands, climbing it is off limits. It is adorned with a wraparound stone staircase, although it is missing some steps. Legends abound that the former camp is haunted. More likely the state of disrepair, especially in days before the state owned it, propagated eerie tales, as rings true with many abandoned properties.

▶ Camp Columbia State Park is located off Route 109 in Morris.

Further Other-Worldly Excursions into Pachaug Forest

Griswold, Voluntown, and Sterling

Maud

Pachaug State Forest is widely known in paranormal circles for the tale of Maud. In one version, Maud is a holistic healer who helped many village people not having access to doctors; but one day, a boy she treated died. She was called a witch and her punishment was to be buried alive, with the assumption that if she were truly a witch, she would fly out of the grave and save herself. Maud's identity changes depending on who is telling the story, but one commonality is that she is said to still inhabit the deep woods of the forest. In reality, Maud Reynolds was a girl who died at a very young age.

For a village that has been out of commission for over eighty years, numerous stories abound. The area was first settled in the late 1600s into the early 1700s. In addition to the foreboding legend of Maud, the area has unsettling place names like Hell Hollow Road and Mt. Misery. The disconcerting names derive from the poor quality of the area for farming, not due to an ungodly presence. Today's overgrown forest still has remnants of the lost village with stone walls and foundations.

Lilacs

One village resident named Mrs. Gorton was quite the horticulture enthusiast, or at least she enjoyed her precious lilacs. The lilacs, whose aroma can still be smelled today, brought her joy beyond belief. She was so partial to them that she vowed death upon any lilac thieves. Jacob Myers, a typical self-centered teenage boy, decided that it would be fun to take some of the beloved lilacs. Not thinking that Old Mrs. Gorton would actually make true her words, Jacob sneaked up to the Gorton homestead and picked her flowers. The next morning, an enraged Mrs. Gorton noticed her prized possessions were gone and stormed into town, seething mad. Soon after, she saw a group of teens laughing, yelling, and altogether being obnoxious, with lilacs in their hands! Gorton pulled Jacob out of the crowd to question his whereabouts during the previous evening. He, of course, had an alibi and denied ever being near, never mind picking her flowers. She pulled him by the collar and shook him, just to see if that would jog his memory, but it was to no avail. Feeling downtrodden, she walked away from town and no one in the village heard from her for months.

During October of the same year, Jacob Myers decided to go fishing in the ponds behind Mrs. Gorton's house. That was the last that anyone ever saw of Jacob. His fishing pole was all that was left of him. Some say that Jacob got lost in the woods and never made his way back to town; others say that Mrs. Gorton fulfilled her promise and that a corpse lay buried underneath her lilac trees. To corroborate the second premise, locals mentioned noticing the placement of fresh dirt.

Although Jacob may have met his untimely fate in the backwoods of eastern Connecticut, Mrs. Gorton seems to have remained. Even today people have mentioned seeing an old woman tending to her favorite lilacs. In 1925, a man noticed an old woman crossing the road and then noticed the smell of lilacs lingering behind her. Gorton is said to roam near the area of present-day Bailey's Pond, close to the Rhode Island border. Just follow the scent of the lilacs.

The Gorton home can be seen on a map of the forest from 1869.

Knocks

The next story involves Mr. and Mrs. Dixon, who owned a farm in Voluntown, close to the southern edge of Hazard Pond. An unusual disturbance outside called Mr. Dixon's attention. Gun in hand, he carefully opened the door to see who or what was there. Much to his dismay, there was no one. Much to Mrs. Dixon's chagrin, Mr. Dixon decided to venture out into the blustery autumn evening, lantern in hand. Soon Mrs. Dixon started frantically yelling for her husband to come back inside. Mr. Dixon did not respond, even when the wind eerily stopped blowing. Petrified, Mrs. Dixon hastily closed the door, but stayed glued to the window until the glow of her husband's lantern could be seen. Mrs. Dixon heard a knock at the door, but through the window could not see anyone at the door. She surmised that it was her husband playing a childish trick.

She pleaded with him to stop the foolish nonsense of scaring her, but still did not see anyone by the door. Completely flabbergasted and terrified, Mrs. Dixon found refuge in the haven of her bedroom. Even hiding under the bedcovers did not prevent her from hearing the ever-present knocks. Yelling at the door and equipping herself with a knife did not help, as the knocking continued. Mrs. Dixon swallowed hard and decided to face whoever was outside the door. She twisted the handle and the old door creaked open. The empty front porch was basked in the moonlight, but suddenly the bright harvest moon became hidden behind the passing clouds, which left the rural Voluntown landscape shrouded in the deepest black. All of a sudden Mrs. Dixon was face to face with her husband's lantern, hanging in midair. The floating lantern entered the home. An understandably petrified Mrs. Dixon hid. The hovering lantern was suspended as if it were being carried by an invisible person. The lantern and whatever was holding it crept farther into the home and near the place where Mr. Dixon kept his pipe. Now, with pipe and lantern in tow, the force made its way back toward the front door, but first shined the light under a table to discover where Mrs. Dixon was hiding.

Mrs. Dixon hoped that if she closed her eyes and then opened them, this nightmare would be over. When she finally built up her courage to look, there was no sign of lantern or pipe, nor did she see anything outside. In the morning light, Mr. Dixon was finally spotted, although not inside the house. He had fallen into the well located nearby. The original disturbance was caused by an unhooked barn door, blowing in the blustering wind. After she processed the events of the evening, she felt that the knocking came from the spirit of her husband, saying goodbye to her and returning for his two favorite possessions, his lantern and his pipe. After her husband's passing, the smell of cigar smoke would on occasion waft through the home. Even today, the odor of cigar lingers around the southern edge of Hazard Pond.

Standing Guard

Although the remnants of the first two spirits manifest themselves by their aroma, the next is by sight. The story takes place on Breakneck Hill Road, which is technically in Griswold. The road intersects with Hell Hollow Road, which makes anyone living at the corner of Hell Hollow and Breakneck Road have quite the address! A soldier is said to keep march on this road still today. Holding a rifle and dressed in a colonial soldier's garb, he stands as if on guard. The soldier is said to be from King Phillip's War.

Weeping Woman

The final tale involves a family of Native Americans fleeing for their lives from colonial soldiers. Military men caught and slaughtered four children and the father, but the mother escaped. Understandably distraught after seeing her family executed, she began to weep uncontrollably even though her cries gave away her location. She was soon discovered and killed.

Throughout the years, witnesses have heard ungodly cries emanating from the very same woods, on the edge of Hell Hollow at the hour of the family's demise. This region may have been named Hell Hollow due to the torture of trying to farm the poor soil, but tales of ghostly wails have made the name even more apt. The woman's cries can be still heard in the loneliest sections of Pachaug's Hell Hollow.

Pachaug State Forest has many a tale to tell. Along with its most popular legendary figure, the oft disputed Maud, its ghostly sights, sounds, and smells will creep out any unsuspecting visitor. One word of warning: one end of Hell Hollow Road is an extremely desolate road (the other has houses). The road is incredibly beat up and is actually closed in the harsher winter months. So if you decide to venture down to the fiery inferno yourself, make sure to take care on the cracked pavement. Now you would not want to be trapped out there when, all of a sudden, you get a whiff of lilacs and cigar smoke, start hearing desperate crying, and see the ghost of a colonial soldier!

Salmon River, Comstock Bridge, and Day Pond State Park

Colchester, East Hampton, Hebron, East Haddam, and Marlborough

Originally, the first places that I explored and then eventually wrote about for the first volume of *Connecticut Lore* had been places I had been familiar with for years, either by reading about them or by word of mouth, stories that had been passed down to me by family members or other acquaintances. One of my favorite aspects about speaking at book events is the ability to connect with the audience. Just as in my childhood when my grandmother would tell me certain tales or legends, readers and audience members have given me many leads for this collection of stories for which I am grateful. One young man mentioned to me a sight that he saw that stayed with him: an abandoned car in the woods of Colchester's Day Pond State Park. In following this lead, I was able to piece together a few entries all within the same geographic region.

Starting at Day Pond State Park, my adventure began with a walk around the

The picturesque Day Pond State Park in Colchester.

pond on a temperate day for December. This site was settled by the Day family who used the water in the pond to operate a sawmill during colonial times. Close to the pond, stone walls, an old pump, and a dam can be seen. More modern amenities, like bathrooms, an outdoor fireplace, a pavillion, and picnic tables, offer the modern visitor needed facilities. Visiting in the winter the park was quiet, but the beach bordering the pond is known to be popular in the summer. Trout fisherman enjoy casting in the stocked pond. The brook that is fed by the pond is a tributary of the Salmon River. Many trails wind their way through the state park property, but the main one is a loop around the pond. The Salmon River Trail connects to the nearby Salmon River State Forest. On this trail is where foundations can be seen along with the rusted old car, which was my impetus in traveling to the park in the first place. The biggest question that remains about the mystery junked car is: why? Why is it there? How was it put

there? In any case the juxtaposition between the natural beauty and the decrepit automobile provides a stark contrast.

In seeing Day Pond's close proximity to the Salmon River, it is only fitting to mention the notorious Black Fox of Salmon River. Although the tale harkens back to the days in which Native Americans fished the waters of Tatamacuntaway and the salmon ran freely upstream in the aptly named river, it became widely known by the works of two poets, John Brainard, who first mentioned it, followed by an expanded version by John Greenleaf Whittier. Arguments ensue about the spookiest area of the state, with some voting for the greater Fairfield area where many of Lorraine and Ed Warren's stories have taken place and of course is the location of Connecticut's most notorious graveyard, Easton's Union Cemetery. Others argue that the greater Sterling area has the most ghostly associations, with the tale of Maud and the other spectres of Pachaug State Forest. My vote would be the greater East Haddam area. Where else could a castle, a town reverberating with seismic activity (or angry gods), an abandoned living history museum, and a ghost of a black fox be seen in the same general area? Whittier expounded on the tale of the Black Fox to include other legendary figures of Connecticut folklore. He mentions Hobomoko, the angry god said to have created the rumblings underfoot in Moodus, and Miantonomo, sachem of the Narragansett who met his fate by the hands of Mohegan sachem Uncas.

The banks of the Salmon River are protected under the aegis of the Salmon River State Forest today. It flows through the towns of Marlborough and Colchester, forming the border with East Hampton, on to East Haddam near the village of Moodus, and eventually emptying into the Connecticut River. Smaller rivers and brooks like the Blackledge River, Safstrom Brook, and Pine Brook find their termini in the Salmon. The Salmon is a favorite spot for fly fisherman. The Airline Trail passes through the state forest, which provides one of the state's most popular biking trails. The geography, including valleys, waterfalls, and glacial rock, afford gorgeous natural vistas.

The Black Fox

Popular today for fisherman, the native people who used to inhabit what is now known as Middlesex County also found the waters of the Tatamacuntaway prime fishing grounds. They also hunted animals and birds along its banks. One of the most elusive creatures to stalk this area was and possibly still is, the black fox. For the native hunters, seeing this beautiful animal, with its lustrous black coat, was too tempting to pass up. A crazed desire for the capture and kill of this fox led to the demise of many men. For some, the fruitless fox hunt could last days; those less fortunate never returned from the hunt. Arrows clearly shot at the beast with direct hits never punctured the fleeing fox. Frustrated,

the hunters would try time and again, but to no avail.

When English settlers moved into the area, the local Native Americans showed them the natural bounty of the region. The abundant salmon swimming freely upstream (which eventually provided the river with an English name), the birds flying overhead, the game roaming the grounds: this was the settlers' paradise. When told of the black fox, the settlers laughed the matter off. Quite surely the failure of the fox hunt was due to the indigenous people's primitive weapons, for their bows and arrows could not compare to the muskets of the settlers. What at first was a laughing matter quickly became point of frustration for the English. Just as the Native Americans had warned, when hunting the region, the settlers were driven crazy by the allure of the black fox. Musket balls that clearly punctured the flesh and should have sunk deep in the heart of the fox were passed through, as if it were a ghost. The area's new inhabitants similarly were driven to great lengths in pursuit of the fox, eventually leading to unsuccessful hunts and worse, death. If you are visiting and see the little guy, do not get fooled into following him for it will be for a lost cause.

Comstock Bridge

One of the great landmarks of the Salmon River is the Comstock Bridge (sometimes referred to as Comstock's Bridge). One of Connecticut's only three remaining covered bridges and the only one in the eastern part of the state, it crosses the river separating East Hampton and Colchester. Although the year of its construction is unknown for certain, it is estimated at being built sometime within the mid-nineteenth century. Since the creation of a concrete bridge just downstream in 1932, eliminating the daily use for traffic over the bridge, Comstock is solely a pedestrian bridge. The bridge is named for a beloved postmaster in town. A truck accident caused major damage to the bridge in the

1920s. Legend has it the truck was carrying liquor that was contraband during the Prohibition years. The folks in town clearly did their best to collect the remaining runoff in buckets, being mindful that it would not seep into the river below!

The Civilian Conservation Corps rehabilitated a great deal of the bridge in 1936, repairing much damage caused by the truck accident. The bank of the river beside the bridge is a favorite place for fly fishermen.

While You're There!

One of my favorite places to go after a long day swimming in Day Pond, hiking on the trails, fishing in the river, riding my bike on the Airline Trail, and chasing after that elusive fox is Nunu's Bistro in Colchester. Nunu's, located in a house just off the Colchester Green, is the perfect quaint Italian restaurant. Their home-made pasta is incomparable. One of my favorite dishes ever is Seafood Linguine. The fresh seafood liberally served over the aforementioned pasta is simply superb. Perfect for a date, its close quarters and welcoming decor add to the memorable experience. Bring a favorite bottle of wine or a few well selected beers with you, since Nunu's is BYOB. Nunu's is located at 45 Hayward Road in Colchester.

Captain Grant's Inn 1754

Preston

Inns are common places to encounter ghosts. Many inns and bed and breakfasts of New England are located in historic homes that highlight their storied pasts. Some, like Captain Grant's in the Poquetanuck section of Preston, embrace both of these aspects of its heritage. The bed and breakfast is in the heart of southeastern Connecticut's "casino country," wedged almost equidistant between Foxwoods and Mohegan Sun at 109-111 Route 2A. The property includes a few buildings. In addition to Captain Grant's is the Avery Home and the Stagecoach Inn, both dating from 1790, which together create a mini village of lodging. The inn was used both as a garrison during the American Revolution and as a stop on the underground railroad. The innkeepers are Ted and Carol Matsumoto. *Yankee Magazine* agrees that this bed and breakfast is worth a stay and gave it the prized "Best of New England/Editor's Choice" award. It has also been featured on national productions including HGTV, CNN, *Maxim Magazine*, and *USA Today*. The property was added to the National Register of Historic Places in 1996, the same year that its rehabilitation was completed and it was turned into the present-day bed and breakfast.

Each of the historic rooms is furnished traditionally with hardwood floors, four poster beds, and fireplaces, but thankfully all include private baths (and modern amenities like televisions and even a gratis decanter of sherry). The wall near the front staircase is adorned with a mural depicting a view of Poquetanuck in 1825. Each guestroom is emblazoned with a woman's name. Weary travelers may find themselves in either Marie, Holly, Margaret, Collette, Amy, Adelaide, or Elizabeth's room.

The most notorious is Adelaide's room. Named for the wife of Captain William Gonzales Grant, Mercy Adelaide Grant, this accommodation is the paranormal jackpot, chock full of mysterious noises, shapes, and otherworldly occurrences. In Adelaide's room a woman in full colonial dress has been spotted, and other strange events have happened, including a shower curtain being torn down, beds moving, blankets being hastily ripped off guests, the television turning on and off, and unexplained knocking being heard. Other guests have complained of footsteps walking overhead, but the attic space above is only used as a storage area for building materials. Captain Grant died, aged only thirty-two, at sea en route to Honduras. He left behind a pregnant wife, two sons, and a daughter. Mercy lived into her eighties. The nearby cemetery is the final resting place of the captain, the son he never knew, who became the second Captain Grant, and Mercy.

Although the colonial woman has been suspected of being Mercy and has been seen with a child, other specters have been associated with the building. Some say that Captain Grant's spirit arrived back home and that he is one of the inhabitants, maybe the one pacing in the attic. Others blame the inn's proximity to a graveyard for its uninvited guests. For whatever reason, and whoever they are, they seem to enjoy the Matsumotos' hospitality and do not seem to be leaving anytime soon! For a place that has seen so much history and incarnations, it is no wonder that it has such extensive ghostly associations.

It is thought that the ghosts are benign and are protective of the property. Guests' interactions with ghosts have been mainly positive. The ghostly encounters have proved a positive attraction for prospective visitors. The owners have openly acknowledged their inn's permanent guests and welcome prospective ghost hunters, often for overnight stays.

Luckily, the beautifully furnished and meticulously decorated inn lures the visitor for repeated stays. Come for the ghosts, but stay for the gracious hospitality, including a scrumptious country breakfast and relaxed country feel.

While You're There!

Maple Lane Farms, also located in Preston, is the perfect place to pick your own blueberries, raspberries, strawberries, and cut your own Christmas trees. In the fall, Maple Lane offers hayrides and pumpkin picking. If you're thirsty, make sure to pick up a bottle of their fantastic black currant juices. The masterminds at Maple Lane have recently started their own Maple Lane Spirits, distilling the popular Foggy Harbor vodka as well as a black currant-based cassis and a gin with a touch of black currant. Maple Lane Farms is at 57 Northwest Corner Road in Preston.

Curtis House Inn
Woodbury

Not many locations in the country, never mind the state, have as much of a reputation for the paranormal as the Curtis House Inn in Woodbury. With its existence predating the founding of America, the Curtis House Inn is oozing with history. Located at 506 Main Street between Orenaug and South Poperaug Avenues since its construction in 1735, it has functioned as an inn or public house of some kind since 1754 and is touted as "America's oldest inn." Its motto reads: "Every modern comfort, every ancient charm." I'm guessing the "ancient" refers to the presence of its oldest guests, the ones who never left.

The inn was built by Reverend Anthony Stoddard for his son, Eliakim. Stoddard's grandson, also named Anthony Stoddard, turned the house into the Orenaug Inn in 1754. Guest rooms were on the first floor while a banquet hall and tea room were on the second. In the nineteenth

The sign for the Curtis House, Connecticut's oldest and one of its most haunted inns.

century, the second floor was turned into lodging quarters as well. In the twentieth century, under the tutelage of owner Levi Curtis, the inn was expanded with a third-story addition. Before the Masons were able to assemble publicly, the inn harbored them for meetings and was equipped with a secret entrance. The inn features a dining room and the City Hall Pub. Today's inn has eighteen guest rooms, four in the carriage house and fourteen in the main inn. Eight of them have private baths and six share baths. Reflecting the motto "ancient charm," rooms do not have air conditioning or phones.

One of the many specters to haunt the storied inn is Lucius Foote, who in 1856 died one night after winning a large sum at a poker game. After the game, he tried to make his way home by an unfamiliar route, but he never made it there. He was found killed on the property of nearby St. Paul's Episcopal Church (which has its own story to tell!). He is rumored to haunt rooms 1 and 2. After a painting of Anthony

Stoddard was hung up in the inn, it became the epicenter of paranormal activity. Visitors and employees complained of Stoddard seemingly "watching" their every move from his painted physiognomy.

Sally is a ghost of a young woman who longs for male companionship and calls room 16 her permanent home. She has been known to tuck in and even glide into bed with men, but pull the covers off guests of the fairer sex. She has even ripped one female guest out of the bed. In Room 5, other-worldly voices and footsteps have been heard. Others have felt the presence of a former slave. Some guests have felt uncomfortable during stays in room 23. A Confederate soldier has been reported to have made an appearance as well. In more recent times, a former employee of the inn named Joe, who passed away in 1985, has been seen in the basement, eating mashed potatoes (as he would during his lifetime). As per his will, Joe is buried on site. Famed Connecticut ghost hunter Lorraine Warren has stayed at the inn numerous times and pinpoints the second floor and the basement as harboring spectral activity. Donna Kent and her Cosmic Society have also investigated the Curtis House and have had eerie encounters. Others have seen rocking chairs move, beds become mussed, and televisions turn on for no apparent reason. Even scarier than any specter, celebrity chef Gordon Ramsay visited and helped reinvigorate the inn on season one of his television show *Hotel Hell*.

Although the Curtis House Inn is not as well established in the ghostly realms as other Connecticut stalwarts, after all these incidents, it will soon join their ranks. The next time you are in Woodbury and want an unsettling night's sleep, saddle up to the Curtis House Inn.

Haunted Litchfield Inn

Litchfield

The rolling hills of Litchfield County are renowned as a tranquil escape from the heavily trafficked suburbs of New York City. This corner of the state is chock full of country roads, quaint villages, and an altogether slower pace of life. It's an area where couples go to honeymoon, where nature lovers romp amongst its numerous parks and many protected wildlife areas, and antique hunters are offered a plethora of tantalizing options to find the perfect accoutrement.

Historic inns and luxurious accommodations are often staples of picturesque country towns. Litchfield County is no exception to this rule. Litchfield's Toll Gate Inn, Morris's Winvian Resort, and Lakeville's Interlaken Inn are among the more popular of the region. Litchfield, the county seat, is a microcosm

of the best of the whole region. Known for the oft-photographed First Congregational Church on its expansive town green, the town seeps with charm. A trip to Litchfield in the autumn is seeing New England at its finest.

Another town landmark is the Litchfield Inn. The Litchfield Inn is known as a premier accommodation, including its restaurant the Bantam Bistro, a well-appointed spa, and beautiful grounds. Guests rave about their stays at the inn, wishing they would never end. For some lodgers, it never did! A variety of spirits have been spotted enjoying the confines of the inn. Among the most popular permanent visitors is a Native American woman, who is particularly fond of the yard and seems to be summoned by the sound of music. Frequent sightings of her occur in the common areas of the first floor. Inn workers have spotted her peeking out of ground floor windows as well. Other times, mortal guests have inquired why there was a woman in their room when they first opened the door. "What woman?" is the bewildered answer from the inn staff.

Whether leaf peeping, antique seeking, or ghost hunting, Litchfield is an ideal place for jet setting urbanites, honeymooning couples, and paranormal investigators alike. Its quintessential New England charm is certain to draw you in, just as it did its permanent visitors.

While You're There!

In Washington Depot, about a twenty-minute picturesque country ride away from the inn, is a fantastic old restaurant, the GW Tavern, named for old President George himself. The place certainly has ambiance. Its colonial decor sets the perfect backdrop for an autumn or winter meal, with its blazing fire warming the interior and a portrait of the president overhead. It was originally a home built circa 1850. Today, it serves hearty American fare. On my visit, I opted for the steak tips, which were perfect, and my wife ordered the chicken pot pie. It was big enough to feed a family, and since she did not finish all of it, I got to help. Boy was it good! The GW is certainly not a hidden jewel though; weekend reservations are a must! The tavern is located at 20 Bee Brook Road in Washington Depot.

The Windham Inn and the Sad Story of Betsy Shaw

Windham

Whether due to past industry or present revitalization efforts, Willimantic is synonymous with the metropolitan heart of the town of Windham, although this was not always the case. The center of Windham is a few miles to the east and south of Willimantic at the intersection of the present-day Routes 203 and 14. Here is where the town green, as well as a library, church, and inn are found. When Windham was just another blip on the rural landscape of Connecticut, this was the focus of town life. Although today's sleepy intersection recalls images of a bygone era, this corner of Windham County has not always been the picture of perfection. Here at the courthouse the fate of a young woman with pronounced cognitive delays was sealed.

The story of Elizabeth (Betsy) Shaw is a stain on the history of colonial Connecticut. Different sources produce conflicting dates, but essentially the time of her baby's birth and Betsy's death range within the years of 1774 and 1775. The Shaws were a large farming family who lived a few miles from the center. Betsy was seen as a nuisance around the home, since she could not help provide for the family. With the father unknown (although some speculated that it was Elizabeth's own dad), Betsy bore a child. Not having full mental capacity, Betsy carried her child out to a cliff in the nearby town of Hampton where she left it, with the infant perishing due to exposure. One version of the tale puts her father at the scene of the crime, witnessing the abandonment. Her father committed her to the local authorities who then made her face a nine all-male jury to determine her innocence. Betsy was found guilty of infanticide, which was punishable by death. The execution was to be held publicly with a holiday-like atmosphere surrounding the borough of Windham. Although the public display of her death happened on a cold day, it did not deter a sizable crowd from gathering.

The location of Gallows Hill where she gasped her last breath is debatable. Some sources pinpoint it close to the river (presumably the Shetucket), while others say it was carried out in a field near the town green. Either way, Betsy arrived at Gallows Hill sitting atop her own coffin in a horse-drawn carriage. Her nervous fingers thumped the outside of the pine box that spectators described as sounding like nails being driven into the coffin, as she was yelling, "Oh Jesus, have mercy on my soul." Betsy was hanged, but her place of interment is unknown. Her execution date has been disputed as well, some placing it in September, others in November, and still different sources dating it in December. Either way, it explains why her presence is more active during the autumn months. As a last minute effort, one variation of the story has her father attempting to rush to government officials to ask for a reversal, but falling short due to inclement weather.

A spirit of a young woman in white has been seen in the area of Plains Road

The Windham Town Green with the haunted Windham Inn in the background.

near the intersection of the two major routes. November has been a prime viewing month. It is as if the ghost is searching for something as she meanders down the road. Could she be looking for her long abandoned child? She has been witnessed by many individuals, including a professor, who stopped to see if she needed a ride. Others have noticed her at the Windham Inn, located across the street from the green. The inn is now an apartment building, which, at the time of this writing, looks to be in a state of disrepair.

Betsy's ghost frequently visits young, single mothers living at the inn. Stories abound. In one, a normally well-behaved baby, after moving into one of the apartments, morphed into a colicky, troubled young child. He only reverted back when his mother and he moved out. The whole time the duo lived in the apartment the mother felt a sense of constantly being watched. Another woman arrived home to the unwelcome sight of her door and window completely open,

smashed frames containing ruined pictures of her child, and the September calendar page torn from the binding. She has been seen in the corridor as well. The ghost of Betsy cannot be described as docile!

The inn is the location of yet another tale of infanticide. Betty, a former maid at the inn, gave birth to a child in the inn's attic and left it there to die. When her sin was discovered, Betty was tried, found guilty, and hanged as well. Her ghost is also known to frequent the Windham Inn.

When the days grow shorter and there is a chill in the air, Windham Center is bathed gloriously in shades of orange, yellow, and red from the turning trees. Be on the lookout though for restless spirits, searching for their predeceased children, since these spooks' activity heightens between September and December. The tale of Betsy Shaw is a dark blemish in the history books of Connecticut's forefathers, but her phantom will not let her tale be forgotten.

Yankee Pedlar Inn

Torrington

Classic hotels located in town and city centers have a certain mystique to them. Whether they are recently rehabilitated to look shiny and new or dilapidated and falling apart, they do conjure up images of years gone by. The vast number of strangers who once slept for a night or two inside the same room also gives a sense of mystery (or cooties). Unlike blank, nondescript chain hotels, these beauties have character. Rooms are not cookie cutter and offer different amenities. Most city centers had one or two such hotels, but unfortunately many have met their fate via the wrecking ball or redevelopment into something else. Torrington, the largest (and only) city in Litchfield County has a small urban center marked by a main street with glimpses of the past. A stately library, classic theater, and the Yankee Pedlar Inn, a hotel from a bygone era, are all concentrated in the downtown. These once-vital assemblages have found a renaissance in Torrington center.

The Yankee Pedlar Inn started its continuous run as a hotel when it was built in 1892 as the Conley Hotel. Its name was changed to Yankee Pedlar in March of 1956. The downtown hotel, which is full of history, is quite large with fifty-two rooms. Beware of Room 353, though; this is where original owner Alice Conley died. Room 353 along with the attic, basement, and hotel's secret staircase are hotbeds for paranormal activity. Even a group from New York, the Glory Haunt Hounds, held a public, overnight ghost-hunting event in the hotel. Unfortunately, they were not able to attain hard evidence, although otherworldly presences have been detected throughout the hotel's existence. Such was the reputation of the Yankee Pedlar that a recent B-movie, *The Inn Keepers,* was filmed there.

Torrington is a perfect location to use as a jumping-off point for the beautiful Litchfield Hills. It offers many cultural activities, such as live theater, restaurants (including a pub on site at the Yankee Pedlar), and art galleries. For the traveler who wants the natural beauty of the surrounding area by day, but entertainment by night, Torrington is an ideal location to reside while visiting. Looking for the classic downtown hotel, with a twist of the paranormal? If so, then the Yankee Pedlar is the place to stay.

Tales of Norwichtown

Norwich

Norwichtown, the oldest section in the town of Norwich, is the perfect place for a ghost story. Its colonial houses encircle the town green. The neighborhood is punctuated by the stately Congregational church and high cliff, adorned with a cross, behind it. Behind the row of houses on Elm Avenue is the old burial ground with the earliest stones dating from the 1600s, but most from the eighteenth and nineteenth centuries, including the final resting spots of Samuel Huntington and Benedict Arnold's mother. Next to the graveyard is the expansive Lowthorpe Meadow, public land, which is an exquisite backdrop for a walk.

Although picturesque, this neighborhood's underbelly was exposed in the first volume of *Connecticut Lore*, with ghostly visitations including Benedict Arnold's yearly trip to see his mother on Halloween night, a bygone wake scene witnessed by an out-of-towner in a nearby home, and unexplained cold spots sporadically encountered in the meadow. Hold on to your hats because that was only the tip of

Gravestones protrude at every angle in the Norwichtown Cemetery.

the iceberg. The historic village has many more secrets to be revealed. This neighborhood is so charming that its former residents do not seem to want to leave.

Huntington Lane

On Huntington Lane, which runs into East Town Street, is a lamp post near where several people have seen the image of a sea captain, while others have seen him reflected in the glass. His presence has led certain individuals to avoid the street entirely, even if it means traveling extra miles out of the way to avoid it.

In one house near said lamppost, a gentleman has been seen in the living room. The intruder was witnessed by one guest at the foot of her bed. In the same house a lady wearing a gown has been spotted.

Another figure, a Revolutionary War soldier who some speculate as General Jedediah Huntington, has been spotted walking a few inches above the ground on this road, from the middle of Huntington Lane to its intersection with East Town. The road used to veer off, connecting farther up on East Town. The man has been seen walking through the former road site.

From another very historic home on Huntington Lane, screams have been heard reverberating from an underground well that is connected to another nearby home. Legend has it that someone long ago was thrown down the well to meet an untimely demise.

A home on the corner of East Town and Huntington is the rumored site of the suicide of Faith Trumbull Huntington. Daughter of Governor Jonathan Trumbull (see the chapter on the Lebanon Green for more information on the Trumbull clan), Faith was a troubled young woman whose husband, Jedediah, was off to fight for the Continental Army during the Revolution. She went to Massachusetts to be closer to her husband, but was confounded by the horrors of war. Some accounts say she witnessed the Battle of Bunker Hill, but others say she was only perturbed by the events happening around her where she was staying in Roxbury. She was sent to nearby Dedham where she ultimately took her own life. Other legendary variations depict her suicide happening in the back yard of the family home on the corner of East Town Street and Huntington Lane; other accounts claim it happened in Hartford. If the Norwich version were true, the residence in which the lady in the nightgown is said to haunt would be on her former home's backyard property. For a short street, Huntington Lane has much paranormal activity!

Elm Avenue and East Town Street

At the Simon Huntington Tavern, up the road a bit on the corner of Elm Avenue and East Town Street, many ghostly happenings have occurred. Walking by, onlookers have witnessed a face appear to them in the window. A former proprietor of the home was combing his hair in the bathroom when he noticed his face was not the only one looking back.

Another man dressed in Revolutionary War-era garb was also combing his hair in the mirror as well! The home owner said to the stranger, "Hello Simon," at which point the figure disappeared. Simon died of a snake bite at age twenty-two. Visitors to the house have witnessed figures out of the corners of their eyes. When modern paintings were displayed in the historic home, something was irked, for when the family returned from an outing, the paintings were tilted. This distortion only ceased when the paintings were transferred to a modern part of the home. A local medium, who will be called John, has seen the figure of a heavy-set woman wearing a long white cap and apron, possibly a former innkeeper's wife, on the premises.

Psychically Speaking

Speaking further with the medium, who is very familiar with Norwichtown, gave much insight into the neighborhood. Each time he walks into a home near the corner of Mediterranean Lane and East Town Street he has seen a gentleman waving at him and the spirit of a woman and a little girl next to the stove in the kitchen. He asked the homeowner if the smell of burnt cookies ever permeated through the house. She replied yes, even though the stove was broken. The medium believes that the house was subject to a possible fatal fire and the girl fell victim to smallpox. The homeowner has felt the workings of the little girl by her child's toys being moved around without explanation.

At the First Congregational Church at the head of the green he has seen fifteen to twenty people from the other side sitting in the pews. At the Johnson Home, located across West Town Street from the church, he has witnessed many strange goings-on. He has seen a man wearing gloves and a hat at the home for elderly women. When mentioning the apparition to a staff member, they brought him to see a portrait in the home. The portrait exactly showed the figure he had been seeing, but he had never seen the painting before. He also saw a hole in the floor that he believes was for storing liquor during an earlier incarnation of the building.

One house on the green, which was formerly used as a storage facility, has many otherworldly associations with it. John has seen a gentleman sit by the fireplace holding a Bible. He made special note of the man's buckles on his shoes. It seemed as if the man was a former owner of the home. Chairs have been seen moving on their own. Animals in general can sense presences that many humans cannot, and spirits are drawn to animals, the medium went on to say. The current homeowner's canine companion has been on alert to something unseen in the air.

The Samuel Abbot House on East Town Street has more stories associated with it than those outlined in *Connecticut Lore* Volume 1. John mentioned the family dog here staring off seemingly at nothing. He also took note of a scratching sound in the walls upstairs and seeing orbs around the area of the front door. He spoke of strange occurrences with doors shutting and lights turning on and off. When John spoke to me, he did not look straight into the house; instead he had his head tilted as if to understand better the activity that was going on in the home. The medium talked of a figure walking down the front staircase who had long gray hair and was wearing a tuxedo. This phantasm relayed to John that he tolerates the music being played in the home, although sometimes it is too loud. The ghost also inquired to see if the family could smell the cigar smoke that accompanies his presence. John made it clear that the spirit wants the family to know that he is there. Hours later a smoke smell was detected, but it turned out to be a bonfire next door. The medium also asked if a dog in the house had been sick with an upset stomach and vomiting within the last few days. Pepper, the dog that was visiting the home, did in fact deal with a bout of vomiting for a few days. John said it was due to the dog eating makeup out of the trashcan. He mentioned an African-American man being buried underneath a large tree or near the garage in the backyard. The man was in his thirties or forties and dressed in rags. He was a visitor to the home or neighborhood. A metal stake is near the top of his head, although it could have been severed (which alludes to the story of the man decapitated in that very swamp as written in Volume 1). Others have felt uncomfortable in the evening in an upstairs room. Someone else mentioned feeling a ghostly presence at nighttime in the area between the living room and dining room

as well as in the back yard. She reports of being scared when she has been alone in the home at night.

John has seen things roll across the floor of the school house on the Norwichtown Green without provocation. At the Governor Huntington Home (see the chapter on the Welte family for more information), he mentioned observing the spirits of presumably important people, as well as of a servant on site. The Lowthorpe Meadow behind the Huntington home has seen its share of ghostly visitors as well. John has seen spirits marching towards the meadow, as it was a popular gathering spot in the bygone era. A phantom rider on a white horse frequents the meadow, in addition to Benedict Arnold who visits his mother high atop a white steed every Halloween night. In the adjacent cemetery, the medium has felt a tapping on his shoulder and a slap on his back. In another East Town Street home the medium has witnessed a woman in a ball dress walk down the front staircase.

Also on East Town Street is a house haunted by a benign "healing ghost." Two previous owners, who had had family tragedies prior to moving to the home, found their lives changed for the better in their new environment. When the current owners moved to the house, the oldest daughter would wake up around three o'clock in the morning and start to talk to someone. The parents have also heard voices around that same three o'clock hour.

Norwichtown is much more than a collection of antiquated homes and municipal buildings. Bearing witness to centuries of history, its former inhabitants do not want to leave. Justly so, since this quaint village is a perfectly preserved look into colonial New England.

Tales of a Medium

Norwich

In many places John the medium visits he comes in contact with the departed who once trod over the same parcel of land as we have in the present. Ever since he was a boy, he realized that his ability was precious. Most individuals, even when sharing the same space as him, do not witness what is actually happening in the room. We are lucky to have him share some of his stories with us.

Norwich Parks and Recreation Department's Cemetery Division

While working at a job at the Norwich Parks and Recreation Department's cemetery division, John's vocational duties often included digging graves in preparation for burial. Although much of the real estate within the Yantic Cemetery was claimed years ago, now and again it serves as the location for a recent arrival. As the cemetery worker was excavating the resting place, a dead man approached the worker and told him to dig the hole six inches over from where the hole was currently being dug. The foreman on the project became perturbed over why the worker was not following directions and was starting to dig half a foot from where he was directed. As the medium protested his case, the foreman dug a spade into the assigned spot only to detect the presence of a wooden casket. The project continued albeit six inches from the foreman's initial orders.

While working for the cemetery department, John often saw people from the other side standing around their earthen place of eternal rest.

A Young Visitor

As mentioned, this special power of sorts has been with John since he was a child. At eight years old he shared a room at Yale New Haven Hospital with a young boy in an oxygen tent. One day, alarms went off in the room around the boy. The boy looked at him, winked, and died. A few years later, a relative asked him who the boy was whom he was playing with. It was the boy from the hospital room. Another medium mentioned to John that there was a boy in his truck, the same boy from the hospital. No matter how many years have passed, his deceased roommate still accompanies him. John recounts that whenever he smells what he describes as "oxygen tank plastic," he knows the boy is close.

Sightings

A few years later as a teenager, an apparition of Mary Magdalene came to him in his bedroom and talked to him. John levitated above his bed and after she shared her words, he was put back down. The ability of seeing people from the other side he shares with his mother.

Once, in Taftville, John was in a new house, speaking with a young nurse. He could see her deceased husband who had died tragically. When John inquired, the nurse told him her whole story. Other times he has warned individuals, "Don't get in the car; the tire is loose." Sure enough, the tire was loose. Some have heeded his advice, while others, ignoring his warning, have lost a tire mid-drive.

He has seen apparitions of a male and female child at the Broad Street School. They were happy and just wanted to stay in school, he says. John hears voices when he walks into certain buildings. In most houses, spirits want to stay and, in most cases, they are benign. Other times they appear due to unhappiness or domestic fighting in the home. In front of the Benedict Arnold house (which is a modern home on the Arnold home plot on Washington Street), he has seen in a picture the silhouette of the original structure.

Overall John feels his ability is a gift. The capability to interact and listen to people from the other side has been beneficial to both the departed and those on earth. He finds Norwich an especially intriguing town, one steeped in history and with mystery around every corner. Small family cemeteries like the tiny one on Old Salem Road add to the intrigue. Norwichtown oozes colonial history and the other time periods are represented in the town's variety of neighborhoods.

The Demon House

Enfield

Many notorious hauntings in the state come from years ago, even when talking about highly active spots, such as Union Cemetery and Dudleytown. One of the most memorable and horrifying ghost tales of the present day comes from Enfield. This is the story of the Yaple family. Jay and Elke Yaple had recently moved into a home in Enfield, a place where they would eventually raise a family and care for their two beloved Yorkshire Terriers. Enfield was the seemingly perfect location. A picturesque town just beyond the suburbs of Hartford and Springfield, Enfield is a desirable town for a young family to call home.

The first time that Elke walked into her future home, her reaction was not a positive one. She said it was a place that "you do not want to be (in)." The couple's two Yorkies were extremely nervous in each room they went into, constantly barking, nipping, and growling at seemingly nothing, at least nothing that could be seen with the naked eye. This was the first indication that something was awry in the home.

The first incident that directly affected a family member was when, seven months pregnant, Elke fell down the two stairs that led from the screened-in porch to the outside. Her "fall" was more like a push from phantom hands. She fell squarely on her pregnant stomach; luckily the children were not harmed. Elke was to have twins. In the weeks prior to their birth, her doctor put her on bed rest. While in the home, she constantly observed the restlessness of the two dogs who had never acted that way prior. One day she heard noises while she was lying in bed. She thought her husband was creating the ruckus until she noticed a figure of a black dog from the corner of her eye. Just as quickly as she saw it, the form vanished.

The presence of a black dog harkens back to the tales of the hellhound, a prominent forbearer of death, evil, and wretchedness. This creature is found in the legend of Robert Johnson, purportedly selling his soul to the devil, who cannot shake the "hellhound on his trail." The Black Dog of West Peak in Meriden is another variation of the misery-bringing beast.

Soon the twins were born and the house became calm for a while. But then activity began again and was observed by the twins' babysitter, Michelle. She heard unusual noises and what sounded like someone running up the stairs. The problem was that no one else was home and the young children were fast asleep. Another similar incident occurred when she was playing with the children on the first floor. They pointed to the stairs as the same running sound reverberated from them. She saw shadows on the staircase. This was the final episode witnessed by Michelle, as she could not bear being in the home and quit her babysitting job. Not even the generous hourly wage paid by the Yaple family would keep her in the home another day! A new babysitter was hired to take care of the twins.

One evening Elke heard something she will never forget over the baby monitor while both children were sleeping. At first she heard banging noises followed by, "You're all going to die," clearly stated through the device. When she and her husband checked on the twins, luckily no one, or no-thing was in the room with them, but bloody handprints were discovered on the cribs. As the months progressed, Elke's once jovial and carefree personality took a sharp turn. She started feeling understandably on edge. Her dogs continued to take the brunt of the attacks as well, as they were kicked and pushed.

Jay was baffled by the whole state of affairs. He contacted the town historian to get answers. In working with the historian, Jay found out that the house, which had been built in 1771, had much tragedy associated with it. There had been many deaths connected with the home, from carbon monoxide poisoning to pneumonia to death from complications from an injury. Other freak accidents in the home included a child who choked on their own vomit and someone else being badly burned. In 1919, a woman named Elizabeth fell down the stairs (similar to what happened to Elke), broke her arm, and eventually died. A man named Charles, who lived in the house during the 1930s, was having an affair with a married woman. One day he fatally stabbed her and her husband. Upon his return home, he shot himself dead.

Eventually, the couple contacted a paranormal team from Enfield. One individual from the group felt negative energy at the house and even recorded a dog's bark on the tape recorder (a gruff bark, not a Yorkie yip). While they were there, a loud crash was heard, and the parents rushed up to see blood all over the children's room, but luckily they were not injured. A lamp falling and light bulb breaking caused the smash. There was no explanation regarding the source of the blood.

The chaos was deemed to be demonic in nature. Father Bob Bailey, who is an expert in this realm, was called in as well as members of a Connecticut paranormal group. The EMF meter, which reads energy, was getting responses. Medium Paula O'Brien was also brought in. The energy level was different on the second floor and their video devices even spotted a flying orb. The orb traveled from the master bedroom to the dog. The family dog became possessed, going into a state of shock, convulsing and flailing about. After prayer was directed at the dog, its episode ceased. Two weeks later though, the dogs were acting strangely again, as they were barking, running around, and growling in the middle of the night. One of the two began showing signs typical of rabies, foaming at the mouth and acting dazed. It eventually snapped out of this state as night became morning.

The paranormal team came back to the house and felt a strong presence on the second floor, most emphatically in the girls' bedroom. On EVP (electronic voice phenomena) "Get Out" was clearly heard. Bob Baker, a member of the group, felt severely sick on this visit. As Father Bailey walked through the house, he sprayed holy water in each area. After the administration of blessings and holy water, it seemed that the presence had disappeared. The family still lives in the house and thankfully there has been no reported activity since this time.

While You're There!

A mysterious statue adorns a grave in Broad Brook.

Visit the Book Club in Broad Brook. This is a small independent bookstore with a big heart. This book store has many events, including author readings and book club meetings. It has helpful displays that showcase a certain theme, for example, local interest reads, books by female authors, or books about the Boston Red Sox. It has a well-stocked children's section as well. The Book Club is located in Broad Brook, a section of East Windsor close to the border of Enfield.

Not far from the bookstore is a cemetery where there is a copper statue of a shrouded woman emerging out of a gravestone marked by the last name "Morton."

Makens Bemont House/Huguenot House

East Hartford

The Makens Bemont house, which is also referred to as the Huguenot House, is a fine specimen of eighteenth-century New England architecture and happens to be haunted. The home was built in 1761 by Edmund Bemont and today is located in East Hartford's Martin Park, along with a War World II memorial, the Goodwin Schoolhouse, and the Burnham Blacksmith Shop. All of these structures are owned by the East Hartford Historical Society, with the Bemont House being the oldest. The Bemont House escaped the wrecking ball and was moved here in 1971 from its former location on the corner of Burnside and Tolland Avenues. It was only since the move that this home, in which tragedy was never documented, became restless.

The two main culprits of the ghostly sightings are the Blue Lady (because she wears a blue dress) and Benny, who was nicknamed by workers at the house and who likes to cause a lot of ruckus by banging and clanging around. While the home's location was being transferred, the noises started to occur. What sounded like hammering was such a common sound that the project's foreman eventually gave the spirit a "to do" work list. Sounds often come from the basement and the living room, but also a faceless ghost was seen in a window in the early 1980s by a young girl in Martin Park.

So who are these ghosts? Some speculate that they are the ghosts of the former builders and that the move awoke their desire to work. Others think that the lady in blue is Abigail Bemont, wife of original owner, Edmund, and that Benny is their son. Even the name "Huguenot House" is highly disputed. Legend says that the original Bemont owners were Huguenots, part of a French Protestant sect who were persecuted by the Catholics, which in turn led many to flee France. The reputation that Huguenots had as woodworkers also contributed to the idea that the ghostly noises were caused by the clanging of hammers. In actuality though, the Bemonts were documented to be living in the region since 1654, in Enfield, which at that time was part of Massachusetts. Records do show the name "Bemont" being changed to "Beaumont" in the 1800s to make things sound a bit fancier, which could then have led to the Huguenot claim.

Either way, Bemont or Beaumont, French or English, what we do know is that other than a ghostly reputation, the house is a prime example of New England colonial architecture equipped with fine furnishings from a moderately wealthy family. The Bemont house was in the family until the mid-nineteenth century and the name "Makens Bemont" refers to Edmund's son, who raised his own family in the house.

Makens did quite well for himself as a saddle maker and the period furnishings from his family home during the eighteenth and nineteenth centuries reflect that. The one-and-a-half-story house is painted red with a gambrel roof. Many of the structures are original, and those that are not, are still very old. The interior has wide floorboards and interestingly enough, many closets. It even has on display a wooden yoke that milkmaids would use.

The home is open by the historical society only in the summer months, although if you are walking through Martin Park and see a face in the window or hear an incessant hammering, you will know that although the inhabitants of the Bemont House are long gone, their spirits still resonate today.

Pettibone Tavern

Simsbury

One of Connecticut's most venerable ghosts stems from one of the state's most gruesome murders. In a jealous rage, John Pettibone beheaded his wife, Abigail, after she was found in the arms of another man. Pettibone's Tavern, currently named Abigail's Restaurant, is located at 4 Hartford Road, in the Weatogue section of Simsbury, at the intersection of Routes 10 and 185. The building dates back to 1780, when the tavern was a major stagecoach stop on the route from Albany to Boston, situated in the shadow of Talcott Mountain. Built during the American Revolution, Pettibone has seen the likes of John Adams, George Washington, and Ethan Allen lodge within its walls. During later years, Harriet Beecher Stowe is said to have frequented its guest quarters. Although the tavern has been given different monikers over the years, most famously Pettibone Tavern, it has also been known as the Chart House and most recently, Abigail's. The restaurant's previous incarnation shuttered due to a fire in 2008, the second in its history, as it was also set aflame by hostile Native Americans in the year 1800.

Pettibone Tavern was named for its first owner, John Pettibone. Pettibone earned his keep as a whaling captain. Returning home unexpectedly from a voyage out to sea, he found his beloved wife, Abigail, committing adultery with another man. Not only did Pettibone decapitate his wife with an axe, but he chopped her male companion into miniscule pieces with the weapon as well. Following their murders he cut the head off every portrait of Abigail in the house, including one painting that depicts Abigail as a child sitting on her mother's lap. Abby's head was precisely glued back onto the body in the aforementioned painting in 1973. The portrait is on view at the

Pettibone Tavern is now called Abigail's, named for its resident ghost.

restaurant and can also be seen on its website with clear markings of where the head was reattached.

Although the story of Abigail and her lover's demise is on the horrific side, her ghost borders on the mundane. Its manifestations have included turning on lights unexpectedly, lighting candles, reconfiguring furniture, and the most malicious incident, splintering an antique chair to bits in the dining room. The location of Abigail's murder was Room 6, now the upstairs ladies room. Strange noises have been heard emanating from the water closet. Some visitors have heard a disembodied voice call their names. Others have witnessed shadowy figures, cold spots, and have had the feeling of being watched. Paranormal experts have conducted investigations. Some have been fruitful, calling Abigail's Restaurant home to more than one spectral resident, while others have come up empty-handed without any supernatural findings.

Ghost or not, Abigail's and before it the Pettibone Tavern revel in its phantasmic associations. (Hence the name of the restaurant alone!) If the thrill of spotting Abigail has brought you into the tavern, its oysters, steaks, and pasta dishes will keep you coming back! The classic American fare has been recognized as some of the region's finest. When traveling to Simsbury for ghosts, "while you're there" stay for the food!

Connecticut's Haunted Campuses

Willimantic, New Haven, and Other Statewide Locations

The haunts of Connecticut's educational institutions, be they university or high school, are numerous. New Haven's Yale University and Albertus Magnus College are home to notorious ghosts. Eastern Connecticut State University in Willimantic and high schools in Avon, Plainfield, and Colchester are also known to host paranormal activity. Whether it is from the stress of a challenging curriculum (like today's Common Core standards!) or the stress of a student's social life, school can be a burdensome place!

Eastern Connecticut State University

A reader of mine who attended Eastern shared a story that he had heard around campus. A student named Gertrude "Trudy" Beer jumped from a window at Burr Hall, a dormitory on the campus of what is now Eastern Connecticut State University around the year 1912. Her last words were, "Don't tell my mom," uttered before the leap. Trudy could not deal with the academic and social stressors of college. Since her untimely demise, her spirit haunts the residence. A haunted house was even set up in her honor in the autumn of 2011.

In my research, I found the truth behind this well-known ghost story. Although not far removed, the reality changed things a little. It is true that a student named Gertrude Beer, nicknamed Trudy, jumped from a third-story window to meet her fate on the concrete below. Although the legend speaks of the year 1912, Trudy ultimately met her maker in January of 1940, on the twenty-fifth of the month. Trudy was born in Aliquippa, Pennsylvania, which today is a suburb of Pittsburgh, close to the airport. During her youth, she moved to Rockville, Connecticut, where she graduated from high school and was an active member of the drama club. Her father passed a year before she started college. She decided to attend what was then called Willimantic Teacher's College to pursue her dream career of

teaching. Trudy was known for her bubbly personality and, generally speaking, for her jovial manner. During the school year though, she became withdrawn and depressed. Her social and academic life took a turn for the worse. She felt as though she was an outcast. When she *could* sleep, she was often discovered sleepwalking in the corridors of Burr Hall.

Although the pressure of campus life, along with the stressfulness of college-level tests, caused Trudy much concern, what happened on the early morning of January 25, 1940, still came as a surprise to those who knew her. Rumored to be suffering from social anxiety coupled with the untimely death of her father and academic pressures, Trudy stepped out of a third-story window at Burr Hall. Her body lay crumpled on the concrete walkway below as her screams woke up other dormitory residents. She had multiple compound fractures and her body lay in a state of shock. She was taken to a nearby hospital in Windham only to leave this earth in the early hours of the afternoon the same day. Although the legend places Trudy on campus before she was actually born, her campus life and death were true.

What has followed in the wake of her suicide is the haunting of the residence, even some seventy-five years after her death. Local ghost hunters, with Trudy's help from beyond the grave, say that she is not the only spirit in the residence. Events with unknown origin are commonplace. Toilets flush themselves, lights flicker or turn on and off, heavy breathing is heard, and images of specters are seen in the rooms in Burr Hall. Legends tell of three other girls who all met their fate in the same dormitory: one died from stab wounds, another hanged herself, and the last one was choked to death. Yet another ghost story details the account of a cleaning lady having a heart attack and dying in a broom closet in the dormitory. Ghost hunters speculated that

Trudy is of a benign nature, whereas the others are the ones stirring up the mischief in the student residence.

Today's students are afraid of roaming the halls late at night due to their spectral roommates and are especially unnerved when studying in the common area. Although Trudy last set a physical foot in the hallway of Eastern Connecticut State University many years ago, her presence is still felt today!

Yale University

The state's most prestigious institution, Yale University, may turn away most of its applicants, but it cannot deny its ghostly inhabitants. The most well-known of the school's phantoms is particularly fond of the Newbury Memorial pipe organ in Woolsey Hall, a popular concert space on campus. The organ can be heard playing even when the concert hall is void of human life. Many attribute the ghostly notes to former organist Harry B. Jepson, who was the instrumentalist in the early years of the twentieth century. Even after death, he did not want to be separated from his favorite musical device. The welcome center on Elm Street is also supposed to be visited by someone returning from the grave.

Other Schools

In addition to these well-known haunts, many other campuses throughout the Nutmeg State have ghostly associations. Most schools, especially those that are older than fifty years, may acquire paranormal overtones, heralded or not.

Norwich Free Academy, established in 1854, is said to have a specter who haunts the tower of Slater Museum. The Woodstock Academy also has its share of paranormal leanings. The dormitories of Albertus Magnus are full of visitors from the other side. Prestigious Avon Old Farms School is said to be haunted by a ghost of a girl, ironic for a historic boys-only school! Even the public schools in the area, including Plainfield's public high school and Colchester's, known as Bacon Academy, are said to have their share of unwanted guests. A former student who perished at Plainfield High School is rumored to walk its halls, while the auditorium at Bacon Academy has ghostly connections due to a man who died on site.

The next time I hear of a student "scared" to go to school, I'll completely understand why! All over the state the visitor or prospective school researcher will find something peculiar with their hometown institution of higher learning.

Connecticut's Haunted Offshore Lighthouses
Bridgeport and New London

Lighthouses tend to invoke eerie images, gusting winds, driving rain, and thunder and lightning. The lightning bolt briefly illuminates the sky as only the silhouette of the lighthouse remains. Penfield Reef Lighthouse off the coast of Bridgeport and Ledge Light off the coast of New London evoke even more threatening, isolated feelings, in part because these two unique beacons stand alone in the middle of the ocean. Their deserted location adds to their legendary status. Penfield Reef and Ledge Light are both said to be haunted by former lighthouse keepers who met an untimely fate while keepers of the light.

Penfield Reef Light

Since Penfield Reef Light is more than a mile out to sea, it is disputed what town is actually in command of the lighthouse. Is it Fairfield or Bridgeport? The winner here is Bridgeport. The lighthouse was operated for the first time on January 16, 1874. It led guidance to ships maneuvering around this part of Long Island Sound, which some sailors proclaim as the roughest waters in the whole state. Many a ship had lost its way and was shipwrecked off this troubled coast.

The lighthouse's unique architecture makes it not easy to forget. Its first square floor is constructed of granite with its second floor cast out of wood. The tower protrudes out of the second floor. Its architecture looks as if two lighthouses were haphazardly joined together, sticking the top of a wooden one on the base of a granite one. Rising above the floating waves, Penfield Reef looks especially imposing given its seclusion. Currently, the lighthouse is for sale. Although romantic images of private lighthouse living may appeal to some prospective buyers, under the National Historic Lighthouse Preservation Act, a lighthouse, even one privately purchased, must be available to the public for educational or recreational purposes. Unfortunately Penfield Reef needs much rehabilitation as well. Although the light is technically abandoned, one former keeper still watches over it.

On December 22, 1916, lighthouse keeper Frederick A. Jordan rowed a small boat from Penfield Reef to the mainland so that he could celebrate the Christmas season with his family. Unfortunately, due to the choppy sea and the tumultuous weather, Jordan never made it ashore and was tragically swept out to sea. Worse even was the fact that assistant lighthouse keeper, Rudolph Iten, saw this tragic scene unfold right before him. Due to the immensity of the storm, Iten had to watch, horrified, as nature caused his friend's boat to drift out to sea, out of his reach.

After the passing of Jordan, Iten became the head lighthouse keeper. A short while after the death of his friend, Iten saw a phantom figure come out of Jordan's former room. On another occasion, he saw that his professional journal was moved, and it was opened to the date of Jordan's death. Sporadically, Jordan's ghost has been seen in the lantern room or floating above the reef, especially during squally weather. The light itself is known to have acted tempestuously after Jordan's demise.

Several stories have a positive spin. One tells of a shadowy man rowing a boat and leading a yacht to safety during a rough storm. In another tale, two boys were rowing a boat out by the old lighthouse when it capsized. An unknown man pulled them to the lighthouse and safety. When they were coherent enough to realize what had happened, they could not find anyone around the lighthouse.

Although Jordan may have met his maker due to the turbulent, dangerous waters of Long Island Sound, he seems to be hanging around even in the afterlife.

Ledge Light

Ledge Light in New London rises a stately sixty-five feet high out of the ocean and is a three-story, eleven-room brick structure that sits at the confluence of the Thames River and Fishers Island and Long Island Sounds. Although situated out to sea, driving along harbor roads like Pequot Avenue in New London, the traveler can clearly see Ledge Light. Ledge Light more closely resembles a federal-style house grandiosely stationed at sea, rather than a "typical" lighthouse. Ledge Light was built in 1909 and is located on Southwestern Ledge. It was originally called South Western Ledge Light, but a lighthouse in New Haven already had that name, so a year later it was renamed New London Ledge Light. The Coast Guard took over control of this facility in 1939.

The most notorious story from Ledge Light has to be the one of former lighthouse keeper John Ernie Randolph. Nicknamed Ernie, he married a woman half his age. Legend says that Ernie was not the best husband. His wife was miserable out at the lighthouse, wanting desperately to return to the mainland. Eventually, she ran off with a ship captain to New York. After she left, Ernie's despair led him to slit his own throat "for speaking too much" and fling his body atop the rocks close to the lighthouse.

Although this occurred in the '30s, since his untimely departure strange occurrences have happened throughout the lighthouse. For instance, the foghorn occasionally sounds, even on clear days. Odd noises, electronics turning on and off, doors closing and opening, sheets being torn off a slumbering guest, unusually cold spots, and even a smell like a decomposing body have been experienced. A figure, described as a tall, slender gentleman with a beard, wearing a raincoat and rain hat, has been seen throughout the years. In 1990, a television reporter from Japan visited the lighthouse and was able to hear whispers on tape that were not there in real time.

Stonington's Old Lighthouse Museum

Connecticut's offshore lighthouses are not the only beacons of hope and guidance of note in the state. Stonington's Old Lighthouse Museum is a beautiful structure and is open to the public. Near the aforementioned Pequot Avenue, New London's former Lighthouse Inn is another reputedly haunted locale.

While You're There

If you find yourself tracing the back roads of southeastern Connecticut trying to catch a glimpse of Ernie at his Ledge Light, turn your radio dial to Connecticut College's WCNI radio station which is 90.9 on the FM dial. WCNI plays a bit of everything, from indie and college rock to metal and polka. Make sure to turn into "Uncle Ken's Rummage Sale," which at the time of this writing is on every Tues-

day afternoon from 3:00–6:00 p.m. Be prepared to hear anything from Johnny Cash to Wilson Pickett, "Su-kiyaki" to Sam Smith. Listen in to other great shows like "The Old Wave Show" playing oldies (rock, pop, soul) every Sunday from 3:00–6:00 p.m. I remember as a child fondly listening to this show on our drive home on Sundays from my grandmother's house. Listen to other unforgettable radio personalities like Senslis Killian, Marko, and Gramma. It's a real treat from the preplanned format of most radio stations and can also be found on Internet radio formats such as IHeartRadio.

The Phantom Ship of New Haven Harbor

New Haven

The story of an ill-fated ship that was supposed to bring wealth to the New Haven Colony has remained such fodder for legend that it is still talked about almost 400 years after its supposed occurrence. Although New Haven is regarded through most of its tenure as a successful port city, the early days of the New Haven Colony did not have the same reputation. It was full of mishaps.

Citizens of the New Haven Colony needed some way to bring wealth to their struggling enterprise. They joined together and decided to have a mega ship built in Rhode Island. The townspeople wanted to gather a large collection of goods found in the colony to sell to the folks back in England.

Unfortunately, from the beginning the ship ran into trouble. The boat was massive, but colonists figured the bigger the vessel, the more that could be stored, hence a bigger profit would be paid. There was much hope and currency riding on this voyage. A successful journey meant a bright future for the New Haven Colony. Many individuals sacrificed their livelihood investing for the future to supply the contents of the sellable goods. When the ship was loaded with all the varied wares and goods from the colony, its crew was ready to embark for the open ocean. The journey over the Atlantic would be long and strenuous. The ship left harbor in the winter. At the time of departure, ice had frozen the boat where it was moored. Ice had to be hacked away before it could leave. This should have been a red flag for the crew right away. The large vessel seemed uneasy on the sea as it eventually pushed off from the New Haven harbor. As it drifted into the abyss of Long Island Sound, some folks whispered that the old girl did not seem seaworthy.

The days, weeks, and months were checked off as calendar pages were flipped. As no word was heard about the boat, New Haven's residents began fearing for the worst, thinking they may have lost friends and significant finances that were used to supply the ship with goods. In June, roughly six months after departure (some variations recall the date as a year and a half after embarkation), an apparition appeared during a tempestuous thunder storm. Up in the sky appearing in the clouds was the very boat, albeit a bit worse for wear, tattered and battered. Over the years the same ship has appeared in the sky above the harbor sporadically. So famous was the account that both Cotton Mather and Henry Wadsworth Longellow used it as a focal point in their literary works.

Luckily, the city of New Haven had better luck than the New Haven Colony. Its port was eventually used for trade and transport, making the harbor town successful. Although this event occurred in the 1600s, some folks still say they have witnessed the large ship floating in the sky, seen typically after a thunderstorm with driving winds. If you decide to venture to one of the beautiful or fun oceanside spots, keep an eye on the sky to see if you can witness New Haven's phantom ship.

___

The Search for Lottie Enkin

New London and Old Saybrook

A young girl who was abducted and allegedly killed in the early years of the eighteenth century is rumored to haunt Saybrook Woods. She haunts these woods during the winter months, leaving a trail of bloody footsteps in her wake. Her name was Lottie Enkin, daughter of the proprietor of Wild Goose Tavern. One day, young Lottie went missing. Her vanishing was associated with a curmudgeonly local fellow nicknamed "Old Dreary." After her disappearance, a little girl wearing a blue cape was spotted by folks in the woods. Two men, while hunting, found the decaying remains of Lottie inside a cave. Her arms were broken, her body lay with dregs of food around her, and she wore her blue cape. The legend goes that Lottie still haunts the woods today. If you go walking through Saybrook Woods, watch out for bloodstained footprints in the snow and the ghost of a young girl scampering through.

This story, which can be found in collections of American ghost stories, places Lottie's location in New London in the woods on the west bank of the Thames River. Unfortunately, New London no longer has woods on its riverbanks; it's either commercially, industrially, or recreationally developed. The location of "Saybrook" typically refers to the town of

Old Saybrook, which was originally founded as the Saybrook Colony in 1635. Saybrook Woods Conservation Area does exist, though in Old Saybrook, just off Route 154, across the street from the Exchange Club Skating Pond.

Although the exact location of Lottie's ghost is disputed, beware when walking in the woods of Saybrook Woods Conservation Area in Old Saybrook or on the banks of the Thames in New London.

While You're There!

Visit The Telegraph, a record store in New London, while you are trying to locate the ghost of Lottie. Enjoy searching through the stacks of vinyl for that classic LP or newly released record. Maybe pick up a title by Ghost, The Haunted, or Grim Reaper. Look for live shows that take place in store for indie celebrations like Record Store Day in April; Small Business Saturday, the day after Thanksgiving; or New London's annual indie music showcase, The I AM Festival. Also featured are prominent local artists in the thriving New London music scene. Groups like Fatal Film, Paul Brockett Roadshow, the Can Kickers, and Violent Mae are cornerstones of the small city's music showcase.

The Wonders of Woodbury

Woodbury

Woodbury's Main Street oozes with New England charm. With churches, antique stores, inns, and restaurants, this is a perfect town to visit for the traveler looking for a charming slice of ideal Connecticut. Pulling back the layers of the perfect town, Woodbury reveals its underbelly with tales of ghosts, witches, and public beatings.

The Episcopal Church was founded in Woodbury in 1740, but the present-day building of St. Paul's initial construction was completed in 1785 (although it was not fully completed until the early nineteenth century). The church is at 294 Main Street South, which, if heading from the south, is on the right side of the road. The white church is flanked by an old cemetery to its left. The cemetery is deceptively large, as it continues down the hill with the newer stones toward the back and abuts Glebe House Road.

My trip there was in the middle of a pouring rain storm, which gave the site an eerie feeling. The church itself is opposite, bright, bathed in white paint, and cheerful inside with two rows of pews. The church is noted for its balcony and foyer with chandelier. It is home to many study groups, although the cemetery next door is reputedly haunted by an angry spirit.

Witch of Woodbury

Woodbury is also the home to the "Witch of Woodbury," Moll Cramer. The legend goes that Moll caused unusual events to transpire. For instance, if she were in a particularly sour mood, she could sabotage whatever project her husband was working on without lifting a finger. Her husband, Adam, was a local blacksmith. Eventually, stories of Moll circulated around Woodbury, causing Adam to lose valuable business and eventually led him to kick out Moll and their son, who was also supposedly cavorting with Satan.

Afterwards, she spent years living in the woods in a small hut, close to the present Roxbury town line near Route 317. After her eviction by her husband, she became a beggar in downtown. She was said to curse those who did not comply with her requests. In one particular case, she asked for a morsel of pork. When the passerby did not comply, his swine would

This cemetery in Woodbury has ghostly associations.

not become fat, no matter how much food they ate. During her lifetime, storms never hit the town of Woodbury, but as soon as she disappeared, Woodbury was ravaged by tempests.

The Glebe House

Unfortunately, Moll Cramer was not the only resident to be treated savagely by fellow citizens. The Glebe House was home to the Reverend John Rutgers Marshall. Marshall, suspected of being a Tory during the American Revolution, was routinely beaten due to his beliefs.

The Glebe House is on Hollow Road off Route 6. A "glebe" is a piece of land that is given to a member of the clergy currently in office. This gambrel-roofed home was built in 1740, but is said to have sections of it dating from much earlier. The Glebe House is the birthplace of the American Episcopal Church. In 1783, Reverend Marshall called together a secret meeting of ten clergymen at the house to elect the first bishop of Connecticut and

the American Episcopal Church: Reverend Samuel Seabury. This move helped break the Episcopal Church from the Church of England and led to one of the foundations that America was built on: the separation of church and state. Today's Glebe House is a museum loaded with period furnishings that is open for tours and even has a gift shop!

The Glebe House is full of spirits. Some have witnessed an African-American woman, most likely the spirit of a slave who once lived on the premises. Due to the location of the graveyard across the street (that, as previously mentioned, is haunted), ghosts tend to come and go from one location to the next. Legend says that walkway stones in the garden are actually former headstones that irritated those folks whom the stones once marked. Speculation is that these angry ghosts also haunt the Glebe.

Although known for its specters, the Glebe House is even more well-known due to its Gertrude Jekyll-designed garden.

The famed Glebe House in Woodbury.

Jekyll was a British horticulturist and the premier landscape garden architect of her time. This is the only garden in the States designed by her. The horticultural display includes iris, lamb's ear, and lavender. Jekyll designed the garden in 1926, but her plans were not completely followed until the 1970s when they were unearthed.

While You're There!

Up the road at 860 Main Street South is the outlet of Woodbury Pewter. Inside the store you can view the factory floor where the pewter is made. The store does not only sell Woodbury Pewter, but includes ware from pewtersmiths across the country and other gift items. The outlet has existed since 1952. The company's first outpost was at a blacksmith's shop. Watch the informational videos inside the store, and then look at the historic photos and the newspaper clippings that adorn the walls. Fac-

tory seconds can allow the buyer to purchase a piece of Woodbury Pewter at a fraction of the retail cost. While I was there, I saw pewter mugs, cups, ladles, chalices, candle holders, and dishes with pewter handles. My favorite had to be the pig-shaped butter dish.

Thomaston Opera House

Thomaston

This opera house, even without a resident ghost, would seem imposing. Its Richardsonian Romanesque architecture emphasized by its tall square tower protruding skyward screams, "Look at me." Although today, popular shows and theatrical performances like *The Buddy*

Holly Story, Winnie the Pooh, and *A Christmas Carol* by the Landmark Community Theater grace its stage, rumors circulate that the action on the stage is not the only activity that this theater bears witness to. To add to its reputation, the opera house was built on top of a cemetery!

On my visit to Thomaston it did not help that the backdrop was a gloomy gray October day with spitting rain adding to the foreboding and imposing aura of the opera house. It looks more at home on a European city block in a place like Amsterdam than the centerpiece of Thomaston, a former mill town in Litchfield County. The town is named for Seth Thomas, an entrepreneurial clock manufacturer whose keepers of time adorn world-renowned locales, such as New York City's Grand Central Station. One reason the building looks so reverential is the fact that the three-stories-tall structure almost sits on the sidewalk; there is not much room between the front of the opera house and the nearby swath of concrete.

Thomaston's crown jewel was erected in 1884, designed by Robert Hill of Waterbury. It was used as a venue for live theater into the 1930s, but then spent time as the Paramount Theater, a movie house, only to reopen again as a performance space for live theater by 1938 due to the opening of a nearby movie theater. It has spent most of its life as a theater venue. Placed on the National Register of Historic Places in 1972, the building almost met its fate by the wrecking ball on more than one occasion. In 1963, it was closed due to fire code violation. Citizens rallied together to save its brick façade from a case of urban renewal. By 1968, the opera house was back on its feet with a rededication that took place that year. All of the renovations were handled by volunteers. Just like today, the opera house was a source of extreme pride for the town of Thomaston. In 1991, the building was condemned after closing in 1985, once

The tower of the Thomaston Opera House proudly reaches towards the sky.

again for another fire code violation during a run of the Thornton Wilder classic *Our Town.*

Throughout its existence, the Opera House held various uses, including a dance hall, a meeting space, a high school graduation venue, and a vaudeville theater. Rumor has it that famed opera singer Enrico Caruso's voice once echoed off its walls. The theater seats 564. Inside, its ornate ceilings and walls are truly timepieces. In 1971, the Connecticut Valley Theater Organ Society installed a pipe organ. The building that holds the opera house also contains the town hall. The theater is on the second floor. During Christmastime, its perimeter glows with white lights.

Although the building is impressive in itself (and it really is) its reputation precedes it. Many stories swirl about the premises. Some say a ghost of an elderly caretaker of the firehouse next door haunts the building. Actors and workers have complained of hearing peculiar noises. Another patron, Butch, who does not want to leave, has his own seat that is on the left side of the balcony where a plaque is said to mark his seat. Legend of a fire sweeping through the theater is said to have been the impetus of some of the ghostly apparitions. One employee alone in the theater late at night heard footsteps and saw a doorknob turn only to find no one there. Another story tells of a fireman who hanged himself in the attic of the theater and whose body is still heard swinging to and fro causing loud banging noises that emanate from above. In actuality, these odd noises have been likened to shutters swaying in the wind. Finally, the pipe organ has mysteriously played by itself.

Who exactly is Butch? Could he be the caretaker or the ill-fated fireman? Or is he a hapless soul whose final resting place was taken over by the construction of the building. Either way, he or his minions are certainly creating quite the stir in Thomaston.

Just like other majestic old opera houses, such as the beautiful Goodspeed Opera House in East Haddam and the unfortunately abandoned Sterling Opera House in Derby, Thomaston Opera House ranks among the state's finest. Come to Thomaston to catch fine live community theater, make sure to marvel at the interior and exterior of this gem, but keep an eye peeled for Butch!

▶ The theater is located at 158 Main Street in Thomaston.

While You're There!

The Railroad Museum of New England is a must visit for the train enthusiast while in the Thomaston area. It operates the scenic Naugatuck Railroad, which runs from Thomaston to Waterbury. The train takes passengers on a ride through history as it uses classic railroad cars on a historic track. The locomotives range from steam to diesel. The museum depicts both the area in which the railroad is located as well as notable train equipment and artifacts. It is located in the gorgeous Victorian-era Thomaston train station. Santa even comes for a ride around Christmas. Look out for special tours like the one that stops at the Haight-Brown Vineyard in Litchfield.

Warren Occult Museum

Monroe

Connecticut has a museum for almost everything, from tobacco and cartoon characters to locks and dinosaurs. The state also features a collection of its most notoriously haunted memorabilia. It would be only fitting that its museum of the occult would be in the home of the world's premier ghost hunters, Ed and Lorraine Warren. Although Ed has passed on, Lorraine still lives in the home and still gives presentations on her ghost-hunting experiences. This museum's collection represents artifacts culled from their years investigating some of the most notorious paranormal cases ever. The museum is a mish-mash of items related to their ghostly investigations.

The Warrens' resume includes the *Amityville Horror* house, Union Cemetery in Easton, and the Perron family case in Rhode Island, which became the basis for the film *The Conjuring*. Their most extreme demonic possession investigation comes directly from the latter case, which focuses on a Raggedy Ann doll, "Annabelle." This doll is said to have caused human death and personal injury. In the film, it was a creepy, lifelike female doll, but in actuality it is a commonplace Raggedy Ann. After one visitor taunted the doll, he perished in a motorcycle accident on the way home.

The doll first appeared odd to a young woman and her roommate after it was given to her by her mother. The doll would shift positions while they were out. Soon after, the doll began to write messages. Eventually, the girls contacted a medium who found that the possession of the doll was by the spirit of seven-year-old Annabelle Higgins. The doll attacked a male friend while he was sleeping in their home.

The Warrens were called in by the urging of a priest. They found that this doll was not actually inhabited by a little girl, but instead by an inhuman demon. The maleficent demon was trying to find a human host! The Warrens extricated it from the house to put in custody in their museum. The doll still moved by itself inside their home. It is now protected under glass in their basement collection.

A visit to the museum is by appointment only; for more information log on to www. warrens.net. The website also features information regarding talks given by Warren. Other pieces in the collection include mannequins, paintings done by Ed that are all inspired by cases the demonologist has worked on, and seemingly normal statuary. The case files of their ghost hunts are also housed in the collection, as well as an organ that played by itself. The Warrens were devout Catholics, who had complete faith in God, but conversely knew the forceful pull of evil. Spirits are often conjured by Oujia boards. Many times these "games" are the reason why negative energy is brought into a home. Although the malevolent ghost encounters become the most publicized, many are benign.

From one corner of the state to the next, unusual museums dot the landscape of Connecticut, although none as wicked as the Warren Occult Museum. The Warrens have become the fabric of the folkloric landscape of Connecticut. This museum is not only a showcase of items associated with their cases, but also a tribute to the legacy they have left. Before shows like *Ghost Hunters*, *Ghost Adventures*, and a slew of others, there was Ed and Lorraine. Today their daughter and son-in-law follow in their footsteps and assist with Lorraine's presentations. For a long look into the life and artifacts of this intriguing couple, a visit to the Warren Museum is a must.

Jesus Trees, An Elusive Golf Course, and the Lincoln Oak

Danbury, Wallingford, and New Haven

Jesus's visage has appeared everywhere from toast to windowpanes. Connecticut has three different trees where he has shown up. Down the road from the most celebrated site is a golf club that is rumored to have cult-like associations; and in New Haven, when an old tree fell, skulls and bones, along with its ancient roots, were unearthed.

The stretch of road that begins as Federal Hill Road in Brewster, New York, and becomes Joe's Hill Road in Danbury has its share of eerie associations. Locals in the Danbury area remember seeing a tree that looked like Jesus crucified on the cross as they drove from the New York border into Connecticut. The dead tree, located in the Aunt Hack neighborhood of Danbury, was a must-see for those growing up in town in the '70s and '80s. Unfortunately, it was cut down in the '90s, although legend says that when it was removed, a red blood-like substance emerged from its core. Twelve other trees that flanked the Jesus tree, equally spaced apart, are thought to represent Jesus's twelve Apostles.

The road also has ghost stories associated with it. Nearby Farrington's Pond has been the final destination for motorists distracted by something on the road and unintentionally landing in the water. One of those hapless drivers was a young girl on the way to her prom. On certain moonlit nights it is said that a prom dress can be seen hovering over the shimmering surface of the pond. A man was also found in a car, dead via gunshot wounds, by the banks of the pond.

Although the Jesus Tree has been removed and the other legends could be chalked up to just that, the elusive Morefar Back O'Beyond Golf Club still remains— as mysterious as ever. The story goes that this was the estate built in the 1960s, of Cornelius van der Starr, founder of what would become AIG, whose golf course was designed for his golf-loving wife. Today, the former estate, still containing an impressive sculpture garden, is a golf club, albeit an extremely prestigious one. Those golfers who have played on the nearby public course in which certain holes of Morefar can be seen, never see golfers on the greens of the secretive club. Although still open, it has no website and is reserved for only a few golfers, typically heads of big businesses and banks. It is under the control of Starr International headed by Maurice Greenberg, former CEO of AIG. These greens and clubhouse are utilized more for business deals than utilizing the 1-wood. Given its clandestine nature, satanic and cult practices have been associated with the property. Rumor has it that the golf club is a front for the real goings-on happening there. The estate, said to have been built by Chinese workers, has a curious name. The hypothetical reason for the name harkens back to its construction; when asked how far the estate was, the workers with little grasp of the English language would say "more far."

Continuing the Jesus theme, a branch of a tree was cut on North Main Street in Wallingford. Two years later, in the notch left by the missing branch, the face of Jesus appeared. The bearded visage is said to have been created by the tree's sap.

New Haven's Wooster Square, known for its cherry blossoms and close proximity to the nation's best pizza, also has a Jesus Tree. This one is best seen at night illuminated by a nearby light and depicts Jesus on the cross. His face is outlined in a knot of the tree while his outstretched arms are represented by off-shooting branches.

This is not New Haven's most famous tree though. The Lincoln Oak, named for the former president, was planted in commemoration of his 100th birthday in 1909 on the town green. This green actually has thousands of unmarked bodies underneath it. The stones were moved to the Grove Street Cemetery in 1821, but the remains were never reinterred. [For more about this, see the chapter "Center Church on the Green" from the original *Connecticut Lore*.] Superstorm Sandy did much damage to the state when it hit in autumn of 2012. On the evening before Halloween of that year, a woman walking on the Green noticed that a large oak tree had toppled due to the storm. The tree, later to be identified as the Lincoln Oak, had something unusual sticking from its unearthed root ball. The police were called and a group of spectators gathered. What was at first assumed to be animal bones was proved more grisly when a human skull, rib cage, and teeth were soon uncovered. All in all, seven individuals' resting places were exposed when the tree toppled. The last bodies were interred here in the 1700s, and the thought is that these seven dated from the 1790s. The remains included men, women, and children, who experts believed could have succumbed to a disease outbreak like the rash of scarlet fever cases that hit New Haven in 1794. The former cemetery that is now the Green was said to have also been a secret location of small pox burials. In addition, two time capsules were brought to light with the tree removal. One capsule contained memorabilia relating to Abraham Lincoln, while the other's contents included coins, a medal, and letters. Former State Archeologist Nick Bellantoni led a panel discussion on Halloween 2013 regarding the discoveries made from the Lincoln Oak. In the place of the fallen Lincoln Oak, a pin oak sapling was planted.

While You're There!

Over the years, the Keeler Tavern in Ridgefield (which is close to Danbury) has traversed the path of American history, but it is literally embedded with British history. The building, which dates from 1713, was turned into a tavern in 1772 by Timothy Keeler. It had seen use as an inn through different incarnations until famed architect Cass Gilbert bought the property in 1907. He added the extensive brick-walled, sunken garden that is ornamented by a statue of a cherub in 1910 and a garden house. Among Gilbert's noted designs are the Woolworth Building in New York City, the Detroit Public Library, and the United States Supreme Court. After the Gilberts' tenure in the home, the building was eventually bought by a group of concerned citizens in 1965 and turned into a museum the following year.

History abounds at the tavern and museum. Jerome Bonaparte, who was the youngest brother of Napoleon, even vacationed at the inn for his honeymoon. The building's most notable feature though is its British cannonball lodged into a post, which can be seen today. The Battle of Ridgefield was fought here in 1777. The Redcoats fired upon the tavern since the basement was used for musket ball manufacture.

Today's museum has extensive archives and documents on the Keeler, Resseguie (another inn proprietor family), and Gilbert families. It also houses period pieces and artifacts from eighteenth and nineteenth centuries when the tavern and inn were in use.

The Tell Tale Apples

Franklin

Have you ever seen or tasted a "Mike" apple? When you take a bite of a Mike, its interior reveals a red spot, somewhat reminiscent of a drop of blood. The nickname Mike comes from the story of Micah Rood, a Yankee farmer who lived in what is now Franklin, Connecticut, in the early 1700s. Franklin is a rural town, with only a few roads bisecting it. Much of the town even today is comprised of farms and woodland. Rood lived in an area of town close to the center known as Peck Hollow. This heavily forested area is cut through by the Susquetonscut Brook.

In 1759, Franklin was still part of the town of Norwich. A peddler came to the hamlet to sell his wares. As the night was beginning to fall, he realized that he needed a place to stay for the evening, for the center of Norwich was miles away. Some local residents suggested that he ask the local farmer, Micah Rood, if he could house him for the night. Rood was a reclusive, hermit-like farmer, but obliged in housing the foreign salesman.

The next morning, the peddler was found dead next to an apple tree in Rood's orchard. He had been beaten, with his head split open, and his goods had been stolen. Many speculated that Rood had done the dirty deed, but it could not be proven. Some said that the traveler was French due to his accent and that Rood was especially belligerent towards Frenchmen since his father had been killed in the French and Indian War. One theory was that Rood thought the peddler was actually a spy from Canada. As the days slipped into weeks, no one was ever charged for the death of the salesman, and eventually the grisly murder was nearly forgotten by the townspeople. The winter came and went. When spring arrived, the blossoms on the apple trees in Rood's orchards were streaked with red. In the autumn, when the very same trees bore fruit, each of the scrumptious apples had red blotches staining the interior. The trees in his orchard were silent witnesses to Rood's heinous act whose apples showed proof of Rood's guilt. Some say the apple trees of Peck Hollow still bear bloody fruit today.

Although the fact that the apples still have red interiors is up for argument, what is fact is that there are still apple trees growing in Peck Hollow. The apples are not the only otherworldly happening in this small, rural area. Along the road, there is a foundation and a well that is said to belong to a witch. Move the stone over the top of the well and listen for the eerie sounds.

While You're There!

Nearby Bozrah is home to one of the state's greatest farmers markets. The Bozrah Farmers Market runs every Friday evening during the warmer months. It has an eclectic mix of food vendors—from gourmet grilled cheese to Hosmer Mountain Soda, from Lazizah Bakery to farm fresh produce. There is nothing better on a gorgeous summer evening than wandering from booth to booth, sampling the delicacies of the market.

Musical entertainment provides a backdrop and wagon rides are enjoyed by visitors of all ages. Dogs are allowed, and even encouraged, as it seems most visitors bring theirs. The volunteer staff are very friendly and there is a good chance you will make a friend or two before you leave! In the past, one evening has featured an "Authors Night" where local authors showcase their work. The location at 45 Bozrah Street in Bozrah also has trails perfect for walking those pooches while the market is in session and even when it is not.

Great Hill (Hookman's Cemetery)

Seymour

As a teenager, legend tripping was one of my absolute favorite activities. I would spend days with friends traipsing to all corners of my home state. I was able to combine my love for exploration and travel while finding places that had eerie undertones due to their accompanying lore. I was well versed in the subject: Did I know about the White Lady of Union Cemetery? Of course. Dudleytown? You really think I don't know about that one? The Green Lady of Burlington? Uh-huh. As the years passed and my interests shifted more to food and nature walks than ghosts and goblins, I could never forget one notorious location that I had been told about years earlier: Hookman's Cemetery.

During one of my trips gallivanting from one side of Connecticut to the other, I stumbled upon Hookman's. En route to Union Cemetery from Carousel Gardens

Restaurant (also reputedly haunted, also in Seymour) our party had to stop to refuel. Maybe a bit loud, boisterous, or dare I say it, obnoxious, one of us proclaimed to anyone listening that we were going "ghost hunting." (Attracting so much attention, even at that age I found myself becoming embarrassed.) My friend's decree did not fall on deaf ears. One young woman overheard his remark while washing the windows of the gas station convenience store. She proceeded to tell us about Hookman's Cemetery, which in her variation included the slaughter of a family (named Hookman) that took place either at the cemetery or elsewhere, with the family buried at the cemetery. In either case, the massacre of the family led to macabre hauntings. The young woman we spoke to had not seen anything yet, but her friend's brother was witness to a maleficent spectacle where he left barely escaping with this life. (Why is it that a friend of a friend always witnesses these fantastic events?) She stressed the importance of the care that we needed to take if we dare seek this out.

We didn't want to stray from our itinerary since the White Lady was the crème de la crème of our journey, but months later we ventured back to Seymour in search of the notorious Hookman's Cemetery. At this time, when it took half an hour for an Internet page to load, any search for this haunted locale online came back fruitless. I also had not read about it in any books. After a bit of digging, I found directions online that were vague. When we finally arrived in Seymour, we searched and searched, but could not locate Hookman's Cemetery. (Oh the days before GPS!)

So what really is the story of the Hookman family and their cemetery? The cemetery is actually called Great Hill Cemetery; it dates from the 1700s and is where many of the town's settlers are interred. So why the Hookman name? Numerous variations of the story appear, with seemingly similar features to the original tale that I heard at the gas station. A similar spin on the tale I heard featured a son who murdered his whole family and lived in the house behind the cemetery that used to belong to the caretaker. One variation includes a cemetery caretaker with the last name of "Hookman" who was unjustly accused of committing a crime and then hanged himself. Another version depicts the cemetery caretaker with a hook for a hand, who allegedly killed a boy by hanging him from a tree with a hook impaling him. Yet another take is that a man was killed and was found hanging, dangling by a hook.

The caretaker today said that the stories are nothing more than "fairy tales created by teenage vandals." If anyone should be upset, it should be he since in almost all the variations, the cemetery caretaker gets a raw deal. Marian O'Keefe, the town historian, said she was unfamiliar with any haunted tale and only knew it as a cemetery with many historical connections. Those who have witnessed strange goings-on at Hookman's have attested to seeing figures hanging from trees, ghostly presences, orbs, and scratching sounds, possibly from a hook.

The Hookman story is Connecticut's take on the classic urban legend of "The Hook." The tale begins that one evening while parking, a young couple became startled by a "Breaking News" story on the radio. The broadcast spoke of a killer who had just escaped an asylum for the criminally insane and was on the loose. A scraping sound is heard on the side of the car, and the girl insists that her boyfriend take her home. When they arrive at her house, they see that there is a bloody hook dangling from the door handle.

Whichever variation you believe (or do not believe), Hookman's is a must for any ghost hunter.

UFO Sightings

Statewide

Was the giant cigar-shaped object that was seen floating above the skies of Meriden for thirteen minutes on July 28, 1956, truly a spaceship from another planet, a piece of aerospace technology, or a hoax? Unidentified aircraft have been viewed in all corners of the state. From Bethel and Torrington to Franklin and Suffield, these oddities are seemingly everywhere! UFO enthusiast John Greenewald has painstakingly researched accounts of unknown objects from outer space on his website, The Black Vault. Declassified UFO case reports by the government have been released as Project Blue Book. The Air Force has looked into many of the cases and were able to discredit most of them. Of the 12,000 cases listed, 701 of them remain without a proper explanation.

Speculated UFO sightings increased after World War II, as the military was in earnest testing new flying technology. Unusual-looking objects were spotted in the sky. Many of the cases were linked to the military testing, other aircraft, or were simply hoaxes or hallucinations. Or were they? Some folks think that the government does what it can to shield the public from the knowledge of true UFOs. Although there may have been a burst of sightings post World War II and during the Cold War, the witnessing of UFOs continues today.

Connecticut's more well-known cases stemmed from the 1950s and '60s. In 1968, a Cheshire man named Sterling Jewett witnessed an unusual object hovering about forty-five feet in front of him on Mount Sanford Road. In the Norwich area, on March 28, 1954, what looked like a metallic object was seen spinning in the sky. Not only was this seen by folks in Norwich, but also in Moosup, Jewett City, Plainfield, Danielson, Wauregan, and Goodyear. Observers reported that it was

flying for over an hour and was so bright that they needed to cover their eyes. Others said that it was leaving a trail of red fire in its wake. This case became newsworthy due to the length of time and number of individuals who saw the unknown object. The Air Force emphatically stated that it was not a craft from another planet, but instead was either a meteor or a weather balloon. In July 1956, a man in Windham witnessed two crafts collide.

The hydroelectric dam on Waldo Road in Scotland is an imposing structure. I remember as a teenager on a drive stumbling upon it and being in awe. The area of Waldo Road near the dam has been the site of unexpected occurrences and unknown eerie lights. Due to this phenomena, some citizens of Scotland believed that the dam was actually used as a charging station for UFOs! Nuns who worked in Baltic used this road while traveling from Scotland. They saw something on this road that they would never discuss, although after the event, they never drove on Waldo Road on the way to Baltic again! Other old-timers from Scotland witnessed similar spectacles and would not talk about what they had seen either.

From one end of the state to the other, although the government has ruled out the possibility, UFOs have been spotted. Windham County has been a hotbed of this activity. Add the presence of UFOs to the long list of other abnormalities that already include ghosts and locations with satanic associations that have been witnessed in this corner of the state. The next time you go for a drive on the back roads or highways of Connecticut, keep one eye on the road ahead and the other on the sky. You'll never be sure exactly what you may spot!

Dens of the Devil

Sterling, Plainfield, Weston

I was a guest on the *Colin McEnroe Show* on WNPR, Connecticut Public Radio, Halloween 2013. He posed the question to state historian Walter Woodward, author David Leff, and yours truly about what we thought was the most haunted section of the state. A few ideas were tossed around. The Warrens typically consider the Easton/ Fairfield/Monroe triangle as the spookiest, with the White Lady of Union Cemetery at the epicenter. I threw out the idea of East Haddam, with the Moodus Noises, Johnsonville, Gillette Castle, and the abandoned resorts all being eerie sites. Colin instead brought up a town that none of the rest of us had thought of: Sterling. Unlike East Haddam and Monroe, which are in more heavily populated areas of the state, today's Sterling is comprised of Pachaug State Forest and farms. After a quick moment reflecting, I felt that the answer made sense. With all of the ghost stories of Pachaug, Hell Hollow Road, and Maud's Grave, he was onto something. In my personal experience on Halloween night 2003, I saw a strange shaft of light rising from the sky (which probably was some kind of spotlight). Colin even mentioned that people had declared to him the presence of a space-time vortex in the town! The area of Sterling, Voluntown, and Plainfield certainly do have their share of otherworldly associations.

The Lair of Satan

Although the following story is not as sci-fi as a space-time vortex, it still showcases another eerie locale within the small town. In colonial days, close to the Oneco center of town was a cave within two clefts in a rock ledge. This odd structure the townsfolk of Sterling conjectured, was the lair of Satan. This 100-foot in diameter cave, unlike Satan's typical abodes, was always cold in temperature. The cave had an even smaller area inside it that was said to be the Devil's clubhouse. The colonials were impressed by the acoustics of the cave.

Devil's Den, Gravity Hill

Devil's Den of Sterling no longer exists due to the quarrying of granite in the area, but Plainfield, the neighboring town, does have its own rock structure also donned with the moniker of "Devil's Den." It is a much smaller cave near the vicinity of Hell Hollow Road. As mentioned in an earlier story, the diabolical place names, including Hell Hollow, Devil's Den, and Mount Misery, were actually in reference to the poor farming quality of the soil and not the presence of evil.

Also in the area of Sterling is what is known as a Gravity Hill, a place where witchcraft associated with a certain area seems to push a car up the hill. At the corner of Main Street and Snake Meadow Road, face your car south on Main Street from that intersection, stop the car, and put it in neutral at the site of the first telephone pole, which is just past the 35 mph sign. The car should start moving uphill all by itself. Some area residents say this is a natural pull where others speak of a witch named Margaret Henry who, through enchantment, causes unwanted cars to be pulled uphill. She even has a nearby road named after her. Is the car actually bewitched? Is the car being pushed uphill or is this an optical illusion? Two of my staff members (my parents) made the trip to the wilds of Sterling, found the spot, and to their surprise, the car started moving up the hill! They found it to be very spooky and had to quell their fear with ice cream cones at Ekonk Hill Turkey Farm's market.

Another Devil's Den is a serene nature preserve on the other side of the state in the town of Weston. The official name is the Lucius Pond Ordway's Devil's Den Preserve. It is run by the Nature

Conservancy and is the largest preserved land in the area. A beautiful piece of land, especially in autumn, it is marked by a large pond, waterfalls, trails, and an assortment of flora and fauna. Devil's Den is where colonists from Redding and Weston hid from advancing British troops. The Devil's cloven hoofprint was left in a boulder in the preserve, which is how the refuge earned its name.

Section 3
Unusual
History

The Norwich Firearm Industry

Norwich

The idea of Connecticut being a hotbed for manufacturing comes as no surprise. Some of the state's largest cities are recognized for the goods they are known for: the Brass City (Waterbury), the Hardware City (New Britain), and the Thread City (Willimantic). Did you know that firearms were a major industry in the state? Hartford is home to Colt and New Haven has Winchester.

Although Norwich's nickname is the Rose City, and its primary manufacture was textiles, a real shock may be that it too was a major manufacturer of firearms. Even though the name "Smith and Wesson" may conjure up images of the Old West, or at least Springfield, Massachusetts, the original home to the industry giant was Norwich!

Connecticut was a prime location for industry, mainly based on its geography. With major rivers, like the Connecticut, Housatonic, and Thames, cutting through the landscape, it had a natural source of power built in. Connecticut is ideally placed between two major metropolises, New York and Boston, and had a steady stream of skilled labor and manpower to work the factories. Norwich's locality was ideal for all of these reasons, but even more so since it was situated at the confluence of three rivers, where the Yantic and the Shetucket join to form the mighty Thames. Steamboat travel and transport ruled the waterways in the 1800s, and the port of Norwich was a major player in this scene. It was ideally located not only on an important steamboat route, but also on the New London-Norwich-Worcester railroad line.

Norwich's once-thriving downtown today is littered with abandoned and semi-abandoned buildings, sparked with sporadic signs of revitalization. Among the permanent vacancies on Franklin Street stands the former Hopkins and Allen firearms factory. Of the twenty gun manufacturers that at one time called Norwich home, Hopkins and Allen was the city's most successful, calling the city home from 1866 to 1915. Rumor has it that the empty factory space on Franklin Street once contained a basement-level firing range and that underneath a nearby paved lot lay piles of defective Hopkins and Allen guns. This company was to supply guns to the Belgian army during World War I, but the country was soon overrun by Germany. Hopkins and Allen did supply the rifles for the Belgian government while it was in exile during Germany's occupation of the country during the Great War. The Norwich company ended up folding in 1915 and was bought by another Connecticut gun manufacturer. In its heyday it made rifles, pistols, and revolvers.

Although Connecticut's most famous gun maker has to be Colt, headquartered in Hartford and whose building is known for its blue onion dome, Norwich was known as the center of firearm manufacture in New England. The first gun was produced in this town in 1798. Also early on, Elijah Backus founded the Norwich Iron Works, which made cannons and anchors for the navy. The gun industry did not blossom fully in Norwich until the 1840s. In addition to Allen and Hopkins, other Norwich gun makers included Smith and Wesson, Allen and Thurber, and Christopher Brand, which made whaling guns. Allen and Thurber started manufacturing in town and stayed until the company moved to Worcester in 1847. An employee of this company was Horace Smith, who later teamed with Daniel Wesson to create their own firearm brand in 1852. Smith and Wesson, in partnership with others, began the "Volcanic Repeating Arms Company." In 1856, they broke away from the company and reclaimed the name "Smith and Wesson." (The Volcanic Repeating Arms

Company eventually became Winchester.)

Richard T. Addison, a writer in the mid 1800s, took a long look at the manufacture of guns by the Norwich Arms Company, describing each painstaking step in the process. It is easy to forget that firearm manufacture was made by laborers who were skilled at a particular job, and not made by machines. The same writer likened Norwich to a summer resort. While the name "Norwich" may no longer appear in the same sentence as "summer resort," the stately mansions he describes still line Broadway and Washington Streets and are reminders of Norwich's former opulence.

Colonel Charles A. Converse is an important figure in the history of Norwich. He was one of the founders of Hopkins and Allen. Converse left a sum of money to the town's high school, Norwich Free Academy, to build an annex to Slater Memorial Museum. This building, named for Converse, houses art exhibits throughout the year. The main gallery in Converse is home to the Connecticut Artists Show, an annual juried exhibition featuring the state's artists. Slater Museum also showcases a large collection of antique firearms. Converse's house is on the National Register of Historic Places and is noted for its High Victorian Gothic architectural style.

Colt Armory

Hartford

Born and raised in Hartford, Samuel Colt brought Connecticut into the age of industry. His legacy in the capital city can be seen within the confines of the community known as Coltsville, as well as in the single-action revolver that was lauded as the gun that "won the West." More than just the usual influx of skilled laborers was needed to run Colt's enterprise; additional expert craftsmen and engineers were employed. Other famous Connecticut inventors, like Francis Pratt and Amos Whitney, were apprentices who both cut their teeth under the tutelage of Colt. Colt's progressive Hartford landscape has given it the nickname of the "Silicon Valley of the era." Although his arms manufacture began in the mid-nineteenth century, the Hartford factory churned out guns until 1994 when its headquarters moved to a modern facility in nearby West Hartford. Colt, known for its historically significant models, is still one of the country's premier gunsmiths. During the Vietnam War years, the company churned out around 10,000 M-16 rifles a week!

Driving on Interstate 91 just south of downtown Hartford, the Colt Armory stands out, as its bulbous blue onion dome rises above the bustling freeway complex. The dome marks the Coltsville section of Hartford; the tract of land that Sam Colt bought abuts the Connecticut River. Gold stars adorn the deep blue of the Russian-inspired onion dome. Perched high atop the dome is a golden sphere with a Rampant Colt (the animal) with a broken spear in its mouth. The colt figure is rearing itself upright on its hind legs. A fire destroyed the armory in 1864, but it was rebuilt in 1867 under the guidance of Colt's wife, Elizabeth, since Sam passed away in 1862. The new building retained many of the same features of the original, including the dome, but was bigger and there was more detail in the design.

Also in the complex is Armsmear, the Colt's mansion which is now a home for elderly women. Built in 1857, located on Wethersfield Avenue, and styled after an Italian villa, Armsmear once featured even more elaborate ornamentation, which was removed after the Colts' occupation. Today's dome is made of fiberglass, but the original gilded wooden dome can be viewed at the Museum of Connecticut History. The Wadsworth Athenaeum also

The Colt Armory is marked with an onion dome; look hard for the stallion on top.

has much Colt memorabilia. The dome was renovated in 1999 after years of neglect. After over a decade of promotion and deliberation, in late 2014, Coltsville was deemed worthy of the title of National Historical Park. The hope is that it can mirror the success of Lowell, Massachusetts. Once upon a time, another down-and-out mill town, Lowell's revitalization has made the former Industrial Revolution beacon a model in the rehabilitation of a factory town. The National Historical Park recognition will include the entirety of Coltsville, including adjoining Colt Park, which includes a statue of Samuel in memorial to him. Also the Church of the Good Shepherd, founded by Elizabeth, will be included under the national park banner.

Today's Coltsville is within the perimeter of the Shelden/Charter Oak neighborhood of Hartford. The neighborhood has historically seen waves of immigration sweep through, from Swiss expatriates hired during the company's early years to the predominantly Hispanic population that resides there today. Many buildings in the complex have already found their way onto the National Register of Historic Places. The revitalization has included the armory being transformed into apartments, classrooms, and businesses. Further efforts will include a 10,000 square-foot visitor center and a museum equipped with an observation platform. Visitors are slated to be welcome in the dome. There is also talk of a garden on the premises reminiscent of one that Elizabeth planted during her years in Coltsville.

Colt's company began in 1851, as he started to purchase land. Operation began in the factory four years later. The complex of buildings totaled twenty. Its Russian-inspired dome was not placed by chance. The Colts were guests at the coronation of Czar Alexander II in 1856, but the dome's materials were manufactured not in Mother Russia, but instead in Hartford, Philadelphia, and even Berlin. Colt was one of the most well-known and most lucrative inventor. As the blue dome of the armory attests, Colt's legacy in his home city and state will not soon be forgotten.

The Ultimate Fall Route

Lisbon, Canterbury, Brooklyn, Pomfret, Woodstock

Route 169 is *the* quintessential New England road. Ironically, it is not found among the Green Mountains of Vermont or in the bucolic Berkshire Hills of Massachusetts. Instead, this National Scenic Byway bisects the Quiet Corner of Connecticut. This road meanders its way among picturesque colonial villages, past farmland and is best enjoyed when the autumn colors are alive and dancing. (A recommendation is to listen to George Winston's solo piano classic, *Autumn* on your journey). The ride begins in the small town of Lisbon and ends close to the Massachusetts border in Woodstock. All of the destinations mentioned are right on Route 169. All of these towns have much more to explore by traveling off the main road, but for the focus of this chapter, we will stick to Route 169.

As a child, 169 was the route that my family would take from Norwich to visit my grandmother in Danielson. Although we didn't make it to the ultimate villages on the trek (Pomfret and Woodstock), we would often take rides from her house into the nearby countryside. As I got older, every year when the air became crisp and a light jacket was necessary to feel comfortable outside, Route 169 was my go-to destination. My focus shifted from the beachside communities of Mystic and Stonington to the countryside of the Quiet Corner. My journey on Route 169 may have only yielded one stop or two,

sometimes even setting foot outside of the car was not necessary, since the foliage on view created a destination of its own.

On a side note, this area of the state offers superb walking tours throughout the month of October sponsored by the Last Green Valley called "Walktober." Many of the towns visited on this trip offer fantastic walks including Woodstock's town cemetery and green, Aicher Hill in Pomfret, and even the mysterious "Village of Voices," also known as Bara-Hack in Pomfret. These walks change from year to year, but some, like the one in Woodstock Center, seem to be offered year after year.

Although Route 169 begins in Norwich, the best starting-off point would be the intersection of Routes 138 and 169 in the center of Lisbon. At this intersection, begin on Route 169 and simply go north. The majesty of the road begins to unveil itself to the unsuspecting driver in Lisbon. Behind every turn one beholds another glimpse at the foliage of the Quiet Corner. The sign that greets visitors to the town of Canterbury will soon be seen. Look for old cemeteries, colonial architecture, and blazing foliage on the ride through these towns. Canterbury's most well-known attraction is the Prudence Crandall House and Museum, where teacher Crandall admitted an African-American student into her classroom, rumored to make it the first integrated school in the country. The stately building is located in the center of town, at the intersection of 169 and Route 14. Soon after this intersection is Canterbury Cones, on the right-hand side of the road—if an ice cream treat is what you crave.

Brooklyn is the next town located on the route. Pass by the Brooklyn Fairgrounds, home of the nation's oldest continuously run agricultural fair. The fair runs at the end of August and features animals, rides, and plenty of fried food. It's a perfect size for kids where it is small enough to be manageable, but large enough to hold their attention. The fairgrounds also host other events sporadically throughout the year. Once past the fairgrounds, notice the statue of Israel Putnam, mounted on horseback atop a large pedestal. This is the final resting place of the famed colonial general. The statue is located in the center of town. Flanking both sides of the pedestal are wolf heads to represent the legend that he slaughtered the last wolf in the state.

Passing through the intersection at Route 6, soon you will come to the well-regarded restaurant, the Golden Lamb Buttery on your left-hand side. This is much more than a restaurant, but an edible experience. Drinks are first had at the red barn on premises that overlooks the pastureland. The restaurant is situated on vast acreage, which includes their farm, stone walls, and of course, the eatery itself. A hayride through the premises is also available. From here, guests are seated in one of Golden Lamb's dining areas inside the former home. The Golden Lamb is truly a memorable dining endeavor, but make sure to plan ahead by booking reservations.

The final two towns en route are autumn at its utmost in terms of their picturesque quality and their unmistakable New England charm. In Pomfret, pass by the Pomfret School with its million-dollar views. For a quicker, but still inspiring dining option, visit the always packed Vanilla Bean Cafe at the corners of Routes 44 and 169 in Pomfret. The Vanilla Bean features exceptional soups and sandwiches in a barn-like building. More than just good food, the cafe is heralded as a premier venue for folk music as well. Also in Pomfret is the ever-popular Lapsley Orchard, where visitors can pick their own apples and pumpkins in the fall. Hayrides are offered and other autumn goodies can be purchased. Off of the beaten path from Route 169 is Sharpe Hill Vineyards in Pomfret on its border with Hampton. The grounds are beautiful and the wine is superb.

After Pomfret comes Woodstock, an autumnal playground for all senses. The route will pass by the Woodstock Fairgrounds, home to one of the country's best, if not *the* best agricultural fair, (Woodstock Fair), which takes place annually over Labor Day Weekend. Just like Brooklyn, it features a fine selection of animals, rides, and fried food. This fair is larger with an extensive Better Living Building and also has nationally known musicians grace their stage. Past performers have included "Weird" Al Yankovic, Belinda Carlisle, and The Tokens. Just past the fairgrounds are the Scranton Shops and Mrs. Bridge's Pantry. Browse a collection of antiques and country home decor at the Scranton Shops and the Primitive Crow or pick up a few British chocolates, a soup, or tea at Mrs. Bridge's. Just before the center of Woodstock, turn in at the sign for Woodstock Orchards. Although pick your own apples and pumpkins are available, it is just as much fun to visit the store. Choose an already-picked pumpkin, all shapes and sizes are available, and don't forget the apple cider and gourds at the shop. The center of town is marked by an expansive green, the dignified campus of Woodstock Academy, and an early cemetery. It is worth a walk around the grounds.

Across from the green is Roseland Cottage. The summer home of Henry Bowen, it is noted for its bright pink hue and its ornate gingerbreading. Feel free to tour the interior and walk around the outside. The grounds are the site of different events throughout the autumn, including the annual arts and crafts festival on the third weekend of October and a Civil War encampment.

If you still haven't eaten yet, another choice is Sweet Evalina's past the center of Woodstock on the left. This features goodies like mozzarella sticks, sandwiches, and ice cream, as well as beer and wine. Sweet Evalina's vibe is a combination of general store and hot dog stand.

The final destination of our trip is the Christmas Barn. The Christmas Barn is just that, a former barn that in the autumn is chock full of seasonal decorations as well as its namesake holiday accouterments. Candles, gifts, and country home decor dominate the interior of this special place.

By now, you are not far from the Massachusetts border. If you feel like you want more, travel down a back road, visit nearby downtown Putnam and its slew of antiques stores, or journey back down Route 12 to see the former industrial towns of eastern Connecticut (only a few mere miles from 169, but will feel like a world away). This region has much to offer, as Route 169 clearly is only a sampling of its attractions. The fall is New England at its finest, make sure to get out there and enjoy it and Route 169 is the perfect place to start! Hopefully on this trip you have witnessed the region's glorious foliage and enjoyed a perfect rambling country afternoon.

Kennedy City

Plainfield

Although as a kid I passed through the many villages of Plainfield every other week en route home from my grandmother's house in Danielson, I had never heard of Kennedy City. Wauregan? Yes. Central Village? Of course! Moosup? Most definitely, but never Kennedy City. After I started exploring the area once known as Kennedy City, I soon realized that I had been through the village unbeknownst to me on those bi-weekly trips. If you are traveling south on Route 12 from Killingly, there is an area before you officially get to Central Village, which, for lack of a better description, looks a bit sad today. It begins close to the intersection at Route 14 and extends close to the heart of Central Village; this is the former Kennedy City. Truthfully, the area looks exactly as I remembered it, although the time I frequently passed by was in the late '80s and '90s.

Just like many of the river-hugged towns of Eastern Connecticut, Kennedy City and most of the other villages of Plainfield were manufacturing towns. Around 1835, Arnold Fenner bought property in this area from John Kennedy (no, not John F.) and created a smallish cotton mill. The Kennedy family was a prominent family in this area in the late eighteenth century and owned a gristmill. Fenner lived at 40 Main Street (also called Manufacturer's Row), which was dubbed the Fenner-Matthewson Mansion and was heralded as one of the most architecturally exquisite homes in the Italian Villa style in the state. It was built in 1855. The striking home is directly across the street from the Plainfield Woolen Company Mill, which was built in 1901 and was the main employer in town. The mansion is painted a striking yellow, with ornate gingerbreading, quoins outlining its perimeter, and has statues along its front. Its yard is sloped as it is built on a hillside with a series of inclines.

Kennedy Mills was located at the western end of Central Village. Also producing textiles, its focus was producing flannel, cotton, and twine. Unusual to factory towns, the nearby homes were not multifamily tenements, but single-family houses, which were and are located on School Street. Central Village still retains glimpses of its once-thriving past. It still has a hotel, restaurant, and a few stores. The Kennedy House can be seen on Black Hill Road (Route 14). The factories in this area derived their power directly from the Moosup River, which parallels these roads.

On my trip to Kennedy Village, I had trouble deciphering where Central Village ended and Kennedy Village began. The main factory (Plainfield Woolen Company Mill) is still in great shape, has an impressive

The elaborate wedding cake house watches over the former Kennedy City.

smokestack, and has been converted into apartments. Exploring the property, a large grindstone of some kind is on display like a sculpture on the grounds. To get to the Moosup River, I took a right on Torrey Lane, near the post office. I walked around the area near the banks of the river, behind the football field, but found no remnant of a forgotten mill or any other structures except something that could have been the last vestige of a bridge or a sluiceway.

The Still River and Saw Mill Park

Eastford, Woodstock, and Ledyard

I wanted to explore the former mill sites along the banks of the Still River in Eastford, but had a degree of difficulty finding them at first. However, in my

opinion the adventure getting there is half of the fun. My directions were primitive, basing the former mill site on the proximity to the river. My first attempt started behind the soccer fields of the elementary school. I found a path marked with white blazes. Although this loop proved to be fruitless, it was pleasant walking in and out of a pine forest with benches along the way, with stone walls meandering through the property. Although Route 198 is not by any means a major thoroughfare, it is the most populous route in town. This path was not far away from Route 198, albeit on the other side of the Still River. I enjoyed the wildlife on my walk and chipmunks and horses on a nearby farm, though I did not see any foundations. The Still River is a small river that combines with Bigelow Brook farther south in Eastford to become the Natchaug River.

On my way out of Eastford, I ended up stumbling upon the sought-after foundation—on the opposite side of Route 198, just across from the area where I had

The foundations of a building on the banks of the Still River.

been walking was the former mill site. The concrete base of the former mill exists. A bridge over the river leads to the still-standing warehouse that is close to the road. On Route 198 a nearby sign says "Still River Mill."

Another feature of Eastford is the town pound, located on Pound Road, which is off John Perry Road. The town pound is small, the walls about four feet in height and square shaped, consisting of an iron gate with two pillars. The enclosed pound has a tree in the middle, a common feature of town pounds. It has a new stone that marks it, and the adjacent area consists of stone walls traversing the landscape.

In the same context as the sites along the Still River is Saw Mill Park in Ledyard, which is on Route 214 between Ledyard Center and the Mashantucket Pequot Reservation.

For a small town that most travelers drive right through en route to Mystic or know solely for its behemoth casino, Ledyard has other worthwhile excursions.

This collection alone mentions Lantern Hill, Jemima Wilkinson, and Maugle Sierra Winery. The eleven-acre park, although marked with a sign that reads "Ledyard Water Powered Up-Down Sawmill," is easily missed. Although I have ventured on this road throughout my life, I never knew it existed until recently! The park is on the National Register of Historic Places and consists of a grist mill, a shingle mill, a blacksmith shop, a mill pond, ice-harvesting tools, a playground, a picnic area, and its namesake sawmill. The sawmill dates from the mid-nineteenth century, built by Israel Brown. The Brown family operated a few sawmills in the Ledyard area. This kind of saw mill is known as an up-down sawmill. The first sawmill on this site was built in the 1790s by Nathaniel Brown and Increase Stoddard. The current sawmill was in operation until 1935. Ledyard bought the sawmill and adjacent land in 1975. It was rehabbed by a team of volunteers in 2014; tours are offered as well as demonstrations of the up-down saw during the spring and autumn months on Saturdays from one to four in the afternoon.

The sawmill utilizes a straight six-foot blade. This is known as a sash sawmill because it is operated like a sash window with its moveable panels. The Ledyard sawmill is heralded as the only machine of its kind still functioning with its original saw mechanism housed in its original location in the country.

The next time you are planning a trip to Mystic Country or one of the casinos, take a trip off the beaten path to Saw Mill Park in nearby Ledyard.

While You're There!

The Chamberlin Mill has been recently restored.

In Woodstock, close to Eastford, is the Chamberlin Mill. The Chamberlin Mill on Old Turnpike Road, close to the large town's Eastford border, is a restored sawmill powered by the Still River. A mill has been located on site since the 1700s. The mill has been featured in the annual Walktober events. On the other side of town,

A classic New England autumn scene in Woodstock.

in the center of Woodstock is the Woodstock Hill Burying Ground. The first stone dates from 1689 making it the oldest cemetery in town. The interred include members of the Bowen family, owners of the nearby Roseland Cottage. Instead of the traditional gray stone, many tombstones have a blackish hue to them.

Connecticut's Coastal Forts

New London, Groton, New Haven, and Old Saybrook

Given its shoreline and its history, it only makes sense that Connecticut has four prominent forts that helped defend the state and country's coast from enemy threat. Unfortunately, as history shows, one of the most tragic events in the state's past happened at the site of two of these forts. Fort Trumbull showcases a true fortified structure where the other three are remnants of one kind or another.

Forts Trumbull and Griswold

Forts Trumbull and Griswold are on opposite sides of the Thames River. The port of New London, which is near the mouth of the Thames River was protected historically by these two. New London was used as prime arsenal storage for the colonists during the Revolution. Norwich native son and traitor Benedict Arnold knew of this fact and led the burning of New London by the British in what is known as the 1781 Battle of Groton Heights. Forts Griswold and Trumbull witnessed this firsthand. The obelisk monument, built in the same vein as the Bunker Hill Monument, at Fort Griswold commemorates those who lost their lives in the bombardment. Fort Trumbull was sieged by Arnold and his troops, which left the city in shambles. A huge percentage of colonists were killed as the soldiers defending New London rowed across to the safety at Fort Griswold in Groton. Just like many place names in the state, the fort is named for Governor Jonathan Trumbull. A lesser known Mark Twain short story "A Curious Experience" takes place at the fort.

Although this has been the location of a fortification since the colonial days, the current fort is the third structure on this land. The present structure was erected between the years of 1839 and 1852 in an Egyptian revival style. The blockhouse, which dates from 1796, is the oldest structure on site and is also in the same architectural style.

Although the fort had not seen direct combat since the American Revolution, it has been utilized by the United States military throughout the years. Fort Trumbull was the first site of the Coast Guard Academy between the years 1915 and 1932 when it moved farther up river into New London. The *Barque Eagle*, which is a tall ship that is used by the Coast Guard, is stationed here when in port. Fort Trumbull provided a vital strategy for the United States during the Cold War. The Navy located an underwater sound laboratory there in which they perfected sonar for submarines to counteract the German use of U-boats in World War II. It was the premier facility for underwater

sonar research. This practice lasted until 1996. The park was opened in 2000. The fort is at 90 Walbach Street in New London.

Fort Griswold Battlefield State Park

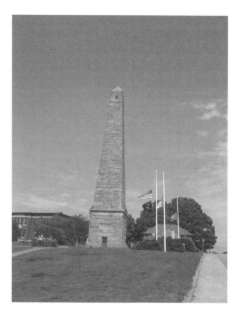

Fort Griswold memorializes those who died in the Battle of Groton Heights.

Across the river is Fort Griswold Battlefield State Park. It is most notable for its granite Battle Monument built in 1830. The British dodged the gunfire from this fort during the Battle of Groton Heights to strategically attack New London. The fort partially remains. The public can walk around the remnants. View the monument, the Ebenezer Avery House, and the Monument House Museum. It affords the visitor a fine view of the New London harbor and is a perfect place to walk the dog or have a picnic. The fort is on Fort Street in Groton.

Black Rock Fort

Black Rock Fort was the original fortification on site defending the colonists from an attack on New Haven harbor. The British, led by General Tryon, captured and set the fort ablaze. It was restructured and renamed Fort Nathan Hale that protected the Connecticut coastline during the nineteenth century. Years after its decommission, the defense post has been remade and today is a state park. The fort is at 36 Woodward Avenue in New Haven.

The Saybrook Fort

The former Saybrook Fort in Old Saybrook can also be visited as a park today. This was not a fortification against the British or other enemies of the country, but instead by the British settlers against the native inhabitants of the land. Although no original structures remain, the site can be viewed with informative descriptions of the history of the Saybrook Colony, the original settlement in Connecticut. The park is at Saybrook Point in Old Saybrook.

For a journey through the early defense systems of the state, visit one of these four forts. With places like the Naval Submarine Base and General Dynamics Electric Boat (where submarines are manufactured) and the Coast Guard Academy in New London being vital to the success and financial stability of the region, it is important to take a moment to reflect on the history of defense in the state.

While You're There!

Also located near the mouth of the Thames is one of the best seafood shacks around, Captain Scott's Lobster Dock. It's located at 80 Hamilton Street in New London. Even though the GPS is seemingly taking you in an area of abandoned buildings and warehouses, keep going; it is not leading you astray. After a turn in the road is the lobster dock. Unfortunately, this once hidden gem is not so hidden anymore. Expect to wait, but it is worth it for the succulent fried clams or hot lobster roll chock full of tasty meat. In this area of Connecticut, the hot lobster roll is the lobster roll of choice. Move over may-

onnaise in the lobster salad roll, this is the real deal! Captain Scott's is purely seasonal, as all of the seating is out of doors.

Falkner Island

Guilford

The idea of the weather beaten island, stranded against the raging sea with its waves lapping against its rocky side, is an image often conjured up when thinking of historic New England. The hardened lighthouse keeper, face punctuated with a long white beard, braves the driving elements in his yellow protective raincoat. Island lighthouses strike many different chords in people. They elicit a vast range of emotions, from romance to depression; whatever the sentiment may be, most individuals do connect with the lighthouse in some way. Coastal mainland lighthouses like those in New Haven or Stonington are well known, but it's the state's offshore beacons that add an extra touch of the intrigue. Although two others (Ledge Light in New London and Penfield Reef Lighthouse in Fairfield) are in this collection, their focus is more on its haunted notoriety. Although in slight passing a mention of a ghost or a pirate has been associated with Guilford's Falkner Island (sometimes written as Faulkner), it is more closely tied to wildlife and structural preservation, although the island and light have borne witness to amazing events.

Located three-and-a-half miles south offshore in Long Island Sound from the mainland town of Guilford, this three-acre island has seen its dominion decrease yearly due to the constant pressure of erosion. The island is capped with the lighthouse. The stone tower, painted white, is the only remaining structure. A 1976 fire leveled the former keeper's house and burned the tower. Although the home was charred beyond salvaging, the tower could be saved.

The island's light had been in existence since it was commissioned by Thomas Jefferson in 1802. It has witnessed its share of historic, tragic, and heroic events on the island. Early lighthouse keeper Joseph Griffing discovered the bodies of seven seamen who had wrecked nearby. Solomon Stone, the keeper during the War of 1812, was approached by the British, but ultimately left in peace due to the strategic and necessary service the light provided to both sides of the battle. Eli Kennedy was the keeper at Falkner for thirty-three years and known for his jovial personality, providing a warm welcome for its many visitors. Most well known was Oliver Brooks, whose family of musicians kept watch over the sea from 1851 to 1882. During his stay as keeper, the light oversaw the wreck of over 100 ships. He won a Gold Medal award for saving five individuals from a schooner that had wrecked on the coast of the island in 1858. This part of the sound is known for choppy waters and rough seas.

Today, the island is part of the Stewart McKinney National Wildlife Refuge and is a primary habitat for the roseate and common tern. Other resident fauna include seals and rabbits. Restoration efforts have been ongoing, including a major overhaul in 1999 with further rehabilitation since. Visitors are only allowed to the island via tour in September sponsored by the Falkner Island Light Brigade, a non-profit group founded in the early 1990s whose preservation efforts have spurred the current conservation effort. For a small parcel of land, the island has a threefold preservation attack: the historic lighthouse, the tern population, and the curtailment of further erosion of its beaches and shorelines. Erosion was responsible for a few feet a year being taken from the island. The tower was once known as "the

Eiffel Tower of the Long Island Sound" due to its astounding presence. From the island, Hammonasset Beach can be seen to the north, Long Island to the south, and a few of the Thimble Islands to the west.

Luckily, through tireless conservation efforts between biologists, the National Park Service, and the Falkner Island Light Brigade, the island and light still stand tall today, proud to be appreciated by another generation of Connecticutians viewing it from the shores of Madison and Guilford or passing by on boat. Connecticut is proud of its coastal heritage and Falkner Island and light are prime examples of why it should be.

___

Town Pounds

Statewide

One summer my family was vacationing in Maine. We piled into the car to explore the town of Harpswell. On the way, my wife yelled out, "There's a town pound; stop the car!" "A what??" was the primary reaction from the rest of us. "A town pound." She said it so matter-of-factly that I thought a "duh" was going to follow out of her mouth. As we turned the car around to view the seemingly ordinary structure, my wife brought us up to speed about town pounds.

Agriculture was the way of life for the majority of New Englanders in the eighteenth century. It was a society of farmers growing their own crops and raising their own livestock. The town pound was a holdover from medieval Europe. Today, we often think of a pound as where stray or lost dogs are put. During the era of the town pound it was cattle, horses, and other livestock that were held there. When an animal broke loose, it was held in the town pound until the owner

The town pound in Eastford is a classic example of the once ubiquitous livestock pen.

claimed it. The pound was built to hold livestock on the lam. It had four walls with a gate, often made of granite or another heavy duty stone. The walls were not high, enough that the animal could be held in, but low enough a passerby could see it without entering the enclosure.

Although the idea of a location for the communal herding of stray animals seems quaint, it was a necessity in agrarian colonial society. The owner whose cow broke away had to pay a fine to take the bovine back. The farmer also had to pay for any destruction the stray animal might have caused before it was brought to the pound. Each town appointed a pound keeper. Many early New England town pounds were made of wood, but durable stone overtook as a more popular choice. Town pounds' heyday was the 1700s into the 1800s, with an emphasis on mid- to late-1700s. Typically, the pounds were located in the town centers. Even today visitors can see a pound next to a church, meetinghouse, and/or cemetery. Often a single tree was planted in the enclosure to provide shade. The gates both kept the animals in and the owners out, to make sure a farmer did not sneak back to steal his livestock without paying the fine. The downfall of the town pound was in part due to constructing better cattle pens and New England marching away from agriculture and into industry, which simply led to fewer farms.

Connecticut had its share of town pounds: from Goshen in the west to Preston in the east, from Hebron to Killingly. Towns like Franklin and Lebanon still retain their village-like charm and the sight of the town pound is understandable, whereas in towns that are now bedroom communities of Hartford, like Hebron and Enfield, town pounds seem out of place today, as the morning rush of commuters crawls by. Although out of the scope of this book, southern New Hampshire and Massachusetts have their share of town pounds also.

Why town pounds struck a chord with my wife remains a mystery to me, but whenever we venture out for a Connecticut adventure, she checks to see if the towns we visit have a town pound. On other occasions, we have traveled to quiet parts of the state just to take in the sight of the town pound. Unfortunately, as in anything antiquated, some town pounds have not stood the test of time and have been removed, demolished, or destroyed by nature. Other town pounds are re-creations of originals. Some are in immaculate condition, where others have seen better days. Eastford, Goshen, and Lebanon have prime examples of town pounds that are still standing and in good shape.

The next time you are out on a country drive and pass a town center with a small sign that reads "Town Pound," pull the car over and take a glimpse at an integral part of New England's agrarian past.

Lantern Hill

North Stonington

The 238-million-year-old quartz of Lantern Hill sparkles and shines in the sunlight. The hill rises 600 feet above the outlying forest. Located on the reservation of the Mashantucket Pequot Native American tribe, Lantern Hill has been a strategic locale throughout history. Sassacus, the great Pequot sachem used it as a lookout for any trace of the rival Narragansett. On a clear day, one is able to see five states: Connecticut, Rhode Island, Massachusetts, New York (Long Island and Fisher's Island), and reportedly, Vermont, as well as far into the Atlantic Ocean. On my visit, I am not sure how many states I was able to see, but I could clearly see the Mashantucket Pequot Museum and Foxwoods Resort Casino.

During the War of 1812, Lantern Hill earned its nickname. The residents of Stonington were on around-the-clock watch for any sign of the enemy in the harbor. Fear was heightened in the summer of 1814 after the British attacked at Essex. Tar was brought in large barrels to the top of Lantern Hill. On lookout for any sign of British action in the harbor, once spotted, the barrels would be lit. On August 11, 1814, Lantern Hill earned its keep. The townsfolk's watchful eye from the top of the hill saw the arrival of British ships. The barrels were lit like lanterns lighting up the night sky. Stonington's women and children packed up and traveled inland as the town's militiamen ventured to the harbor to prepare the cannon for use against the rival navy. In the morning, the British, in hopes of docking, were instead greeted by a suitably prepared regiment awaiting their arrival. Stonington's watchfulness proved fruitful as it led to the stunned British circling the harbor, firing cannon, but never landing. Eventually, they left Stonington frustrated without ever setting foot on land. This event gave the hill its common epithet as well as its other pseudonym, "Tar Barrel Hill." In 1870, the hill was used as a quarry where silica was mined. The quarries eventually closed when the land was given to the Mashantucket Pequot.

Today's Lantern Hill may not be used to spot approaching enemy ships or rival campfires like Sassacus did, or even to mine silica, but it is utilized by hikers looking for a steady climb with rewarding views. Lantern Hill is one terminus of the twenty-one-mile Narragansett Trail, with its other end at Ashville Pond in Hopkinton, Rhode Island. The area around Lantern Hill is bisected with marked trails, but one of the more popular ones that circumnavigates Lantern Hill is the Loop Trail. This path takes the hiker up to the top of Lantern Hill, up an easier incline and down a circuitous, rocky route.

A primitive wigwam at Lantern Hill.

A steep jagged edge greets the hiker at Lantern Hill.

Start your visit to Lantern Hill by parking behind the Two Trees Inn, across the parking lot from Foxwoods. The path starts out easily enough, past a wigwam. On both of my trips to Lantern Hill I ended up getting lost. Although the trail is blazed, it meanders a bit with signage that is not always clear. On the loop trail there are two options. One takes the hiker alongside rocky, steep cliffs on a path that can be narrow, full of loose stones, and dangerous. It also has rocky outcroppings that the hiker needs to shimmy up or down, depending on the direction. The other pathway to the top is much more gradual and not on the edge of the cliff. This is written with warning because those traveling with children or older folks may want to avoid the cliffside route. The route starts off deceivingly easy, but soon narrows and becomes treacherous. Although for those who can safely handle it, the steep quartz inclines and the dramatic drop-offs, coupled with the scenery, are certainly impressive. Either way, though, the top of Lantern Hill affords fantastic views no matter which trail is taken. On my first trip, fellow hikers told us afterwards that a copperhead was spotted on the narrow trail by the cliff.

Other than the previously mentioned man-made sites seen from the top of the hill, I saw a hawk soaring below the mountaintop. Lantern Hill is one of southeastern Connecticut's best-kept secrets. Only a poker chip's throw away from the hustle and bustle of Foxwoods, but in ideology a world apart. The natural beauty of the area does get interrupted with the turquoise and green colors of the casino, but happily, even after the development of the Foxwoods area, Lantern Hill remains untouched by development and is still allowed, encouraged even, for hikers to enjoy its trails.

While You're There!

Although from the top of Lantern Hill, its observation tower does protrude mightily from the low lying trees, the Mashantucket Pequot Museum is a must see. The museum highlights the history of the tribe from the sixteenth century to the present with exhibits presenting historical depictions of aspects of life such as hunting and creating weapons. There is a re-created coastal village on site and the visitor can walk through. The museum is informational, but also interactive and eye catching.

Cedar Hill Cemetery

Hartford

Hartford is known for its architectural gems. Whether it's the Wadsworth Atheneum, the state capital, or the Old State House, Hartford has its share of remarkable sites that are testaments to the prestige and the wealth that the city once held. Leaders of industry, such as Samuel Colt, built prominent mansions to reside in. Although Mark Twain satirized the idea of the Gilded Age, he resided in a veritable palace in Hartford's Asylum Hill neighborhood. It is only fitting that in death, as in life, Hartford's upper crust be laid to rest in a striking setting.

Cedar Hill, along with other pseudo museum cemeteries like Mt. Auburn Cemetery in Cambridge, Massachusetts, and Swan Point in Providence, is a collection of thoughtfully sculpted and beautifully arranged monuments to the deceased. If a typical cemetery can be likened to a sprawling housing development of subdivisions, resting places like Cedar Hill are more like mansions that sweep the countryside.

Jacob Weideman, the landscape architect who also designed Bushnell Park in Hartford, designed Cedar Hill in Hartford's South End, which opened its gates in 1864. Among the monuments, the Gothic revival superintendent's cottage circa 1875 and a chapel are on the 270-acre grounds. The stones mark the lives and legacies of many famous Connecticut-ites, including actress Katharine Hepburn; women's activist Isabella Beecher Hooker; artist Paul Zimmerman; aviation businessman Donald Lamont Brown; politician John Moran Bailey; Dr. Horace Wells, the inventor of anaesthesia; industrialist Samuel Colt; politician and president of Major League Baseball's National League Morgan Gardner Bulkeley; and most notably, financier J. P. Morgan. The latter, whose grave is a red granite rendering of the Ark of the Covenant designed by George Keller, who also built the Soldiers and Sailors Monument in downtown Hartford, is in stark contrast to the next most distinguished of the interred, Katharine Hepburn. Her grave is a simple granite marker in the family plot denoted by an oval-shaped rock with the Hepburn name engraved on it. Other ornate monuments include a pyramid with a life-sized angel in its midst. It is not uncommon to find visages carved in stone, or for that matter actual sized statues. One particularly creepy figure is a shrouded woman standing on a pedestal. Another startling effigy is the monument for two-year-old Cynthia Talcott with a life-sized stone portrayal of her face.

Yankee Magazine calls Cedar Hill one of the most beautiful cemeteries in New England. During the Halloween season, be on the lookout for a "haunted" lantern light tour, where a costumed guide leads visitors to important sites throughout the rural burial ground. Cedar Hill is a must see for a look into the way Hartford's elite have spent their eternal sleep.

While You're There!

Visiting Cedar Hill at dusk during December, other than being atmospheric and cold, has another perk; it is next to Goodwin Park. Goodwin Park is the home to the Holiday Lights Fantasia yearly. Drive through the winter wonderland with your car radio tuned to the listed station and enjoy a two-mile festive jaunt through the paved roads of Goodwin Park. Holiday lights adorn archways and sparkle alongside the car with favorite Christmas characters and other well-known symbols and figures, like Santa, his reindeer, the Statue of Liberty, and Spongebob Squarepants. All proceeds go to the Channel 3 Kids Camp. Goodwin Park is located at 1130 Maple Avenue in Hartford.

Long Society Meetinghouse

Preston

Have you ever seen a colonial broadside meetinghouse? Do you want to? (Of course

you do!) Take a trip to the town of Preston. Located on its border with Norwich, on the aptly named Long Society Road is the Long Society Meetinghouse. The building looks like a typical structure of the colonial era, with no intricacies or particularly striking ornamentation. Quite simply, it resembles a house. Its white façade is a little worse for wear. Its peeling paint and adjoining cemetery give the building a bit of eeriness. This meetinghouse was the second, rebuilt between 1817 and 1819, replacing one on the same spot.

Originally, this part of Preston belonged to Norwich. It was known as the "Fifth Society" and was sometimes referred to as "East Norwich." The farmers from this region advocated for their own parish house as early as 1698. At this time, going to services was mandatory and lasted the better part of the day. During Puritan times there was no avoiding church, even when the closest house of prayer was miles away! The folks who lived in this area had to travel all the way to Norwichtown for their weekly devotional service. This meant a four-and-a-half-mile journey that crossed over rivers and up steep hills. Eventually, this distant area of Norwich was granted a meetinghouse in 1721, with the building established in 1726. The Reverend Jabez Wight called the meetinghouse home until his death in 1782, when the building's use also declined. Four years later, the Fifth Society of Norwich became part of the town of Preston. This new land area was deemed the "Long Society" since its tract of land stretched all the way from the village of Poquetanuck in the south to Plainfield in the north. Originally, the town of Griswold, which is situated between these two towns today, was part of Preston. The thin parcel of land bordered the Thames and Shetucket Rivers on their eastern banks.

The meetinghouse as it stands today began construction in 1817. It utilized some of the original building's wood. Instead of being used solely for Congregationalists, it became a house of

The Long Society Meetinghouse in Preston is known for its architecture and variety of grave stone carvings.

worship for all Christian denominations. Additionally, the building was used for civic functions, such as town meetings and elections. Long Society is the only standing example of a colonial broadside meetinghouse in the state, and there are roughly only a dozen left anywhere. Instead of much ornamentation, like in many churches, the Congregationalists believed that the congregation was not the building itself, but instead the group of people who were gathered for worship, which was in stark contrast to Catholic churches adorned with much decoration and elaborate architecture. Although the building's architectural design aligned itself with strict Puritan ideology, when it was built, the state no longer mandated religious participation by its citizens via the Connecticut Constitution of 1818.

Today the 29 by 33 foot building is used for historical society functions. The white meetinghouse is painted in a pinkish hue in its interior. Its arched windows are perfect for glancing at the gravestones outside. The meetinghouse is noted for its width; instead of many churches that are much longer than they are wide; this is the opposite. It has an area in front where service was conducted, but not an elaborate altar or place for clergy to sermonize. The balcony wraps around the upstairs, with wide floorboards. The downstairs has sets of benches or pews, while the balcony is equipped with freestanding chairs.

The cemetery that borders the meetinghouse on three sides is a perfect example of a colonial graveyard. It has many different types and styles of gravestones, including the foreboding death's head. It is worth it to take a walk among the stones, stop to read an epitaph or two, and take notice of the drastic differences in styles of the graves. Reverend Wight is buried here—in the shadow of his beloved church. Long Society Meetinghouse can be appreciated in any season, but visiting in the autumn or the winter adds something extra. Whether it is the colorful leaves,

Peering out the window at the Long Society Meetinghouse.

looming over the cemetery or being crunched underfoot, or new fallen snow surrounding both the meetinghouse and the accompanying stones, visiting during these seasons is like a trip back in time.

▶ The meetinghouse is located across the street from the former town hall and current senior center on Long Society Road in Preston.

—
Gurleyville Gristmill

Mansfield

For all you "girlie men" (quoting *Saturday Night Live's* Hanz and Franz) who go to the supermarket to get your flour, check out the Gurleyville Gristmill to see how flour was manufactured in a bygone era.

Tucked away in the woods geographically close to the University of Connecticut, but light years away in other regards, is a small enclave of early industry along the banks of the Fenton River. From UCONN's center campus, take the aptly named Gurleyville Road that follows Bundy Brook that originates in the school's Mirror Lake. The brook travels alongside the road until it eventually crosses and spills into the Fenton River. This river begins in Willington and eventually empties into Mansfield Hollow Lake. The road travels downhill with the stream flowing over rocks and passes by Torrey Preserve, a nature sanctuary on land once owned by the Torrey family. Gurleyville Road intersects with Codfish Falls Road on the left and Chaffeeville Road on the right. Take Chaffeeville Road for a brief moment followed by a right on Stonemill Road to get to the gristmill.

The gristmill is on the banks of the Fenton River, which provides a serene backdrop for the area once inhabited by primitive industry. The Nipmuck Trail winds its way through this area as well. By the mill, a stone bridge spans the river. An old grindstone is used as steps in the front. On my visit I was able to look inside the windows of the mill, but the building was not open for tours on that day, especially since the oncoming winter was causing the river to become icy. Nature trails meander their way around the area of the mill.

The stone structure is in fantastic shape, given that it dates from the 1830s and was in use until 1941. It is a perfect example of a nineteenth century gristmill. On the location originally was a sawmill dating from 1723 as well as the initial gristmill circa 1750. The funny-sounding name of "Gurleyville" is derived from Ephraim Gurley, who owned the property at one time, although Benjamin Davis was the first proprietor. The nearby miller's cottage was the birthplace of four-term governor of Connecticut, Wilbur Cross (known today for the parkway bearing his namesake). Cross's family operated the mill.

When visiting, my original intention was to visit the Gurleyville Gristmill, but unbeknownst to me on my way out of the area, I stumbled across the remnants of other former industrial sites. In this area of Mansfield, along the Fenton, was a series of silk mills, including the Royce Silk Mill. Most of the mills operated for a few years, but then were left to battle the elements, often to succumb to fire or other destructive forces. Further on Chaffeeville Road is the site of the Chaffeeville Silk Mill. Although the sign marks the location, all that remains are foundations and a rock dam.

Nearby is Mansfield Hollow Dam, a tremendously large man-made dam that helps prevent flooding in the Quinebaug, Shetucket, and Thames Rivers. Water goes down through holes on the other side of the dam. It is a fantastic place to take a walk as the dam pens in Mansfield Hollow Lake. The view from the top of the dam presents a 360-degree panorama of the surroundings, with the lake on one side and the impressive stone Kirby's Mill on the other with power lines crisscrossing the on the hillside on the horizon.

While You're There!

The Hosmer Mountain Soda sign greets visitors at the Willimantic location.

With the craft beer movement taking a stronghold on the state's palate, soda has found itself relegated to the back of the fridge. Although fellow "Connecticut connoisseurs" may be reaching for a double IPA instead of an Orange Dry soda, Hosmer Mountain Soda knows that trends come and go, but since 1912, their product has been in high demand. Heck, these soda kings have been around since before alcohol was made illegal and provided a tasty alternative throughout the Prohibition years. With its main warehouse location in Willimantic and satellite soda shop in Manchester, Hosmer Mountain has a stronghold on eastern Connecticut's soft drink landscape. Rightfully so, Hosmer Mountain schools the competition, diminishing the national brands to flavorless carbonation. Each variety of Hosmer Mountain has a distinct and unique taste. Their variety ranges from classic flavors like Root Beer (which won fourth best overall in the Great American Root Beer Showdown) and Cream Soda to more adventurous tastes like Lime Rickey and their take on an energy drink, Red Lightning. My personal favorites include Orange Dry, Ginger Ale, and Root Beer. Taking Route 289 south from Willimantic, Hosmer's facility is on Mountain Road on the right just before the Lebanon town line. Its facility is unassuming, inside and out. The visitor can either take home a six pack or a case of their favorite flavor or devise their perfect soda combination by purchasing individual bottles, which are arranged in cartons. Environmentally conscious, Hosmer uses all recycled glass bottles. Instead of recycling your empties at home, bring them in for a cash deposit. Even though Hosmer's facility has a certain antiquated quality about it, in an era when the idea of farm to table and independent business is in vogue, a throwback such as Hosmer feels just as much 2015 as it does 1912. And most importantly, the soda tastes great!

Liberty Hill Village

Lebanon

Liberty Hill Village was once the hotbed of commercial activity in the town of Lebanon during the latter part of the 1800s into the 1900s. Granted, using the word "hotbed" may be a bit of a stretch in talking about a town whose rowdiest event is the annual Antiques Fair. Go north on Route 87 from the town green and soon you will pass through Liberty Hill Village, most likely without even noticing that you drove through it (unless you notice the green

village sign or the handful of places still adorned with the "Liberty Hill Village" name). Once upon a time, this section of town held two general stores and a post office. It was truly Lebanon's marketplace for travelers en route to Hartford and Norwich.

Today, the area is best known for Uncle D's Log Cabin restaurant and the Liberty Hill Farm. The plant farm, which has been in operation since 1966, is famous for its great selection of hanging plants. It is located on forty acres of land and comprises six green houses. Uncle D's, commonly known as The Log Cabin, has favorite dishes like pizza, grinders, salad and steak, but their ribs are legendary.

Hidden in plain sight is the best way to describe the Liberty Hill Village Cemetery. Although I had been there before, and knew precisely where it was (on the right hand side when traveling north on Route 87), I passed it by three times. A bit of folklore is attributed to one of the interred of this graveyard. The cemetery is classic New England in style. Its stones seem to be scattered in a not completely symmetric way. The older gravestones are leaning a bit, as they sink into the earth at varying degrees. It dates from 1812, but our story's gentleman found his resting place here in 1865. Captain S. L. Gray of Lebanon was commanding a whaling ship named the *James Murray* out of the New London harbor along with his crew, his wife Sarah, and his oldest daughter, sixteen-year-old Katie. In the midst of his venturing, the *James Murray* ran into enemy fire along the coast of Guam. The captain was lethally struck in this skirmish with the southern ship, the *Shenandoah*. (Some variations say that Gray died of diphtheria aboard the ship instead.) Grief struck and unhappy over typical ways of handling a dead man on a boat a long way from home, his wife Sarah demanded that he be entombed in a full barrel of rum. The rum barrel was opened, Captain Gray's body was inserted

Open gates welcome the newly deceased to the cemetery at Liberty Village.

inside and then the barrel was sealed back up. When the ship returned to the New London harbor, Gray's barrel and body were postmarked to Lebanon. Upon arrival in his hometown, Gray's body was left inside the rum barrel, buried six feet below the ground in the family plot in the Liberty Hill Village Cemetery.

In addition to the intoxicatingly strange fate of the captain, five of his sons and daughters all passed away around their second birthday, many locals believed due to the mishandling of some sort by their mother, Sarah. Eldest daughter Katie escaped the grip of her mother by sailing with her father, but she too would die only four years after him. Sarah lived for twenty more years, but eventually found eternal rest next to her family members who predeceased her. The Gray family plot can be found at the cemetery. Mother, father, children, and a barrel of rum.

The next time you are passing through this section of Lebanon, on the way to destinations like the Buckland Hills Mall in Manchester or Dodd Stadium in Norwich, you may want to slow down or even get out of the car to enjoy the wonders of oft forgotten Liberty Hill Village.

Lebanon Green
Lebanon

Unlike most town greens in New England, which are small tracts of land surrounded by a cluster of homes and municipal and commercial buildings, some of which are authentic and some of which have been re-created, the town green of Lebanon clearly demonstrates its agrarian past. Although it also is surrounded by a cluster of historic homes, the sheer size and untamed landscape harken back to its original agricultural use.

The green is separated in its southern portion by Route 207, with the south part

A wide view of the Historic Lebanon Town Green.

of it retaining a small quintessential New England feel, with the larger northerly section sprawling until the intersection with Route 289. Route 87, also known as East Town Street, forms the green's eastern border with West Town Street flanking to the west. The green totals a mile in length and about 500 feet in width. A one-and-a-half-mile loop walking path is a popular destination for joggers and dog walkers. The federalist style Congregational Church is on the green, along with many historic homes, including the William Beaumont House (moved here from another section of Lebanon), Wadsworth Stable, the Trumbull House, and Revolutionary War Office. The former Alden Tavern remains as a foundation.

The green was important during the years of the American Revolution as French soldiers used the land as their campsite for six months starting in the winter of 1780. The small town of Lebanon was nicknamed the "Heartbeat of the Revolution" due to the contribution of its citizens to the war effort. In total, 677 men from Lebanon served in the continental army, which was roughly half of the number of adults living in town. Those who did not fight, served in other ways, as Lebanon was known for all of the provisions gathered and donated to the war effort, a main reason why Connecticut became known as the "Provisions State." William Williams's house (great name by the way!) is on the green. Williams was a member of the Continental Congress and also a signer of the Declaration of Independence. A Liberty Pole was raised on the green by a local organization of the patriot group the Sons of Liberty during the Stamp Act. Jonathan Trumbull, the only colonial governor to then become a state governor, also lived on the green. George Washington and the Marquis de Lafayette were known to have visited Lebanon; friends with Trumbull, Washington's nickname for him was "Brother Jonathan." The Trumbull family's store became the Revolutionary War Office, which is available to visit today. Trumbull was so influential that a town in the western part of the state was named for him. The problem with the Trumbull family was that many of them all had the name of Joseph, Jonathan, or John. Many of them went on to important positions and fame, so the chronology of the J-named Trumbulls can be tricky. For instance, the Governor Jonathan Trumbull House was built by Joseph Trumbull, his father, but is also called the John Trumbull birthplace, named for Jonathan's son who became a famous painter. Not to make things more confusing, but Jonathan had a son named Jonathan Jr., also a politician, and another son named Joseph! In any case, the house is now a museum and is opened in the warmer months along with the war office. In addition to all the Joseph, Johns, and Jonathans, the UCONN Huskies' beloved mascot, Jonathan, is named after Governor Jonathan Trumbull Sr. Imagine the first conversation between the Trumbull and the Williams families after William Williams asked for Mary Trumbull's hand in marriage? It would be harder than "Larry, Darryl, and Darryl" from the cast of *Newhart*. "Hi my name is Mary Trumbull, my grandfather was named Joseph, and so is my brother and so is my nephew. My father's name is Jonathan, and so is my brother's, and then there is my other brother John." Then her future husband pipes in, "Well my name is William Williams, my parents liked our last name so much, that they decided to use it twice."

Jonathan Sr. had six children, including Mary who married William Williams; Jonathan Jr., who was the first comptroller of the United States Treasury as well as Washington's private secretary; and John, whose paintings include four scenes from the Revolution that adorn the rotunda of the United States Capitol Building. He also designed the First Congregational Church in Lebanon and is considered one of America's greatest artists.

If Lebanon has not already been presented as the colonial America walk

of fame, it will be now. William Beaumont, whose house was relocated to the green, is considered the father of stomach physiology. Noted for work as an army surgeon stationed in Michigan, he was called to aid a man who had accidentally shot himself in the stomach. In dire straits, the man, Alexis St. Martin, eventually healed, except for a remaining hole in his stomach. Through his unusual deformity, for years Beaumont was able to study the process of digestion through work on his ongoing patient, St. Martin, eventually publishing his findings and leading to scientific breakthroughs regarding human anatomy and the process of digestion.

While You're There!

A yearly tradition taking place during the last weekend in September is the Lebanon Antiques Show where tons of antiques are available to purchase on the historic Lebanon Green. Over 100 antiques dealers showcase their wares. From small knickknacks to large furniture, there will be something to take home. For hungry bargain hunters, food is served, including chowder, grinders, and burgers.

Mark Twain House & Museum

Hartford

Although often associated with the town of Hannibal, Missouri, which conjures up images of riverboats cruising the Mississippi River along with jumping frogs and painted fences, Mark Twain actually spent many of his most productive years as an author living in Hartford. Twain was born on November 30, 1835, as Samuel Clemens in Florida, Missouri, but by the age of four had moved to Hannibal. Throughout his early adulthood, he held a variety of jobs, including writing articles in New York City and Philadelphia, working as a riverboat pilot back in Missouri, and newspaper writing in San Francisco.

Twain first moved to Hartford with his wife, Olivia, in 1872. By the time Twain had his elaborate mansion erected in 1874, he was already a bestselling author with books like *The Celebrated Jumping Frog of Calaveras County, Roughing It*, and *The Innocents Abroad*. Wife Livy drew up her vision of her dream house. This mansion became a reality in 1874 when the Clemenses moved into their new home at Nook Farm, built by Edward Tuckerman Potter. The structure has twenty-five elaborate rooms and would be the place where Twain would write some of his best known works, including *The Adventures of Tom Sawyer, The Adventures of Huckleberry Finn, A Connecticut Yankee in King Arthur's Court,* and *The Prince and the Pauper.* He would consider his years at Nook Farm some of his happiest and most fruitful.

Unfortunately, the good times had to come to an end. In 1891, Twain and his family moved to Europe as his fortune was declining after a series of bad invention investments. Twain and his family still owned the property in Hartford and would venture back until tragedy struck in 1896. His daughter, Susy, died from meningitis while visiting Hartford. Although Twain held his home dear to him, he could not bear to ever go back to Hartford. The family ended up selling their home in 1903.

Even though the Clemens family would never return to their beloved home, the building would not stay vacant for long. Physically it would change uses from a boarding school to a library and eventually to the museum that it is known for today. In 2003, the Twain Museum Center opened adjacent to the house, which includes a rotating exhibition hall, a gallery, a store,

and café to accompany the glimpse into the world of Twain afforded to visitors in the house. The house is furnished with period pieces, and the mansion is restored to the grandiosity that Mark and Livy knew. Ornate details including the woodwork and exquisite furniture highlight the tour. A popular spot for visitors is Twain's elaborate billiard room on the second floor.

For some visitors, the architecture and furnishings are not only the piece of living history. Since tragedy overcame the home when Susy died, the house is rumored to have permanent guests. A young woman in a white dress has been spotted wandering the corridors. Could this be Susy? Visitors have reported feeling a tug on their clothes. Others who have walked by the stately home have seen faces pressed against the glass window panes. For some, nothing has been seen, but otherworldly noises have been heard reverberated through the Victorian mansion. Reputedly, the ghost of former butler George Griffin haunts the Twain House, welcoming guests from today to an era long ago.

The house is a fantastic look into the life and home of one of America's most celebrated storytellers and is one of the state's premier attractions. Do not miss the museum and spectacular gift shop during your visit.

▶ Tours are given by knowledgeable guides throughout the year. The Twain House celebrates its notoriety for its supernatural aspects and does give ghost tours, including the hour long Graveyard Shift tour.

While You're There!
Visit the home of fellow author Harriet Beecher Stowe (of *Uncle Tom's Cabin* fame) next door.

Welte

Norwich

Growing up in Norwichtown, I could grasp the uniqueness of the old cemetery, the Norwichtown Green, and Lowthorpe Meadows, but had always taken for granted what was always known as "United Workers." On East Town Street in Norwichtown is a yellow mansion that was the home of Governor Samuel Huntington, fifth president of the Continental Congress and signer of the Declaration of Independence. The name "United Workers" came from the building's use as a community health care provider. Although I always thought the lion statues out front and the marbles embedded in stonework on the property were cool, I took for granted what a mystery this former estate really was. To me the United Workers building was nothing more than the hill that I would go sledding on and the path I would use to walk the dog. Its parking lot was where I learned how to

ride a two-wheel bicycle and its side yard saw many games of home-run derby. It was not until many years later that I realized how unique my childhood was, walking across the street and having a Revolutionary War era cemetery, town green, and former estate being my playground. Daily walks "behind United Workers" took me on small bridges, one even labeled Minnehaha Falls (after Longfellow's *Song of Hiawatha*) over brooks. Along the edges of the stone bridges and in other places around the property was the word "Welte." I simply figured that this was the name of the stonemason who chiseled out the estate's bridges, benches, and walkways. The first time the name really even registered with me was after a friend of mine hit his head on a railing of the stone bridge. He looked up and there in uppercase block letters was written "WELTE." We joke because soon that very thing would be swelling up on his head—a welt. It was only a few short years ago that I inquired about the history of the estate. When I got word that the Welte family owned it, it finally

The prominent Welte family etched their name into many pieces of their property.

dawned on me why that name was strewn all over the property; Welte was not the stonemason or a warning against hitting one's head, but instead the surname of a prominent family who owned the Huntington home. The first stories I heard were secondhand tales of Mrs. Welte flaunting her wealth through lavish cars and clothing.

The stately home overlooks East Town Street. For as long as I have been alive it has been painted yellow. It is a large colonial, although with pillars out front and a two story portico, adding a Greek flair to its American roots. Additions were made on the back. The building has eight rooms downstairs and an additional eight upstairs. My favorite feature growing up was the two "Big Roars" as I nicknamed them, or the two marble lions, imported from Italy that stood guard presiding over the front of the building. To preserve their integrity, the lions were covered with large boxes during the winter months years ago, and their removal was one of the first signs of spring. The home's interior includes marble mantles and revolutionary-era doors. Although best known for being the home of Governor Huntington, I always thought it was peculiar that a bust of the Mohegan sachem, Uncas was carved into the granite chimney. Many of the ornamental features, such as the inscriptions in stone, the carved Uncas, the lions, and the embedded marbles originated during the tenure of Carl and Annie Welte during the early part of the twentieth century. When the etched Uncas was erected, it was an issue of contention in town. Huntington, a revered hero, some thought was disgraced with the placement of Uncas on his former home's chimney. Even into the twentieth century, the image of Native Americans as inferior, savage heathens persisted. This was illustrated in a newspaper article written in 1935, which described the image of Uncas as being "disturbing" and referred to the sachem as "flesh eating" and a "redskin,"

The bust of Uncas adorns the chimney of the former Welte estate.

(the flesh-eating describing when Uncas ate the shoulder of Miantonomo, as outlined by the legend of "Indian Leap"— see the original *Connecticut Lore*). The bust of Uncas is twenty-six inches tall by twenty-two inches wide. Carl Welte worked tirelessly to find a true image of Uncas, which could then be etched into the chimney. He consulted an ethnologist from the Smithsonian and the director of the Peabody Museum of Archeology at Harvard.

The Welte family had their own interesting story to tell. The story starts off in Bavaria where Michael Welte creates a musical clock. Michael was born in 1807 in Vohrenbach, Germany. In Freiburg he started a company "M. Welte and Sohne." His son, Emil, born 1841, also in Germany, represented the clock and automatic instruments section at the London Expo of 1862. Emil was sent to New York City to install an orchestrion, the self-playing organ which the company was well known for. Here Emil opened a shop on the corner of 5th Avenue and 22nd Street with another on East 14th Street a little while later. This became a branch of the company from

Germany, this one called M. Welte and Sons, which was active until the World War I years, where German goods were not looked at in favorable light. Emil moved to Norwich in 1867 and married Emma Marguerite Foerstner, who was born in 1853. Also with a music background, she studied at the Music Vale Seminary and Salem Normal Academy of Music in Connecticut. In June of 1871, Emil and Emma were married. The family lived in Norwich, but soon after son Carl was born in 1872, they moved to New York City. Carl was born at the former Huntington house, which was at that time the home of Emma's aunt, Phillipena. When he grew older, Carl was to continue in the family business. Emil had another son Emil Jr., who only lived a few short years. Emil also studied music and started working with M. Welte and Sons in 1889. Emil and Carl presented their automatic organ at the World's Columbian Exposition in Chicago in 1893. In addition to working with the New York branch, he also became a member of the Freiburg branch in 1901. He was married to Annie Easter Morgan, in November of 1903. They had one son who only lived a year, named Carl Jr. In 1944, the Welte company was obliterated in the allied bombing of Germany.

The estate came into the Welte family via the Youngs. Charles Young, another Bavarian, married Phillipena Theresa Fronica Young (yes, it was her maiden name too and on top of that her father was also Charles Young). In 1848, the newlyweds moved to Norwich from Germany. Charles earned a wage as a moulder and Phillipena as a dressmaker. The Youngs ran a hotel at the corner of Main and Franklin Streets, appropriately named "Young's Hotel." They then purchased their home, the former Stedman property (the Huntington house). While the Youngs lived there, greenhouses were added, and on the property they grew fruit and vegetables. The remains of grapevines can be seen sloping down the hill behind the house. They had a daughter who died at birth, so without any direct lineage, their estate was left to Phillipena's niece, Annie. Both Youngs are buried in the Yantic Cemetery in the large "Young" vault.

Annie Welte lived until 1950 and Carl until 1955. The house was deeded to the United Workers per request of the family as a thank you for providing help for Annie during her last years. By the late '50s, the United Workers, now known as United Community and Family Services, began operation at the former Huntington Home. Originally, Huntington bought the lot from Lieutenant Thomas Tracy, one of the original settlers of Norwich. The house across the street at 41 East Town Street was bought by the Weltes. Legend says that Emma requested that the home not fall into the hands of the "maid." The maid could refer to Annie. If Carl passed before her, the Welte estate would be passed down through the Morgan side of the family since Carl had no direct heir. Or the maid could refer to Annie Houlihan, who was employed as a servant in their home. In the end, the point was moot since Carl outlived Annie.

Saplings planted on the property blossomed into massive trees. Elms were on site in the nineteenth century. The lamp post in the front used to be operated by gas and was made on Ferry Street in Norwich. Stone benches and walls had marbles embedded in their rock, but unfortunately have been dug out. Also ornamental rocks in the shape of stars adorn the walls. The lions still flank the doorway to the house. Large hemlocks separated the property from the adjacent burial ground. When these were removed a few years ago, old pottery and bottles were found. Bygone names were carved into the trees.

The property today is still in the caring hands of United Community and Family Services that has expanded throughout Norwich and the greater Norwich area.

The path behind leads into the Lowthorpe Meadow, which offers fantastic walking trails. The WELTE inscribed bridges can be found at the end of the path behind the house. Look for other ornamental features like pillars dotting the perimeter of the path, stones sticking out of the former garden plots, and the remnants of a rainbow-colored kite in an old tree by the road. A local medium has seen figures in the hallway of the Huntington home.

Denison Homestead

Mystic/Stonington

For many travelers, Mystic is thought of more for its ice cream, aquarium, and specialty shops than its history. For the other set, Mystic *is* most certainly associated with history, albeit the seafaring industry and other depictions of bygone New England life at Mystic Seaport. In contrast to the fame of one of the state's primary tourist attractions (the Seaport), the Denison Homestead located up the road at 120 Pequotsepos Road showcases the stages of Mystic's past, but on a much smaller scale.

A visit to the Denison Homestead, correctly known as the Pequotsepos Manor, is a close view of the many stages of Mystic's history. The home, built circa 1717, welcomes visitors to tour its rooms, each representing a different era of the building's past. The home is set on 160 acres of land that was originally given to Captain George Denison in 1654 for his tenure in the service. Generations upon generations of the family abided in the home until the 1930s. Interesting historical tidbits are presented here about the family and Stonington, the town where the museum resides. One former family member, fourteen-year-old Elisha, was a cabin boy on an armed privateer docked in Stonington. The ship was captured by British troops and poor Elisha died on board a British prison boat. His family acquired his remains and interred Elisha in the Denison cemetery on Route 1.

The rooms of the home represent the progression of time from its years as a colony of the crown to the 1930s when the home was given to the George and Ann Borodell Denison Society for preservation. In 1946, the home was restored by noted colonial revival architect J. Frederick Kelly to make it into a museum.

Noted rooms of the home include the kitchen, bedroom, and parlor. The kitchen is presented in a colonial fashion from the 1740s and is where Lucy Gallup Denison, her daughters, and servants would gather around the hearth preparing the family's meals. Other activities and chores accomplished in this space, including churning butter, candle making, and grinding corn.

The Revolutionary War-era bedroom includes a four-poster bed made of maple built around 1750 and a trundle bed. The rooms progress through the ages. The parlor, with its fancy accoutrements is showcased in the federalist era. The Victorian-era bedroom is presented as it was in 1860 and includes a mahogany sleigh bed. The newest room arrangement is nicknamed "Aunt Annie's Parlor" named for Ann Borodell Denison Gates who helped transform the homestead into the museum as we know it.

This popular mini trip though the history of New England is a frequent location for school groups. So is the Denison-Pequotsepos Nature Center adjacent to the homestead, which features an exhibit of birds of prey, as well as many hiking trails. For a much less crowded, but still educational and entertaining jaunt through Stonington's past, make sure to visit the Pequotsepos Manor, otherwise known as the Denison Homestead.

Elmer Bitgood

Voluntown

As in any subculture, folklore has its own heroes. Figures like Paul Bunyan, John Henry, or Johnny Appleseed represent the crème de la crème of this genre. Some, like Bunyan, are purely fictional; others like Henry are heavily disputed in terms of their actual existence; whereas Appleseed represents the lot that were emphatically alive, albeit with legendary attributes. One popular subdivision in the folkloric realm of legendary individuals is the strongman. Many heroes of folklore, be it fact or fiction, are noted for their inhuman strength. John Henry died in a race against a machine, only to prove his prowess as a steel driver. Gigantic Paul Bunyan and Babe, his blue ox, embodied the strength of a team of lumberjacks. There is a constant fascination with those who display amazing feats of personal performance. Without this infatuation, the world of professional sports would not exist. Be it Michael Jordan, Nolan Ryan, Muhammad Ali, or Wayne Gretzky, these individuals would not have their place in the history books (or have become multi-millionaires). Sheer immensity of certain athletes, particularly in one aspect of the sporting world, professional wrestling, is a key to their fame. Here the world has come to love or hate larger-than-life figures. Connecticut's own World Wrestling Entertainment performers, like Hulk Hogan, Dwayne "The Rock" Johnson, and Andre the Giant, became true celebrities, hurdling over their point of origin into the mainstream of American culture. Fans of professional wrestling become excited over new performers, especially when they are physically immense. Favorites include Andre the Giant, 7'4" 520 pounds, the Natural Disasters, a tag team with the combined weight of roughly 850 pounds, and Giant Gonzalez who was eight feet

tall. All of these men were enormous. Crowds loved to see their sheer strength in action. Before the world of television, the public still had a fervent interest in strongmen. In this corner, weighing in at 350 pounds, standing at 6 feet 4 inches, and hailing from Voluntown, Connecticut, is Elmer Bitgood. Bitgood represents the best of both worlds, an actual strongman who took on legendary status. At one time he was even known as the "strongest man in the world."

Bitgood lived in the late nineteenth into the early twentieth century in rural Voluntown, tucked away in the eastern part of the state, only a boulder toss away from Rhode Island. Elmer was a logger and a handyman; many of his feats were accomplished near the sawmill. Elmer was raised on a farm with siblings, including two brothers, Doane and Paul, all known for their size though Paul was not quite the same stature as the other two. He eventually left town to become a doctor. Doane and Elmer were the pair, a turn-of-the-century Yankee version of Hans and Franz from *Saturday Night Live*. Although Doane was strong, stories circulated identifying Elmer's lifting prowess as inhuman. In addition to their power, the Bitgood boys were also known for their voracious appetites.

The tale of Elmer Bitgood presents an actual historical figure to whom oral tradition has given superhuman strength. Stories passed down through word of mouth tend to take on this quality, similar to the game "telephone" that children play. One whispers a phrase into another's ear only to be passed on numerous times. The end result is hardly ever the original saying and is usually quite amusing. A prime example of Elmer's exaggeration would be his size. Earlier in the passage, Bitgood's measurements were taken at over six feet and 350 pounds. At age twenty-five, in his prime, Elmer's actual height was 5' 9" weighing in at 290 pounds. Still a big boy, just not a giant. Elmer's story blurs where fact meets fiction. Although a newspaper might have reported an event, the paper was not always a reliable source. Certain Elmer anecdotes passed on from person to person are not verified. The fun part about folklore is that the "fact" does not in fact have to be a fact. Stories take on a life of their own no matter the topic. Elmer's accomplishments as a strongman and an eater are based on truth, who knows how much truth, but nevertheless are fun.

Elmer and Doane were never able to hit the gym after work. They were never able to compete in "tough mudder" or in Ultimate Fighting Championships or the WWE. They were not around to see the invention of steroids or in-home Bowflex weight machines. Although not privy to today's body enhancing mechanisms, the Bitgood boys designed their own contraptions similar to benches for lifting and weight machines found in gyms today. Elmer could throw boulders weighing up to 375 pounds ten to twelve feet! As a barbell, he used two barrels; legend says the contraption clocked in between 1,000 and 1,800 pounds! He would demonstrate his lifting ability near the sawmill on Sundays where it would become a regular and well-attended event. Another story recalls Elmer lifting a calf tied with a belt by his teeth. The newspaper reported that Elmer even lifted a railroad car for payment. He did not put the car down until he received his money. When asked directions while plowing the yard, Elmer would lift up the plow as a pointer to guide the inquisitor.

One of the more popular Elmer anecdotes is how he unstuck distressed vehicles. An oft-mentioned tale involves a Model T that was stuck in mud at the bottom of a steep hill. The car was full of tourists. Elmer was called in to make the situation right. He put a harness on and tied himself to the car. He proceeded to pull the car up through brute force by trudging up the incline. Competitions of strength were often held at country fairs in eastern Connecticut. Elmer was known to pull a team of horses and containers of rocks during this spectacle. He was often the anchor for the popular game of tug of war. Typical teams of five faced off between Elmer and one other person. It goes without saying who always won.

Pictures exist of Elmer. They show a barrel-chested man but certainly not a freak of nature by any account. Some show Elmer and Doane lifting boulders with certain weight amounts inscribed on them. Does this verify the weight or could the photos present a hoax, either in weight size or a doctored photo? Newspaper reporters tried as they could to verify the claim that Elmer was the "strongest man in the world." The Bitgoods did not allow their weights to be professionally checked though.

Other than having superhuman strength, Elmer was a kind, easy-going man, the stereotypical "gentle giant." He remained pure, not drinking liquor or using tobacco. Milk was his favorite drink. He likened his power to his clean living and was often compared to Samson from the Bible. Elmer was somewhat of an ineffectual worker, as he completed tasks slowly. He also had a definite speech impediment. The Bitgood homestead was on Wylie School Road in Voluntown, close to Beach Pond and today's Route 165. A collection of his barbells found on nearby Brown Road today were labeled 1,225 pounds but actually weighed between 1,520 and 1,700 pounds! Legends aside, Elmer could emphatically lift an enormous amount of weight.

Second only to Elmer's strength was his capacity to eat. The ironically named "Lil Elmer" was once known to drink ten gallons of milk in one gulp. His mother would prepare forty-five pounds of meat for him and his brothers. Elmer, preparing his plate first, left no one else a scrap. His mother would have to prepare meals for the Bitgood boys in a washtub. Area churches would not advertise for all-you-can-eat suppers in the area because they knew the boys would show up. At one particular baked bean dinner, Elmer and Doane each paid for five admissions to the feast and ate everything in sight. Another popular Elmer anecdote described Doane and Elmer's trek back home from Norwich. They would buy a fifty-five-pound cracker barrel in Norwich and on the sixteen or so mile journey back home eat the entire contents!

Elmer was born in 1870 and lived until 1938. He was a legend during and after his lifetime. Stories of his feats were passed down from one generation to the next and can still be seen in local newspapers sporadically today. Elmer grew up in Voluntown and eventually moved to Plainfield. Griswold, a town next to both of those, has a "Bitgood Road" and Plainfield has a street named "Bitgood Village." Elmer is Connecticut's Paul Bunyan, a larger-than-life fellow whose combination of history and legend has led to his notoriety present even in the modern world.

▶ The Bitgood family gravestone can be seen at the Robbins Cemetery in Voluntown.

While You're There!

Visit Roseledge Country Inn and Farm Shop in nearby Preston after you have traced the life of Elmer Bitgood. Originally the John Meech House, this is now a bed and breakfast that has been lauded by *Yankee Magazine* for the "best garden lover's bed and breakfast" in their annual "Best of New England" issue from 2014. The home was built in 1720 and has a tunnel system on the property that is adorned with stone walls. The shop is open daily and includes such items as candles, decorations, vegetables, and quilts. The inn also offers teatime for the public. The gardens on site are gorgeous. The inn is located at 418 CT Route 164 in Preston.

Jemima Wilkinson, Public Universal Friend

Ledyard?

As a kid growing up in eastern Connecticut I was familiar with the story of Jemima Wilkinson. She was a religious zealot who grew sick and died, only to return from the dead to lead her group of followers through the mid-Atlantic states, eventually settling in upstate New York. Through the telling of the story, Ledyard was consistently the place of her first demise. Even when I did a reading at Ledyard's Bill Library, audience members asked me about Wilkinson. In researching the story I was startled to find out that Wilkinson may not have actually lived in Ledyard, and her "return from the dead" was much more embellished than depicted. A big distinction between fact and legend is the location of Ledyard. Although many texts name-check the town, it was not incorporated until 1836 when the story places Jemima in town around 1776, when Ledyard was part of Groton.

Since this collection focuses on legends and folklore rather than complete factual history, I will present the legendary version first (especially since the historical record does not place her in Connecticut at all) and then outline the historical details.

Southeastern Connecticut had pockets of fervent religiosity in the eighteenth century that laid the groundwork for the story of Jemima Wilkinson, the Public Universal Friend. Wilkinson was born into a large Quaker family in Cumberland, Rhode Island, in 1752. She grew up on a small farm, was uneducated, but could recite Bible scriptures verbatim. Legend puts Jemima in Ledyard somewhere between the mid 1760s and mid-1770s. Looked at as odd by outsiders, Wilkinson's precipitous moment of her life occurred in 1776 when she fell ill and died. The hypothetical account depicts her in the coffin with a slew of insincere onlookers gathered around. A friend opened the coffin lid before she was lowered into the ground and there was Jemima, but instead of a ghostlike pallor, she was rosy cheeked and completely conscious. Wilkinson sat up in her coffin, proclaiming that she had seen "the light," had conversed with angels, and that her mission was to spread the Good Word. She said she was a heavenly prophet, a second redeemer, and she would show those who followed her a way to salvation.

The historical account references Wilkinson as having a fever or a mental breakdown of sorts. Some accounts recall her being in a trance that eventually broke with her then announcing that she had died and come back. In another version, she had a fever, and when it broke, she had her vision. Either way, she renamed herself the "Public Universal Friend" after her episode.

Society took two approaches to the Public Universal Friend. Some followed Wilkinson, becoming a "Jemimaite." Others in the community scoffed at her, spreading rumors based on what they thought were her outlandish religious notions. Some thought she was cavorting with the devil. Others likened her to a scam artist, trying to earn followers. The fact that she was a woman did not help matters any either. Although her religious views denounced sexual relations and promoted abstinence, scandalous stories abounded. Her proclamations coincided with the American Revolution; despite this, Wilkinson and her followers were pacifists and also were anti-slavery. One tale puts Wilkinson in the bedroom of Judge William Potter of Rhode Island, inappropriately cavorting with him when his wife walked in. The historical accounts though, depict Potter as a devoted follower, who opened his house to the Jemimaites and who freed his slaves as a result of his newfound beliefs. One popular folk tale associated with religious leaders was that they could walk on water. Wilkinson fell victim to the same story. When Wilkinson was asked to prove her divine powers by walking on water, a rousing call and response between Wilkinson and the crowd ensued, in which she supposedly asked them if they had faith. Of course the response was a resounding "yes." Then Wilkinson said, "Since you do have faith, that alone will show you proof that I am divine." Cleverly, she didn't have to demonstrate her ability to walk on water. Another slandering account tells of Jemima being asked to raise the dead. A very much alive follower being set in a predetermined coffin in a cemetery was waiting for her to "raise him up." When an army officer offered to prove that it was a corpse in the pine box by inserting his sword through, the follower hopped out of the box and ran away. Stories like this were spread to discredit Wilkinson and may not have actually been said of her, but instead were common tales spun about what some call false prophets.

For whatever the motives were, the Jemimaites moved west, settling for a while in Pennsylvania. Some accounts bring the religious sect outside Philadelphia; others to Tioga County in the northeastern part of the state. No matter their whereabouts in the Keystone State, the group eventually settled, for good this time, on the banks of Lake Keuka. The town they founded would be deemed Jerusalem, and the hamlet where Wilkinson's home was built in 1808 would be named Penn Yan, which stands for "Pennsylvania" and "Yankee," for the places of origin of her followers. Accounts also tell of Jemima placed on a cart that was carried by hand, emblazoned with the initials P.U.F. for the group's journey from Pennsylvania to New York. After her first demise, she spent forty-three years preaching the Good Word. Wilkinson was known for wearing long black flowing robes and, unusually, ate alone in her room. She also required a daily bath and wore clean clothes, very peculiar for this time period.

The Universal Friends Society did not last much longer after she issued her final breath of her "second life." Whether Wilkinson was a harmless religious eccentric or a con artist, her legacy lives in upstate New York, on the banks of Keuka Lake, where her Jerusalem's and Penn Yan's monikers live on due to her and her Jemimakin circle. Despite the question if Wilkinson actually lived in Ledyard or not, her story has found itself attached to the small eastern Connecticut town.

The Jober Midgets

Waterford/Salem/East Haddam

Human beings who appeared different in some way used to have the negative connotation of being called "freaks." Whatever the disability or deformity, be it dwarfism, elephantitis, or hypertrichosis, these individuals often found themselves winding up in sideshows of promoters like P. T. Barnum. One of Connecticut's most famous residents was a little person, General Tom Thumb, who was showcased by Barnum. Thumb, born Charles Sherwood Stratton, and wife, Lavinia,

were celebrities and accrued a large sum of money. After their heyday, another small couple was featured prominently in the Otis Smith Circus.

Nellie Way was born in the East Haddam/Salem area of the state in 1885. She grew up in Salem with ten other siblings. Nellie in full height was recorded at thirty or thirty-eight inches tall; it is disputed depending on the source. Two of her other siblings also had dwarfism, although they died before they reached adulthood. Unfortunately, many individuals in Nellie's position found the circus life the only career opportunity. Here they were able to procure a job, which was not often the case in other career fields. She traveled as part of the circus freak show where she eventually met her future husband, Stanley Jober, from Warsaw, Poland. They were married in New London in 1920. Jober was born in 1888.

Nellie was a talented musician, excelling at the violin, harp, and organ. The duo was billed as either the "Musical Jobers" or "Jober Midgets." Their stage names were Princess Nellie and Major Stanley. Major Stanley was sixteen inches taller than Princess Nellie, standing at forty-six inches. In photos, Stanley is seated while Nellie stands. Nellie was also an accomplished seamstress. They traveled and lived in a converted bus referred to as the "Circus Caravan."

Although many said that this duo were to fill the shoes left by Mr. and Mrs. Tom Thumb, the Jobers' careers never peaked like the Thumbs' did. Much of this was due to the fact that the Great Depression left many traveling circus shows bankrupt, which was the case for the Jobers.

Walter, one of Nellie's siblings, built them a scaled-down home, ten feet by thirty feet on Boston Post Road in Waterford. At the time of construction, this was lauded as the "smallest house in America." The home's location is directly across from Fog Plain Road in Waterford. Today, a small building still stands, although it looks as if it is part of a larger estate.

Princess Nellie found eternal rest in Jordan Cemetery in Waterford, with her epitaph simply etched with her stage name. Her sister is buried nearby. Stanley's whereabouts is unknown, although there is speculation he too is interred at Jordan Cemetery. There is also a contested theory that the Jobers had a regular-sized child.

Thank you to Suzanne Uznanski, whose grandfather's first cousin was Nellie Way Jober, for sharing with me the intriguing story of Stanley and Nellie.

The Old Leatherman

Western and Central Connecticut and Eastern New York

The process of choosing what stories to include and to exclude in a collection like this is harder than it sounds. One of the toughest decisions to make is often in regard to the more well-known legends. For the first book, I opted for Union Cemetery, Dudleytown, and the Green Lady of Burlington, but stayed away from other mainstays including the Leatherman. I decided to include the tale of the enigmatic Leatherman only after much urging by readers. At book talks or other events the Leatherman is asked about second only to Dudleytown. Similarly to the *Reader's Digest* versions of popular tales in the first volume, this Leatherman chapter will provide the basic overview, but not dive deeply into the annals of his existence since the topic has whole books and documentaries chronicling his life.

Similar to the mountain laurel (state flower), the praying mantis (state insect), and "Yankee Doodle Dandy" (state song), the Leatherman is the unofficial legendary

figure in Connecticut (although the former three are official). Deservedly so. Though dead for over 125 years, this luminary in the hermit world still finds himself in the public eye today, including as the topic of a Pearl Jam song, a B-side from their "Yield" sessions called "Leatherman." The folk singer Bob Beers sang a more traditional ballad, named for and about the Leatherman.

During the mid-nineteenth century, rovers scouring the land searching for food, money, and/or work were commonplace. Think of images of the hobo or the tramp wandering from one locale to the next in search of their next meal. Thought of as a nuisance, solutions suggested by some angry citizens included poisoning or shooting the homeless. In a sea of vagabonds, Connecticut's nameless wonder stood out. Not a very tall man, roughly 5'7" and weighing only about 165 pounds, he was remarkable for both his dress and mannerisms. Unlike most though, the Leatherman never begged for money or work, he only desired a meal (and some tobacco). Wearing sixty pounds of patchwork leather made from tops of boots, his coat, floppy hat, pants, and shoes all consisted of the same material. He wore the same outfit no matter the season—under the scorching summer sun or in driving snowy winds of a blizzard. Due to his namesake material he could often be heard and smelled before he was seen, with sun baked leather causing both odor and sound. He did not speak, communicating only in grunts and gestures.

He walked a loop, a cyclical route, each thirty-four days like clockwork, ranging from the Danbury area, east towards Watertown, southeast towards Southington and New Britain, then near Middletown and south to Old Saybrook. Here he started to travel back west along the coastal route. He passed by towns such as Clinton and Guilford, traversing around city centers like New Haven and Bridgeport, since he strayed away from the attention that city centers would bring. He would reach New York State near the Greenwich/White Plains border. At White Plains he would travel north, through such towns as Ossining, Pound Ridge, Peekskill, and Brewster. At Brewster he would head back east passing near the Danbury border of Connecticut. His loop was roughly 365 miles, traveling ten miles a day. Along his journey he would stop at the same farmhouses for a meal left out for him. The Leatherman's timing was impeccable as his visits occurred within minutes of the last one. For instance, if he showed up one day at 10:30 in the morning, he would be back 34 days later at 10:30 a.m. His sojourn would last only long enough to fill his stomach; he would never stay nor even come inside a home. Instead, he preferred lodging in rock caves, huts, and overhanging cliffs. The first sign of the Leatherman was in the town of Harwinton in April of 1858, although records show him most active between 1862 and 1889.

Although intimidating looking, with his large leather get-up, he was known for his reclusiveness and his desire to avoid confrontation of any kind. When approaching a home, he would knock at the door and give a gesture—fingers towards his mouth demonstrating that he would like food. After the meal was provided, he would nod his head in thanks, never uttering a word. The only time the Leatherman was known to yell was when children pelted him with rocks. Fortunately, this was a rare case, as many children took to him and even followed him for a while on his country walks.

There were cases of cruel people interrogating him to try to make him talk. One such event happened in Forestville, where men surrounded him, and threw him in a horse trough with the hope of making him speak. Another time a group of men tried to get him to talk by using excessive libation. When such an event occurred, the Leatherman never showed

up in that area again. Luckily, more often than not, he was treated as a respected guest.

Being a family who fed the Leatherman was an honor to most, a pride instilling gesture. One teacher in Bristol actually used the Leatherman as an incentive for her students. The student with the highest grade was able to bring in a treat for the wayfaring stranger. Class would be dismissed for the day and the students would line up to see him arrive. Along his route, the Leatherman frequented benevolent tanners who would provide him with scrap leather. When one parcel of his outfit wore thin, he would weave another piece in, creating a hodgepodge design of leather swatches. In his leather bag were all of his possessions including a hatchet, pan, tobacco, and matches. He procured his own pipe and the tobacco used was from cigar butts found discarded along his route. Found at the time of his death was a prayer book, written in French. He also carried a walking stick.

The identity of the Leatherman is controversial. Newspapers during his time identified him as Jules Bourglay (the spelling varies) originally of Lyon, France. The story goes that Jules was born into a poor family and, like his father, was a woodcarver. Eventually, he fell in love and had a clandestine affair with Margaret Laron, the daughter of a wealthy leather merchant. Due to differences in social class, the marriage could not be. Monsieur Laron agreed to let Jules apprentice as a businessman for him for a year. For the majority of the year, Jules succeeded, proving to his fiancée's father that he was worthy of his daughter. Unfortunately for Jules, the bottom fell out before the year was over. A series of bad investments as the price of leather dropped drastically left Laron's family business penniless. Another variation tells of a fire, mistakenly caused by Jules causing Laron's business to go up in flames.

Either way, Jules was not allowed to marry Margaret. This caused the lovesick and guilt ridden Jules to wander around the streets of Paris aimlessly. He was then committed to a monastery for mental rest and rehabilitation. Somehow he escaped and boarded a small boat to America where he was soon found pacing the back roads of Connecticut, forever filling his penance for destroying his true love's family business and never gaining her hand in marriage. The sixty pounds of leather were the physical manifestations of his guilt. This legend was associated with the Leatherman, but was found out to be fabricated by the press. At this time, newspapers, competing for readership would include fantastical articles to heighten their audience.

When he died, his grave was marked only by a pipe sticking out of the ground until 1953 when a historical society placed a plaque inscribed with the name Jules Bourglay in Sparta Cemetery in Ossining New York. Only more recently, spurred by exhumation efforts of his tomb by state archeologist Nick Bellantoni and reverence by Leatherman author and aficionado, Dan W. DeLuca, a proper monument now marks his resting place, inscribed with words "The Leatherman." Unusually, when his tomb was opened, nothing was found save for coffin nails. He was assumed to be French due to the prayer book in the language found with him at time of death and by the construction of the clogs he wore on his feet. A more recent speculation was that the Leatherman was actually of French-Canadian and Native American descent as noted by documented travels to Montreal and Vermont.

Unfortunately, the Leatherman's love of tobacco eventually claimed his life. Although he survived tempestuous weather, including the storm of the century, the fabled Blizzard of 1888, by hiding in a cave near Southington, cancer eventually claimed the life of the Leatherman. During his last few years, a sore on his lip multiplied in size and eventually ate away a portion of his mouth and jaw. Story also tells of the Middletown Humane Society picking him up and bringing him to Hartford Hospital where the cancer was diagnosed. One version tells of him with frozen hands and feet, trapped in a snow ditch when the Humane Society arrested him. Told to stay at the hospital, the Leatherman mysteriously vanished from the institution and was back on his march. During his last years, he had to crumble his food into coffee to eat due to his disfigured jaw. The Leatherman was found dead inside one of his caves in the region near Ossining, Mt. Pleasant, and Briarcliff Manor, New York, in late March 1889 by a young man who brought his fiancée to visit the location of the famed Leatherman.

Of course legends even after his death have embellished the tale of the Leatherman. After his death, he was said to have been seen in spirit form guarding many of his caves, especially when treasure seekers tried to find the location of his supposed wealth. Legend prevails that the Leatherman buried secret caches of riches in his cave dwellings. Although much of this could be written off as simply fanciful, copycats donned similar suits after his death, so the supposed ghost of the Leatherman could be in actuality one of his dopplegangers. Stories perpetuated even while he was alive. Some say he was asked, but of course refused, to be put on display as part of a freak show exhibit in New York City. Other accounts tell of the Globe Museum in New York acquiring his leather suit after his death and having an actor dressed as the Leatherman screaming, "I am the Leatherman, give me a child to eat!" In another variation, this same museum housed his leather suit on a wax figure of the mysterious man.

Today, Leatherman caves can be seen through the area of his route. Although seemingly buried deep in the woods now, during his time the land was cleared for pasture and the hideouts were easier to spot. The most popular of the Leatherman caves is in Watertown. With its overhanging rocks, the cave's impressive size could provide appropriate shelter from the elements. The cave is on the Mattatuck Trail.

The elusive Leatherman's true identity followed him to the grave in March of 1889. For a man who lived so long ago, he is still in the hearts and on the lips of those living in Connecticut and eastern New York today. Pictures do exist, taken without his permission. They can be seen easily online as well as in places like the Derby and Bristol Public Libraries. His legacy lives on in song, book, film, and has even become part of the school curriculum in Danbury. When an old timer spots a fire lit in the caves and crevices of eastern New York and western Connecticut, he says it is the Leatherman, taking shelter in one of his hideouts, warming himself by the fire as the smell of tobacco smoke wafts through the air.

Section 4
Out-of-the-Way Locales

Ayer Mountain and Bailey's Ravine

Franklin

Located off Ayer Road, a side road off Route 207 in rural Franklin, is Ayer Mountain. A scenic spot known for its waterfalls, dramatic cliffs, and panoramic views, the path up the mountain was once a major thoroughfare connecting the industrial towns of Norwich and Willimantic. In the days of yore, when horse and wagons ruled the roads, a series of switchbacks led the traveler up Ayer Mountain heading north from Norwich. Near the top, at one certain intersection, the weary sojourners, after a few drinks at a nearby tavern in Baltic, were said to have seen "Indian leprechauns." (Quite interestingly enough, the leprechauns' habitat is not far off from where the

Makiawisag, little people of Native American lore, were said to have been seen by Martha Uncas). On today's journey up Ayer Mountain the indentation of bygone wagon wheels can be detected. Most of the land in this region, although extremely rocky, was at one time used as pasture. It was cleared out and stone walls marked property lines. On top of the hill remnants of barns, farm houses, and even a school house can be found. The Maynard family lived here until the early 1900s. The road is made of a layer of loose rocks that allow water to go through.

Taking a different route down from Ayer Mountain, I followed a marked path alongside what is known as Bailey's Ravine. The steep journey down the mountain is on a much more meandering trail than the one that was used to climb up. It was certainly never used for horse and wagons! Along Bailey Brook, which eventually flows into the Yantic River, many kettle holes have formed as ponds within the rock formations. The whole journey

Stone walls delineate former property lines at Ayer Mountain.

Follow Bailey's Ravine down from Ayer Mountain.

downstream was full of fantastic views of the rocks, waterfalls that weaved in and out of the rocks, and the overall landscape of Franklin. The ravine was created by glacier that in turn led to the formation of the waterfalls that dot the land. One word of warning: this walk is steep and on rough terrain (especially with the weather I had on my latest trip there, torrential rain.) Look out for a rare fern species on your visit.

This area today is a nature preserve that was bought in 1988, known as either Bailey's Ravine or Ayer's Gap. Read the original *Connecticut Lore* for a legend which takes place near by.

While You Are There!

Feeling stressed? Visit Meiklem Kiln Works and Centerspace Wellness Studio on the Bozrah/Franklin town line for a range of activities that will soothe the soul and comfort the mind and body. From yoga to pottery class-es, from massage to acupuncture, a visit here will be a relaxing unwind after a hike in the Franklin woods. Look for other events including wellness fairs, book club discussion groups, and a variety of art classes here.

Aicher's Hill and Fairy Pond

Pomfret

Hidden in the woods of the Quiet Corner is a little known tract of preservation land called Aicher's Hill. Located off Freedley Street near the intersection of Routes 44 and 169, the entrance to the preserve is dotted with small signs that read "Windham Land Trust." The trail clearing is set between a corn field and a meadow, the latter of which is part of the land trust. Walk down this path with the corn field on the left and a meadow strewn with wildflowers on the right. The grass on the path has been beaten down from the tread of tractor tires. A little way down the path you arrive at "Fairy Pond." As soon as I got to the edge of the pond, a seemingly screaming frog dove into the lily pad encrusted waters. The pond is quite large, and must look stunning in autumn. I found this spot to be incredibly peaceful, with only the sound of frogs and insects permeating the air.

In trekking farther on the path, the incessant buzzing of insects swarming my head made me conjecture if the "fairy" nickname came from these ever-present pests. Aicher's Hill is an uphill, sprawling wildflower meadow. Unfortunately, my walk was cut short due to the pesky insects. At this point, I turned around and headed back through the swarm of bugs, past the fairy pond and back to the car on Freedley Street.

While venturing down the back roads (and actually highways, too) of the Quiet Corner, you may see signs that read "Quinebaug and Shetucket National Heritage Corridor." These are rivers, rivers that gave life to much of the region. They provided the basis of industry for the region from the colonial times up to the modern era. Although these rivers (along with their tributaries) are seemingly everywhere, you turn in the northeast part of the state, where do they start? There is a bit of an argument about the official source of the Quinebaug since it flows from a series of ponds. Some say its Mashapaug Lake in the town of Union; others say it is at East Brimfield Lake in Massachusetts. From Union, it flows northward through lakes and ponds of nearby Massachusetts, but then back down through Connecticut, providing power for the corridor of mill towns dotting the landscape until it joins with the Shetucket on the outskirts of Norwich. The Shetucket

begins in Willimantic at the confluence of the Willimantic and Natchaug Rivers. The Shetucket empties, along with the Yantic, into the Thames in Norwich harbor.

Wells Woods

Columbia

Unlike its much published brethren, the "ghost town" of Wells Woods has faded into the backstory of regional history. This could be attributed to its lack of notoriety, other than a myth that a deadly sickness killed off the whole village. Otherwise there are no supernatural legends associated with it. In any case, just like Connecticut's more famous ghost towns (Dudleytown, Bara Hack, and Factory Hollow Village), what remains of Wells Woods today is a dozen or so cellar holes and an old cemetery, although as of 2013, the town owns a portion of Wells Woods, the former Ira Root Homestead, which was deeded to Columbia from the Ramm family. The former home site is to be turned into a historical park called the Ira Root Historic Site with informative signage depicting the rough life of early settlers, with tours to be given by the historical society at times.

The parcel of land now known as Wells Woods is in the southeastern section of Columbia and today lies mostly on private land. Part of the former land parcel can be accessed via the town-owned Mono Pond Recreation Area, but please be cognizant of private property and no trespassing signs. Much of the former Wells Woods has been turned into a housing development. At one time though, it was a thriving village that held roughly ten percent of Columbia's population on about 800 acres and included twelve farms, factories, a cemetery, and a school house. Although trees and woods seem synonymous with the Connecticut's early landscape, this was certainly not the case. Early settlers cleared much of the land for farming. Even in a rural town like Lebanon, which Columbia was part of until 1804, most of the land was utilized for farming, save for 1,500 acres close to the border with Hebron that were owned by the town's second minister, Samuel Welles, in the 1700s.

In 1816, a relative of Samuel, John Welles, inherited the land and decided to subdivide the acreage. He created a highway through the parcel of land from which he would sell off twenty- to forty-acre plots on either side. The highway is now called Wells Woods Road. The families who bought these land pieces were related via blood or marriage and originally hailed from the Montville and Waterford areas of the state.

One of the original settlers, Ira Root, in 1820 at age twenty-seven, bought forty-two acres of land on the highway that Welles created. Root would become a prominent citizen in town, eventually becoming the Columbia representative to the Connecticut General Assembly in 1844, and his land would increase to 110 acres. When he passed, he left his home and property to his great nephew, Ralph Curtis, since Root only had daughters. Clayton R. Root would be the last Root to own the homestead, leaving the home in 1904. The house finally was destroyed by fire in 1934. Root was born in 1793 and died in 1875 at the age of eighty-one. He married Sarah Dart in 1816, whose parents were Stedman Dart and Sallie Wheeler. Root and his by-marriage family of Wheelers settled most parcels of Wells Woods.

The first settler to Wells Woods was a German builder named Gosper Webler, who was related to Ira Root by marriage. Webler's father came ashore to America as part of the Hessian army but deserted. Gosper was the first to settle Wells Woods and encouraged the other family members to homestead here as well. He bought eighty acres of land and soon brought his family—two brothers, his aging parents, and five brothers-in-law plus families who developed another eighty acres. Soon, in 1823, the population grew enough for the need of a schoolhouse. Life was tough at Wells Woods; farming was the main occupation, but soon the soil proved to be too thin and rocky to be sufficiently arable. The village looked to other forms of industry including a saw and shingle mill. The Wheelers were adept at woodworking, building houses and ships, and the dense forest provided ample resources at first, but eventually the landscape was approaching barren. Root was one of the only family members who stayed put in Wells Woods, mostly on the basis of his successful agriculture. Most of the family's sons moved to manufacturing centers of Manchester and Hartford, where jobs were more easily attained and wages were regular.

Webler in time left Columbia to start another settlement in the mid-Atlantic region, but before that he constructed the Congregational church on the green in Columbia. Along with Root, another early settler's family finally left in the early twentieth century, and by the time of the Great Depression, all of the once-proudly standing homes of Wells Woods had either fallen victim to neglect or fire and had collapsed, burned, or stood as empty shells.

Today, the former village of Wells Woods can be seen by traces of its cellar holes and foundations. The Root family cemetery remains. Unfortunately, most of Wells Woods is off limits since the land is private and belongs to families of the nearby houses.

Wells Woods, a town without supernatural leanings, provides the same kind of glimpse into the past as Connecticut's other "ghost towns": an agricultural village with early forms of industry, whose populace left due to aridity of the soil and the "non-dependency" of income. Wells Woods Road was the major thoroughfare of the village and can be traveled today.

Haley Farm

Groton

As a runner in high school one of my favorite aspects of the meets was traveling to the various towns in the region to run on their cross-country courses. Some schools' running trails consisted primarily of running around the high school building a few times, but others utilized their towns' greenspaces. My alma mater, Norwich Free Academy had a difficult course, winding in and out of trails in Mohegan Park in Norwich, through woods, around ponds, and up steep hills. Running against East Lyme brought the team to Rocky Neck State Park, with its gorgeous ocean views, and the state meets at Wickham Park in Manchester brought with it varied terrain in a spectacular setting. Running against Fitch High School in Groton brought the team to Haley Farm, a lesser-known state park along Groton's shoreline, which I remembered as being truly exquisite as well as off the beaten path.

Located between the villages of Poquonnock Bridge and Noank, on the banks of Palmer Cove is this gem of a state park. This land was originally part of Winthrop Neck, a large parcel of land owned by Governor John Winthrop Jr. Most of the time, the land was used as a dairy farm run by Caleb Haley and kept in the family for generations. Haley enjoyed racing horses around "Racetrack Pond." The buildings on site among others included the homestead, carriage house, and ice house. In 1960, the homestead burned down, and when the site was to become a park, the other buildings were condemned and had to be razed. Today, only foundations remain on site.

A visit to Haley Farm allows the traveler peeks of the cove.

In the late 1960s, a developer was looking to turn the area of Haley Farm into Coast Guard housing, but citizens of Groton cried out. A "Save Haley Farm" brochure was created to drum up support. Champion marathoner and Fitch High School teacher and coach John J. Kelley promoted it. Future marathoner Amby Burfoot put together a concert for raising funds. Other fundraising endeavors included bake sales, pony rides, and car washes.

Today, Haley Farm is a serene place to walk a dog, run, jog, or as I saw on my latest visit, horseback ride. The landscape includes red maple and white oak trees, meadow grass, sedge, and sphagnum moss. The terrain ranges from swampy to grassy to ocean front. Haley built incredible stonewalls, not just rocks placed in a strategic way, but instead humongous boulders arranged seamlessly together. Canopy Rock, otherwise known as Jemima's Rock, is an impressive boulder on the property. Views of Long Island Sound with Palmers Cove, originally called Taskegonucke, a Native American word for "shellfishing area" can be seen on a jog or during a cross-country ski through the park. The park became state property in 1970, with more acreage added in 2002. The park is now connected to its bigger brother, Bluff Point, via trail and incorporates part of the Groton to Mystic bikeway within its borders.

In the scheme of Groton parks, with others like Bluff Point and Esker Point overshadowing it, Haley Farm often gets unjustly overlooked. With its natural beauty and varied terrain, this state park is a must visit.

▶ It is located on Haley Farm Road in Groton.

While You're There!

To me, the salt air brings to mind shellfish. Located in nearby Noank, Ford's Lobsters is a no frills, eat outside lobster shack. Just like Haley Farm, which is often overlooked in favor of Bluff Point State Park, Ford's is overlooked by tourist-favored Abbott's. Ford's offers beautiful views of Long Island Sound. The only thing better than the view is the food. Personal favorites include the lobster roll and oysters.

Elizabeth Park
Hartford and West Hartford

Hartford's Elizabeth Park is a must see for any horticulture enthusiast. Highlighted by their 15,000 bushes of roses displaying a jaw-dropping 800 varieties, this municipal rose garden is lauded as one of the best in New England. Designed by famed landscape architect Theodore Wirth, the rose garden has been in existence since 1904, making it the oldest town-owned rose garden in the country. Keep a lookout for "Rose Weekend" or "Rose Sunday" in late June, which is peak viewing and smelling season for the roses. (It is also a *very* well attended event, so get there early.) In the '70s, due to lack of funding, the rose garden was standing in the shadow of a bulldozer. Luckily, concerned citizens stepped in to procure the necessary funds to keep the garden growing for another year. For over 110 years, the public has been able to stop and smell the roses at Elizabeth Park and even better, can do so for free, as there is no admission to the park.

Elizabeth Park is much more than its rose garden though. Other gardens on site include a perennial, a shade rock, herb, and tulip gardens. It has a premier restaurant, the Pond House Café, known for its fresh ingredients, some grown on site! The park has two ponds to visit: Lily and Laurel Pond. Speaking of ponds, the former estate of Charles Pond is the land that the park sits on. After his wife passed on, Charles bestowed upon Hartford his property to be turned into a park named for his wife, Elizabeth. During Pond's tenure, his manor and surrounding grounds were known as Prospect Hill. Today's Elizabeth Park also includes greenhouses to explore, tennis courts to play on, and a takeout window called the Dog House to grab a hotdog. Pond's former mansion became the park's community center. Sunrise Overlook has a phenomenal view of Hartford's skyline.

On the next beautiful summer day, make sure to take a stroll under the rose-covered trellises in Elizabeth Park. Enjoy this urban oasis and thank Mr. Pond for leaving his estate to the city for generations to revel in.

▶ The main entrance to the park is located at the corner of Asylum and Prospect Avenues.

While You're There!

Close to Elizabeth Park in downtown West Hartford is Bartaco. This is the luncheon spot of the famed Barcelona tapas restaurant next door. Bartaco offers small plates as well. I thoroughly enjoyed a sampling of bite-sized tacos. My favorites were the baja fish, ribeye, and chicken. Along with the tacos, I split a salad. It made a perfect size lunch as I washed it down with a Mexican Coke. The hip décor would not look out of place in Brooklyn with its industrial design.

Sleeping Giant State Park

Hamden

For a sleeping giant, Hobbomock certainly gets around. You may remember him from the original *Connecticut Lore* stirring up trouble in Moodus, causing unusual noises reverberating from the ground. Although his name in that story was Hobomoko, it is the same guy...err spirit. Talk about prolific, he is named in Native American lore throughout southern New England. Not only making his mark in central Connecticut, Hobbomock/Hobomoko (there are many different variations of the spelling and pronunciation due to different dialects) is also to blame for killing a woman at Purgatory Chasm, at both locations with that moniker in Rhode Island and Massachusetts. His rampage finally stopped when he ate some bad shellfish.

For the first-time visitor to Sleeping Giant State Park on Mt. Carmel Avenue in Hamden right near the campus of Quinnipiac University, the ridge line of the mountain chain clearly resembles a human figure lying on its back. Since mountains are big, it is not simply any human figure, but the outline of a giant, the aforementioned Hobbomock to be exact. He is likened to the devil, but this idea was only introduced after Christianity was brought into the area. He has generally been considered a malevolent spirit. One story depicts him as a spirit of the Quinnipiac tribe who was perturbed over the maltreatment of his brethren. Being so large, in his fit of rage, his footfall caused the bend in the Connecticut River that can be seen today near Middletown. His adversary, the hero spirit, Keitan, was tired of Hobbomock's outbursts and he cast a spell on his enemy, causing him to forever sleep on the spot where he now lies.

Another variation casts Hobbomock in a very different light. In this story, he seems to be unfairly misjudged by all of the bad press, almost like Shrek. Hobbomock was a spiritual leader of his people as he preserved both land and sea, but he eventually became upset when the over-confident tribe found themselves losing touch with nature and leaving behind their ability to communicate with animals. This made him livid, which created the reputation that he now carries. A local wise man decided he needed to cease the giant's anger for the benefit of his people. This wise man presented the giant with a plate of oysters. Being a sucker for raw seafood, Hobbomock slurped the bivalves, relishing each briny bite. (I wonder if they were Bluepoint oysters?) These tasty morsels were charmed with a sleep-inducing spell. It knocked the giant flat on his back right where he stood, creating the range as it looks today. A last version, with little embellishment, mentions that Hobbomock was a bad giant who was put to sleep so that the nearby population could be at peace.

Whatever the case, or even if it was really put there by glacier (not nearly as fun), Sleeping Giant State Park is today a premier place for hiking in central Connecticut. The 1,533-acre park consists of thirty-two miles on eleven different trails. One, the Tower Trail, leads to the four-story stone tower at the top, which was built by the Civilian Conservation Corps during the era of the Great Depression. This trail runs for 1.5 miles up to the tower. Other than hiking, popular activities include picnicking, fishing (there is a trout pond), camping, and even yoga. There are rhododendron bushes that bloom spectacularly in the late spring, and the autumn foliage is a must-see, looking from the bottom at the range or from the top, peering out over the Connecticut landscape into Long Island Sound. Sleeping Giant is the beginning of the interstate Metcacomet Trail, which winds itself up to Mount Monadnock in lower New Hampshire.

Sleeping Giant is a true Connecticut gem. This beautiful state park, which includes a stone observation tower, is full of recreational activities and even has legends associated with it. That's hard to top! One word of warning: I sure would not want to be hiking on Sleeping Giant when Hobbomock wakes up. He is going to be incensed and hungry for more oysters probably even with mignonette sauce!

The Beinecke Rare Book and Manuscript Library

New Haven

When I think of the architecture of New Haven's Yale University, its Gothic towers, peaks, and arched windows come to mind. Although Yale's building campaigns during the era of modern architecture contradict this notion, the most striking antithesis to the Gothic perception of Yale has to be the Beinecke Rare Book and Manuscript Library that resembles a giant concrete box and whose windowless façade looks closer to being abandoned than holding many of the world's rarest books.

Located at 121 Wall Street, the Beinecke houses some of the most impressive titles known to man. An original Gutenberg Bible, John James Audubon's *Birds of America*, the first four folios of Shakespeare, an original Vinland map that depicts Viking exploration of the "new world," and papers by such luminaries as Charles Dickens, Ezra Pound, and Eugene O'Neill are in the Beinecke. The library was built by Gordon Bunshaft in 1963 of the firm

Skidmore, Owings, and Merrill, the group who also designed One World Trade Center, the Willis (formerly Sears) Tower, and John Hancock Center in Chicago. When first erected, the feedback was overwhelmingly negative regarding the design of the *avant garde* Beinecke; more than fifty years on though, the library has been embraced wholeheartedly. The nondescript exterior is actually necessary for the preservation of the rare books. In the place where windows could logically go are marble panels. From the inside, the marble panels glow from the light of the sun as they protect the invaluable items. Once inside, the exhibition hall of sorts is along the perimeter, while the middle holds a six-story glass encased, locked rare-book stack area. When I visited, the outer display featured Audubon's book, the Shakespeare Folios, and the Gutenberg Bible.

The Yale library system is the seventh largest in the world, and this branch in particular holds millions of manuscripts and 600,000 volumes in its library. Adjacent to the library is a sunken courtyard. In 2005, art thief Forbes Smiley was caught with an X-acto blade. It was soon revealed that he had in his possession stolen maps from the library. In more of the realm of this book, one of the most fascinating legends associated with the Beinecke is that due to its construction during the Cold War, the six-story book case would submerge into the basement in case of a nuclear attack.

The Beinecke is free and open to the public, although tight measures are placed on anyone actually wanting to look at a rare book. Along with many of Yale's other treasures, including the Musical Instruments Museum, Art Gallery, and Museum of Natural History, the Beinecke is most certainly worth a stop, even just to ogle at the presence of such treasures.

On a side note, the statue *Lipstick (Ascending) on Caterpillar Tracks* was originally placed in the library's courtyard, but now can be found at the plaza of Yale's Morse College. It is a bit hard to find, but visiting Lipstick is worthwhile if you are up for a scavenger hunt!

Time Machine Hobby Shop

Manchester

This sign marks the entrance to the Time Machine Toy and Hobby Shop.

Before I begin to write, I make a list of places I want to investigate further, although sometimes my only lead is the name, not knowing anything else about it. One of those places was the Time Machine Hobby Shop. All I had written was the words, but I did not know anything else about it. I knew the store was in Manchester, but being "just a store," I was thinking of skipping it on my research road trip through that area of the state. At the last minute I reconsidered; I was so close by, I decided to stop.

As soon as I ambled into the store, I knew I was in for a treat. This is not just an ordinary hobby shop or toy store, but a two-level (plus another store, a gaming locale across the street) megalith of model trains, board games, and toys of all kinds in an old factory building.

I started my step back in time on the top floor,which is mainly dedicated to model trains. Elaborate train sets, with their locomotives and adjoining cars, meander on tracks throughout the store. Some of the train sets are even held up by original features of the interior of the mill. Trains are run on certain days, at the time of writing, the first and third Sundays of every month. The sets are so elaborate that the display features details like a replica miniature Dairy Queen, Peter Pan bus, and Dunkin Donuts. Signs showcasing train stops like Meriden, Cedarville, and Portland adorn the walls. The store is a terrific use of the old mill with its tall ceilings and duct work. The trains maneuver their way along the perimeter of the second floor. A selection of doll houses is also on the top floor as well as a thorough selection of "Images of America" books.

A separate track features minute versions of circus elements and a Ferris wheel. The Silk City Model Railroad Club holds its meetings at Time Machine as well as the Central Valley N Scale Model Railroad, a group that specializes only in the N Scale railroad cars, which are tinier model trains. As well as the displayed trains, the store offers many model trains and accessories, such as trees and other geographical features to embellish your model train set. Be forewarned though, many of these are collectors items are not typical Toys 'R Us prices. Some single trains were priced at $350, $500, and even $700! The arcaneness of the hobby attracts a small but incredibly devout following.

As much fun as the upstairs was, for someone like me, who is not a train enthusiast (but who does enjoy looking at them), the first floor was where I could actually get some shopping done. Although the first floor features an extensive model collection, it also houses the "this, that and everything else" of the toy world. It was interesting that I did not see any video games or big franchise action figure toy lineups here (although I was pleased to see "Bone Crushing Buddies" wrestling figures including Stone Cold Steve Austin). Refreshingly, the Time Machine Hobby Shop is the anti big box toy store.

The first floor is truly a smorgasbord of fun, the kind of place where families must make annual trips. From Mr. Men books to candy, from Madlibs to educational toys, it has something for everyone (even us adults). Of course they had throwback toys like Lite Brite, Calico Critters, Hot Wheels, and Duplo. The Fisher Price record player, a color changing top, Lincoln logs, Tinkertoys, and erector sets may seem out of place in many mall toy stores, but are right at home here! The board game section is extensive. Intriguing to me was something called "Baseball: The Dice Game" and the "Donuts" game. Their many versions of Monopoly include Nintendo, Metallica, and the Rolling Stones. My parents were extremely happy to see a deck of their favorite card game, Rage, a lesser known cousin to UNO by the same manufacturer. Their educational supplies not only featured elements of art kits like paint and markers, but also Kumon Publishing math word problem workbooks and learning games. The model section included planes, soldier and battleships, Gundam models, and cars. Everything is displayed tastefully. Stock cars and radio control vehicles also occupy a large part of the floor's real estate. The Lego section was large, too. After the record -breaking snowy winter we had, I wish I had bought the snowball maker! My interest was also piqued by the game with the unfortunate title of "Silent, But Deadly."

My purchases that day included a wooden puzzle bought for my two-year-old niece for her upcoming birthday and a backup set of Rage cards. Trust me, the next time I visit I will be targeting some classic toys and a game or two. It is the perfect place to bring a child to see the look of wonder on their face as they experience a truly wonderful toy store, which is a rare thing these days.

Across the street is a separate building nicknamed "The Portal" that features role playing games and is popular with gamers of all ages. Dungeons and Dragons and Magic the Gathering are staples here. An all-day board game session called "Portal Con" also takes place on the premises.

▶ The Time Machine Hobby Shop is centrally located not far from Manchester's downtown at 71 Hilliard Street, right off Route 83.

While You're There!

Take Woodbridge Street east from Time Machine until it meets Route 6, head east, and make sure to grab a bite at Shady Glen, a Connecticut classic. Shady Glen is to restaurants what Time Machine is to toy stores. Instead of soy lattes and spicy tuna rolls, Shady Glen dishes out tried-and-true standards like cheeseburgers, ice cream, and milk shakes served by waitstaff in bow ties and paper hats. The cheeseburger is a true thing of beauty. The cheese spills over the side of the bun and is hardened resembling a taco salad bowl. The crunch of the cheese mixed with the good old fashioned hamburger is phenomenal. Thick milkshakes make the perfect dessert. One of the state's true originals, this diner is a can't miss!

The Garde Theatre

New London

"The Garde," as locals refer to it, is a premier performance venue and movie house in the heart of downtown New London. It is a landmark amongst the ever changing landscape of the Whaling City.

The theater, officially known as the Garde Arts Center, was built in 1926 on the land of the former estate of successful merchant whaler William Williams. Williams's mansion was purchased by the owner of the New London Day, who eventually sold the land that would be turned into the theater. The Garde, named after Walter Garde, a prominent Hartford and New London businessman, was designed by Arland W. Johnson, architect of other theaters, like the Palace Performing Arts Center in New Haven, the Palladium in Worcester, and Proctor's Theater in New York City. The interior's design is in a Moroccan style including murals with depictions of the Middle East that were created by Vera Leeper.

The first film shown at the Garde was on September 22, 1926, and was called *The Marriage Clause*. The theater featured not only movies, but vaudeville acts as well. During the '20s, it was heralded as one of the best theaters in all of New England. Three years later, in September of 1929, the theater was purchased for one million dollars by Warner Brothers. It was one of the venues that was used to lead the "talkie" or talking pictures movement. Throughout the years, the Garde was a phenomenal place to see a movie or a show. A full house watched the premier of the *Godfather* movie in New London, and the Sonny Liston – Cassius Clay boxing match was televised here on the big screen. As the twentieth century progressed and downtown locations were not in vogue, the Garde lost viewership as it tried to compete with suburban retail centers with cinemas.

Unlike many movie houses and theaters that met their maker with the suburban push, the Garde lumbered on, albeit with the wrecking ball casting a dark shadow. The theater closed in 1977 and was sold to a local business owner. Later, the nonprofit Garde Arts Center was formed and purchased the building in 1985.

Since then, the theater has evolved into a whole complex, including the adjacent Mercer and Meridian buildings. Today's Garde even includes the Oasis Room, which is a smaller venue on site.

Since its reincarnation, the Garde has played host to many world renowned acts, including Johnny Cash, Tony Bennett, Loudon Wainwright III, Richard Thompson, Bob Dylan, STOMP, The Flying Karamasov Brothers, and Penn and Teller, as well as independent movie features and a children's theater series. The Eastern Connecticut Symphony Orchestra has called the Garde home since 1987.

Today's New London, chock full of bohemian vibe, bars, art galleries, and music venues, proudly proclaims the Garde as its ringleader of premier entertainment. As well as national performances, the theater can also be rented for events, such as weddings, with the couple's names highlighted on the marquee. In November of 2014, local author Wally Lamb's premiere of his novella turned movie *Wishin' and Hopin'* held two showings at the Garde with much fanfare. Both viewings were greeted by a full house! My fondest memory of the Garde (other than Lamb's premiere) was watching Bob Dylan on his Neverending Tour of 1998, supporting his *Time Out of Mind* album, when a large incense stick, left burning behind Dylan, had ash drop off into a trash can, which caused a small garbage fire, soon to be snuffed out by theater staff. I believe Dylan had no recognition of the event happening behind him as he ripped through an unrecognizable version of "Leopard Skin Pillbox Hat."

▶ The Garde Arts Center is located at 325 State Street in New London and can be found on the web at www. gardearts.org.

While You're There!

For the best Italian food in town and a location across Huntington Street from the Garde, go to Tony D's. Located in an unassuming building (across the street from historic Whale Oil Row, with incredible columned sea captains' houses), Tony D's knows how to do Italian food. My suggestion would be to start with the fried calamari for an appetizer. Breaded, but not too heavy, its squid rings are bathed in a scrumptious mix of herbs, and its chewy texture will leave an unforgettable flavor on your palate. My entrée of choice is the Zuppa de Pesce, a bouillabaisse of seafood impeccably served over pasta. A classic selection, but the tiramisu is certainly worth saving room for. Make sure to pay respects to the portrait of *Seinfeld's* "The Kramer" as you walk out.

Taft Tunnel
Lisbon

The Taft Tunnel is in Lisbon, near the Norwich border, on the rail line that travels from Norwich to Worcester on the banks of the Quinebaug River. The Taft Tunnel is the oldest train tunnel still in use in the country. Trains pass by three to four times a day. Once upon a time, the Norwich-Worcester line was populated by travelers

Look at the entrance and exit of the Taft Tunnel; it is reputedly the oldest train tunnel still in use.

and cargo alike with its freight locomotives pulling up to 100 cars at a time! When laying track north from Norwich, towards Jewett City, the engineers ran into a hulking problem blocking their way. An imposing granite rock face blocked building momentum. This immense granite protrusion sloped directly into the raging waters of the Quinebaug near its junction with the Shetucket. Digging through the granite was the only solution. The tunnel was dug out by using hand tools like picks and shovels, with help from gunpowder used as an explosive (this was done before the advent of dynamite). The project began in 1836, and trains were ready to rumble through in August of the following year.

Lisbon is proud of its tunnel, heralding it on their town website and using it as the cover for the 1996-1997 Annual Report. The tunnel was even used in a scene for the local horror film *Vampyra*. To get to the tunnel, the best bet is to park on the right side of the road if traveling on Route 12 north, coming from Norwich. Although the signs are clearly marked with "No Trespassing," after talking with the folks at the town office, my wife and I were encouraged to visit the site. On the side of Route 12, a few worn paths lead into the woods. We took the path marked by the closed metal gate. After a quick jaunt through the woods, I was soon on the Norwich-Worcester railroad tracks. Walking alongside the tracks, the tunnel is a few minutes' walk north. These tracks did seem a bit eerie. Maybe it was the presence of the rustic hydroelectric plant alongside the Lisbon-Preston waterfall dam or the sign on the Preston side of the river that warned of grave danger. Also disconcerting was the fact that the still active tracks did not give much room on either side if a train came since one side was a steep rockside and the other led to the raging waters of the Quinebaug. An unusual sound reverberated in these woods too which was most likely a bird, but distinctively sounded like a monkey. Once we got to the tunnel, which measures about 300 feet long and 20 feet wide, we started snapping pictures, but did not venture deep inside due to the possibility of an oncoming train. Much to our chagrin, but at the same time delight, a freight train soon passed by! As we were walking away from the tunnel, we heard a rumbling up ahead and soon after heard a whistle and saw the light of a locomotive. Be sure to get official permission if you choose to venture out here!

On nearby Lower Blissville Road is the Keystone Bridge, the last freestanding stone bridge in the country. It currently spans about two feet over a brook. It is near the junction of Blissville and Icehouse Roads. Hurricane Sandy did much damage to the structure, but it is still there, albeit a shell of its former self. The bridge was used as part of a stagecoach road. The stone structure of the bridge can still be seen; the rocks look as if they were glued together and stacked side by side. Much of the area was washed away due to tremendous flooding, but at least a little bit of history remains.

Squaw Rock and Cave

Plainfield and Bolton

Even diabolical place names like Devil's Hopyard State Park or Hell Hollow Road can seem mundane when they are used as part of a normal repertoire of vocabulary words. Growing up in eastern Connecticut, taking a ride to that state park was not out of the ordinary, yet I never stopped to think of the peculiarity of having a family outing where presumably Satan grew an ingredient vital to brewing beer. Although less extreme than Lucifer, other commonplace names were also thrown around in conversation without an examination into their origin. Driving home from biweekly trips to Nana's in Danielson every Sunday, my father would opt for meandering back roads instead of the direct highway option or even the gorgeous Route 169. Instead, we would venture on these passageways that brought us deep into the bowels of Killingly and Plainfield. Ambling down country roads with names like Snake Meadow and Squaw Rock, it never dawned on me that their names could have deeper connotations than a typical "Main Street" would.

Not until presenting at a book talk at the Salem Library was the association of Squaw Rock Road brought to my attention. Although a highway exit off the Route 6 connector in Killingly bears its name, there is little fanfare regarding the street's moniker. Even friends of mine who live on the road knew nothing of its significance. Unfortunately, the gentleman who mentioned Squaw Rock to me has since passed, but from his recollection as well as research into the annals of Plainfield history, I have procured a historical account of the intriguing name. Additionally in my research, I stumbled upon another geological formation with a similar context,

Squaw Cave in Bolton Notch State Park, but first on to the Rock.

Squaw Rock, sometimes referred to in the plural, Rocks, is in the northern section of the town of Plainfield, roughly three miles from the center of Moosup (a village in the town). This region saw its share of Native American battles. Caves in this area were used as hiding spots for squaws and papooses as well as used for a safe haven in the wintertime. Other formations in the geological landmass include Devil's Kitchen, Old Ladies' Stove, and Old Ladies' Arm Chair which are caves. There is a flat rock named the Dancing Floor as well as the Fiddler's Stand, which is also called Pulpit Rock.

Plainfield is not the only natural locale with the title of squaw in the state. Although Plainfield's rocky outcropping has a highway sign giving away its approximate location, Squaw Cave in Bolton is better known. The cavern is tucked inside of Bolton Notch State Park, close to the intersection of Routes 44 and 6 and Interstate 384 (and not far from Shady Glen restaurant—check out "While You're There" in the chapter about the Time Machine Hobby Shop for more information on Shady Glen). The cave is also right off the Hop River Trail. The Squaw Cave is named so for an Indian maiden named Wunnee. She fell in love with and married a cabin boy who worked aboard the Dutch ship the Fortune. His name was Peter Hager. Wunnee was part of the Podunk tribe and the couple's marriage was celebrated in typical Podunk fashion. The ship docked in the area of South Windsor in the spring of 1620. Here young Peter enjoyed spending free time exploring the surrounding forests. This is how he met his future bride. When word got out that Hager had married an Indian princess, Englishmen were sent to capture him. One of the pursuing party was killed amidst a skirmish with Hager. Hager and Wunnee took shelter in a nearby cave.

Eventually, one of the Englishmen shot Hager. He staggered his way back to the cave, but ultimately perished. By the time the party arrived at the cave, Hager's body was gone. The legend veers off at this point with accounts stating that Wunnee brought the body of her beloved husband out a rear entrance of the cave before the Englishmen could reach it. Other variations include Hager buried in a Podunk cemetery in present East Hartford while another account simply states that his body disappeared. The legend has brought with it tales of the supernatural. The ghosts of Wunnee and Hager are both supposed to haunt the area near the cave in Bolton Notch. Others have spotted quarrymen who worked the land. Even the Narragansett chief Miantonomo's spirit has been linked to this area (seems odd since he met his fate by the blade of Uncas's brother Wawequa in what is now the Greeneville section of Norwich). The park is also well known for its superb vistas as well as graffiti-covered rocks.

The Baltic Grist Mill and Sprague Historical Society

Sprague

Baltic is the quintessential mill village, with streets arranged in a grid pattern lined with row houses, the ruins of the mill that once loomed proudly over the town, and the corner store where the villagers bought their necessities. One key component of industrial Baltic was the grist mill, located in the heart of downtown, at 76 Main Street. Like many Industrial Revolution-era buildings, once its function had ceased, its use was discontinued. Fortunately for this grist mill, the town

library took residence on its first floor, but the grindstone and other bits of its manufacturing past had long since rusted over and were covered with cobwebs.

In the present day, long-neglected factory buildings have found a second life as condos, retail spaces, and art galleries. In the grist mill, the third floor, which was used strictly as forgotten storage space for seventy-five years, was turned into the home of the Sprague Historical Society in 2011. The historical society serves as a museum to showcase the past of the villages of Sprague: Baltic, Versailles, and Hanover (interesting to see three European place names that are not of English descent in New England, although Versailles was not named for the palace of the Sun King). The third floor was expertly renovated, exposing the original beams, refinishing the floor, and putting in full view the machinery that ran the mill.

Today's building houses the library on the first floor, a function hall on the second floor where events like wedding showers and private events are held, and the museum on the third floor. Many of the exhibits were donated by Dennis Delaney who was the first historian of Sprague. Delaney lived from February 27, 1929, to December 14, 2003. His daughter, Mary Delaney, is the current director of the historical society. The museum consists of relics of Sprague from the bygone era. Numerous photographs depict Sprague during its years as a factory town. The large Baltic Mill, which burned in 1999, was the lifeblood of the village and is prominently featured as is the waterfall that provided power to the town. Town military memorabilia are displayed, as well as signs that were once used in the mills, and old fashioned dolls in baby carriages. All of the artifacts represent numerous historical facets of the three villages in town. The museum is a popular destination for local school field trips.

Other exhibits include "The First Industrialists of Sprague" and a photo album of pictures through the years from Sprague's annual talent show. Every conceivable talent was demonstrated, from a man wearing a grass skirt doing the hula to another who reenacted Christ crucified on the cross. Of course, the competition features its fair share of singers and dancers to boot. Admission to the museum is free, but donations are gladly accepted. It is wonderful to see a piece of architectural history be brought to life in the twenty-first century.

While You're There!

TJ's Café Family Restaurant. Stop in for a meal at this good old-fashioned family restaurant, which has been in business for many years. It is most famous for their delectable fish 'n chips and tremendous breakfasts. There is a bar separate from the tables and booths. It is often a hangout for softball teams after they play nine innings at the Babe Blanchette Field, which is directly across the street.

B. F. Clyde's Cider Mill

Mystic

Although autumn may be more often associated with the northwestern and northeastern corners of the state, B. F. Clyde's Cider Mill in Mystic is a must visit once the leaves turn red and gold. Visit during their season from September through December for cider-making demonstrations, tastings, and buying all things apple. Clyde's is most certainly a gem, albeit not so hidden. Long lines will greet you on a weekend visit in the fall. The line to buy the cider and cider

doughnuts often leads out the door, down the steps, and out into the yard. Driving by their location at 129 North Stonington Road in Mystic during the off season made me wonder if the venerable cider press was closed for good as the trees were decorated with "No Trespassing" signs. Gladly, I found that I had nothing to fear when the following October the property was teeming with cars. The cider is produced by steam power, which Clyde's heralds as the oldest and the only such press in the country. Since 1881, the Clyde family, now on its sixth generation has produced apple cider that has been heralded as the finest in the country. Other gift items are also available to purchase, including fudge, baked apple goodies, and fall decorations. Clyde's also manufactures its own wine and hard cider, which can be tasted and purchased on premises. The cider press demonstrations are held in the cider mill at the rear of the property while the main building houses cider and baked goods.

The cider mill is on the National Register of Historic Places and rightfully so, since the same cider press has churned out thousands upon thousands of gallons of cider since its inception in 1897. Until the early twentieth century, the term "cider" referred to what is considered "hard cider" today. Colonists brought over apple seedlings from England to be grown in the colonies. Local farmers harvested their apples and brought them to community cider presses to turn their fruit into the alcoholic libation. Benjamin F. Clyde started out this same way in 1881, when he began to use other cider mills to make his product. Six years later, he decided to build his own cider mill. He purchased a four-crew press as well as a cider pump, apple elevator, and apple grater from a manufacturer from Syracuse, New York. The cider press ran on steam power, as it does today.

Clyde's Cider Mill is a perfect autumn destination.

While You're There!

Although Olde Mistick Village in Old Mystic, close to Clyde's, is not really in the scope of this work, their yearly Cabin Fever Chowderfest in February is a can't miss! Olde Mistick Village is a series of shops, ranging from boutique jewelry and a sports memorabilia store to a few restaurants and a movie theater. The setting is a re-created colonial village equipped with its own water wheel, pond, and church. Many food festivals to me are way too crowded. Small spaces lead to shoving and pushing to try to get the particular item, be it beer, wine, chowder, or chili. There is a pressure not only to try to eat enough to cover the cost of admission, but also a rushed feeling of scarfing the said item to barrel your way to the next booth. The Cabin Fever Chowderfest eliminates this entirely. Each chowder, usually from a nearby restaurant, is served in a different store. The chowder may be located towards the back of the store, which leaves room for an orderly line and also allows browsing to be done while waiting for the chowder to be served. Then it can be enjoyed off to the side or outside the store. Although crowded, the relatively relaxed pace of this chowderfest to me makes it the best I have ever been to since you are able to actually enjoy eating the chowder!

Farm Equipment Museums

Woodbury and Colchester

Buz Russell Museum of Antique Tools and Farm Life

The Buz Russell Museum of Antique Tools and Farm Life epitomizes this section of the book that highlights those less-traveled destinations hidden in all corners of our quirky state. This museum exemplifies an "out of the way" place.

The museum is located in a building on the grounds of the Flanders Nature Center in Woodbury. The Russell collection showcases historic farm tools and equipment, as well as antique toys. Flanders Nature Center's roots harken back to 1963 when Natalie Van Vleck acted to turn the turkey farm on her property on Flanders Road into a nature center, thus beginning the Flanders Land Trust. This group has acquired land in the area, which it saves from commercial development, protecting it for posterity. Properties under their banner include Manville Kettle, Plumb Brook Preserve, and Hetzel Refuge. After its initial charter in 1963, the museum and trust has not only acquired more parcels, but has continued its mission to provide educational opportunities.

The museum acquired the collection of farm tools via donation from Russell himself in 2002. This collection was housed in Russell's home before that. Although small by many museum standards, for a personal collection it is quite large. Each area of the museum is labeled for the use of the tools displayed, including "Dairy," "The Ice Harvest," and "The Barn." Each of these areas exhibit tools of the trade and each tool has a handwritten card by Russell himself outlining its use. The museum also showcases the history of the area's agrarian past. Like many collections of antique tools, saws are a major component of the display.

In addition to the farm museum, also on site are animals on the working farm. Kids will love to pet the sheep and horses. The North Barn offers educational activities. The property also contains a community garden and picturesque hiking trails. To satisfy the sweet tooth, the nature center has a maple sugar house. On weekends during sugaring season (late winter/early spring), demonstrations are given and the center even has a pancake breakfast where one can indulge in their homemade confection. The Flanders Nature Center is at 5 Church Hill Road in Woodbury.

Zagray Farm and Museum

On the other side of the state is another farm museum, Zagray Farm. On a recent trip to their revered "Gas Up," I was able to witness the majesty of agricultural equipment firsthand. I do not own a tractor, nor would I need one since my total yard encompasses less than a quarter of an acre. Many of the entries in this book I can associate with on some level. This one I did not, but I was intrigued; I wanted to know exactly what a "spring gas up" was.

For many of my adventures, recruiting friends to accompany me is usually not difficult. When asking for companionship to this farm, answers ran the gamut from legitimate excuses to, "I need to stay home and read the newspaper." Luckily, my wife and mother were up for the experience. The day was gorgeous: sunny, clear, in the high seventies with a slight breeze. I believe they were just happy to take a ride on such a beautiful Sunday. Another perk was that the farm was not far from home.

The Zagray Farm and Museum is on Route 85 on the Colchester-Hebron line. Although I grew up in nearby Norwich, the farm was never on my radar. Originally

reading about the event in an old guidebook, I still had no idea what to expect. The website mentioned tractors, vendors, a parade, and country music. I knew that with our timing we would miss the latter two. In truth, I was picturing a train of tractors, gassing up for the spring.

As we drove from the center of Colchester on Route 85 towards Hebron, the museum is on the right. The event was more like a flea market and craft fair. Many of the wares that were being sold were of a machine-related nature—tractor parts, car memorabilia, and other items that looked to me as if they fit in that capacity. There were tractors, too, with big men riding little lawnmower-looking ones. There were classic tractors polished to perfection and others that were rusted. One of the highlights for me was buying an actual John Deere hat, yes with mesh in the back. Once I popped on my new hat, I immediately felt more at home, and my wife had to explain to me in detail why we didn't need to own a tractor since I typically mow our lawn with an old fashioned push mower.

We did not stay for a lengthy visit, but it was an enjoyable one. Many dogs accompanied their owners and the pace was relaxed. Food vendors supplied carnivalesque treats. The spring show is one of a few seasonal events like this at the facility. We meandered around the museum property for a while spotting the hog house, outhouse, and hen house.

A visit to the Spring Show at Zagray Farm and Museum was a perfect way to spend a Sunday morning in May!

Both the Buz Russell Museum of Antique Tools and Farm Life and Zagray Farm showcase the importance of agrarian life in Connecticut, past and present. Another museum in this vein was the Farm Implement Museum in Bloomfield, which has since closed.

While You're There!

Nestled in the woods of the Litchfield Hills is the grand Hidden Valley Bed and Breakfast in Washington Depot.

For a taste of the European countryside in New England while you are visiting the Buz Russell Museum, book a weekend at the Hidden Valley Bed and Breakfast in Washington Depot. Overlooking the rolling Litchfield Hills, this chateau-styled inn is simply breathtaking, inside and out. It offers three rooms, two on the second floor of the main house and a separate larger room in one of the wings. This room, called the "red room," has its own walk-out patio. I visited in early autumn and was simply blown away by the atmosphere.

Located up a winding driveway literally hidden off Route 47, the end of the steep driveway feels like a world away from its surroundings. We were able to savor a welcome bottle of prosecco on the stone patio as we watched the sun drop behind a nearby hill. The first floor was lavishly decorated with period furnishings, but instead of feeling stuffy, it was quite welcoming. The gracious inn keeper, Regine, made sure we were well taken care of. She stoked the fire, provided area travel literature in the bedroom, and cooked a scrumptious breakfast in the morning. Make sure you're a dog lover since the household pets had the run of the inn.

The charm of Washington Depot and surrounding Litchfield County is not to be missed. Fantastic restaurants, including the White Horse Tavern and At the Corner provided welcome rest stops between wine tastings at the area wineries, meandering scenic drives, and even apple picking at nearby Averill Farm! Do yourself a favor, book a few nights at the Hidden Valley Bed and Breakfast and explore the off-the-beaten path gems of Litchfield County.

The Lock Museum of America

Terryville

Although Connecticut has its fair share of specialty museums (like clocks, carousels, and, formerly, nuts), one of the most atypical of the bunch has to be The Lock Museum of America in Terryville. Locks and keys are devices that many of us take for granted—and only cross our minds when we misplace our keys! Just like baseball card and porcelain doll collectors, in this world there are avid key and lock collectors. If you happen to be reading this and are one of those said individuals, please make it a point to visit this museum.

The museum is at 230 Main Street in Terryville and is housed in a nondescript brick building. Its logo depicts a bald eagle perched atop an old fashioned key, a perfect symbol for the nation's premier lock museum and similar in style to the logo of the Eagle Lock Company that was across the street. The company was one of the most important trunk and padlock manufacturers in the country; unfortunately, the enormous complex today has been whittled to only a few remaining edifices. Inside the museum the visitor will behold a whole world of locks and accessories, including door locks, hand-cuffs, antique locks, prison locks, bank locks, and even keys. Among its eight display rooms with twenty-three different displays are a bank lock room and a room full of Yale locks. It even has a 4,000 year old Egyptian-made tumbler lock and an antique room lock that was manufactured in the 1500s.

Thomas Hennessey, founder of the museum, narrates a guided tour of the facility. His disembodied voice travels from room to room highlighting the collection for the visitor. The museum holds the largest collection of colonial and antique locks in the country!

Locks and keys are in high demand by antique connoisseurs. For those who are interested, a membership to the museum is available and there is also a "lock blog" to read on their website. Every Columbus Day weekend the museum hosts a lock festival of sorts where over a hundred lock aficionados buy and sell their wares at a nearby function facility.

Very close to the Lock Museum on Route 202 in Terryville is the Eli Terry Jr. Water Wheel. Terry, which the village of Terryville is named for, was the founder of the lock corporation that eventually became the Eagle Lock Company. The waterwheel is large and was used to harness the Pequabuck River to power the nearby mill.

Do not get "locked out" of the fun. Make sure to take a trip to Terryville to visit the Lock Museum of America!

The New England Air Museum

Windsor Locks

Where do aircraft go after they have flown their final mission? For many, the scrapheap awaits as they are stripped of salvageable materials, but a select few are saved by aviation preservationists. Although the idea of "preservation" is often thought of in the terms of fine art, greenspace, or wildlife, even former flying machines have enthusiasts who take measures to conserve their craft. A well-known example of this would be the Smithsonian's Air and Space Museum. Connecticut has a lesser-known museum of aircraft close to its primary airport, Bradley International. The New England Air Museum (NEAM) has its share of neat aviation-related artifacts, including its most impressive collection of eighty specimens of aircraft. Unlike other museums highlighted in this collection like the Muhammad Ali Museum or the Lock Museum, which can be housed in relatively small spaces, a museum showcasing aircraft needs to have lots of room. Space is something that NEAM definitely has.

Its various types of aircraft are housed both indoors and out. Its impressive collection is highlighted by many rare models, some that are even the last remaining known type of a certain flying machine. The Sikorsky VS 44a, known as the flying boat because it truly looks like a small cruise ship with wings, is part of the museum's collection. This version, known as the Excambian, is the only surviving model still in existence, although the plane almost met its demise on more than one occasion. The plane's initial run was during World War II followed by passenger use as well as for special trips. It broke down on an unsuccessful trip to St. Thomas in 1968 and was brought by barge to Sikorsky's facility in Bridgeport.

Eventually housed at the air museum, the plane faced a ten-year restoration process by volunteers, many of whom were retirees from the aviation industry, who initially built planes for Sikorsky. The aircraft also almost met its fate again after a freak tornado in 1979 that destroyed the original location of the museum.

The museum also houses a Gee Bee Model R airplane, which was used for racing, highly decorated in red and white paint. The inside of the museum is a hangar. One plane that was used in the Korean conflict was a Soviet-built and Chinese-operated fighter plane by manufacturer Mikoyan and Gurevich (MiG) with the unfortunate NATO codename of "Fagot B." Walking through the airplane hangar you may break out into song reminiscent of *The Wizard of Oz*: bombers, fighters, and blimps, oh my! Also on display are gliders, balloons, and helicopters. Even a Nike missile is on site! Over 100 years of aircraft history is presented, as the earliest craft date from 1909, and reach all the way to the present day. To exemplify this, the collection ranges from the Bleriot X1 monoplane with wooden skeleton and canvas skin and a model of the biplane glider reminiscent of the Wright Brothers' creation to the Connecticut Air National Guard F-100a Super Sabre fighter jet. World War II fighters are in heavy rotation. Both military and commercial planes are represented. The museum does not solely represent United States aeronautical endeavors as Soviet planes and the German World War I era Fokker Dr. 1 triplane are housed within the hangar walls. The comic enthusiast might recognize the latter plane as the craft preferred by the elusive Red Baron, Snoopy's arch nemesis from the *Peanuts* comic. As the frustrated World War I flying ace, Snoopy's thought bubble is filled with "Curse you! Red Baron." Also exhibits of Poland and France's contribution to aviation history are on view. The 58th Bomb Wing Memorial Hangar houses the shiny Boeing B-29 "Superfortress," an Air Force bomber used in the Pacific campaign of World War II. This powerful jet was built in 1944.

Thought of today as novelties hovering above sports stadiums, the blimp once served functional and integral use for the military. Built in 1941–1942, the Goodyear K Class Blimp was used to seek out the location of German U-boats (submarines) as well as to transport allied troops. Likened to a flying whale based on its appearance, blimps were more like sharks as they were equipped with machine guns and explosives during combat years. The blimp is being restored by volunteers at the time of this writing. The progress of renovation of the aircraft can be seen by visitors to the museum. This is the last surviving blimp of this design known in the world.

The oldest built Connecticut plane is also on view; it was flown and designed by a seventeen year old from Berlin named Howard S. Bunce. With the burning desire to fly, Bunce constructed an early pusher aircraft. It was discovered after years of disuse and pieced back together with replica parts. The circa 1870s balloon basket, which was constructed by Plymouth, Connecticut, native Silas Brooks, is featured in an exhibit. This plane is considered the country's oldest aviation artifact.

The New England Air Museum's hangars have been providing the public a peek into the larger-than-life world of aircraft since 1981 at this location, but the Connecticut Aeronautical Historical Association, which operates the museum, has been in existence since 1959. In addition to the silverbirds, NEAM holds a vast collection of all things related to the aviation industry, such as pictures, writings, and artifacts, including its substantial engine collection. The flying boat and blimp are perfect representations of the preservation work done at the museum. Not only does it house a sublime collection of aircraft, but its volunteers painstakingly restore decommissioned or corroding machines. Although similar to the work that an art preservationist might do, in these cases it is often refurbishing decaying metal, parts, or removing hazardous substances used in the building process of the aircraft. The museum is in the process of acquiring a control tower, which was used at Bradley in its Murphy Terminal. The terminal was taken out of use in 2010, which at that time was the longest-used currently operational terminal in the United States. The museum appeals to visitors of all ages, with much or little knowledge of aircraft. The sheer size of its contents will leave both adult and child in awe. Also, video presentations and flight simulators as well as a whole kid-centric area will draw in the youngsters (they will also like the obligatory gift shop, chock full of all types of airplane merchandise). While in the greater Hartford area, make sure to visit since this is the premier venue for aircraft in the New England region; it will satisfy your lofty expectations and make you feel like you are flying high.

▶ The New England Air Museum is located at 36 Perimeter Road in Windsor Locks right off Route 75 near Bradley International Airport.

Trash Museum

Hartford

Thirtieth birthdays are typically celebrated in some kind of fashion: dinner, drinks, a get together with friends, a trip to the trash museum, a sporting event. Hold up; a trash museum? To honor my first thirty years, my wife planned an all-day surprise itinerary for me with stops at the Thomas Hooker Brewing Company and Bidwell

Tavern, but beginning at the Connecticut Resources Recovery Authority (CRRA). A complete surprise, I had no idea what area we were heading to (even by the time I got there, since I do a fantastic job at falling asleep in the passenger seat as soon as we hit the highway).

CRRA is an agency that oversees environmentally sound ways to eradicate the problem of the state's solid waste. The CRRA used to manage both the Trash Museum and the Garbage Museum in Stratford. Unfortunately, due to the economic recession, the Garbage Museum closed its door in 2009. It was best known for Trash-o-saurus, a dinosaur composed of depleted material, including street signs, license plates, and parts of vehicles. The much loved refuse-laden dinosaur resembled an apatosaurus, but with a large grinning head. As of the time of this writing there has been talk in Stratford of reviving the museum based on the incorporation of private funds.

The remaining museum in Hartford is best known for its large fort of household garbage. Here smaller scale household items are stuck together such as CDs, soda cans, and toys in a canopy of garbage. A scavenger hunt is available to help the viewer pinpoint certain items. The point of the museum is to help its visitors understand the impact of garbage and to educate them on the reusing, reducing, and recycling that can be done with their own two hands. There is a large hands-on area for kids and the museum often hosts school groups. The kid-centric scope of the museum and of the CRRA's educational aims even includes the use of a mascot of sorts, Phillup D. Bag, who has his own website that has trash-related trivia on the main page. The museum is at a working facility. From the main part of the museum a ramp allows access to a second level to view the workers doing their job at the plant. From the observation area the visitor can watch trucks unload trash and other workers sort through it.

If anyone ever calls Connecticut a trashy place, I would stand up for our proud little state, but after my trip to this museum, I would have to agree with them. The difference is that the trash here gets to reinvent itself to something new with the advent of progressive recycling programs.

While You're There!

Thomas Hooker Brewing Company in nearby Bloomfield was the next spot that we visited on my surprise birthday trip, but with its proximity in nearby Bloomfield, it is the perfect place to cleanse the palate after sifting through so much trash. Hooker is named after the founder of the Connecticut Colony and not the world's oldest profession, although the label emphasizes the last name instead of the first. In an ever-changing landscape of craft beer, Hooker has become the venerable statesman. Its lineup includes the popular Watermelon Ale, the autumn seasonal Oktoberfest, and a Munich Style Golden Lager. Make sure to check out their collaboration with local chocolatier Munson's with their Chocolate Truffle Stout. Just as their playful slogan says, this is one hooker you want to be caught with! For more information about Thomas Hooker and other Connecticut breweries, read the Connecticut Beer Trail chapter in this book. Also read about Bidwell Tavern in the original *Connecticut Lore*.

The PAST Antique Marketplace and Museum at Nature's Art Village

Montville

Marked by the big T-rex out front, which is the reason why Nature's Art made it into the first volume of *Connecticut Lore*, the complex here on Route 85 in Montville keeps expanding. What started out as a shop and small hands-on museum has turned into an assortment of businesses and activities in the miniature village. On my latest visit, I traveled back into the PAST Antique Marketplace and Museum. As I walked from the parking lot to the entrance of the store, I noticed the old-fashioned water pump outside.

The antiques store on the premises was built in the last few years and is inviting, the antithesis of the old dingy secondhand shop. First of all, the place is huge! Its selection of wares range from a life-sized Elvis statue to Ross Perot '92 campaign buttons, from a tandem bicycle to a carousel horse. The variety is truly spectacular. All of the items (at least on my visit) were in good shape. Typical antique pieces like clocks and tea cups are offset by larger pieces such as a shoe-shine chair and dinosaur gasoline memorabilia. There is a room entirely dedicated to tools with ice picks and a two-man saw available for purchase. The store covers two large floors.

Adjacent to the store is the PAST Museum. Walking through the doors is like stepping into the past. The interior resembles a colonial town; storefronts greet the visitor. Shoe repair, laundry service, and a barbershop can be viewed, looking as they would in a bygone era. A large mural of the New London harbor is an impressive sight as well. A curator is available for tours of the museum. The "alive museum," which was being built at the time of my visit, will feature all kinds of steam-powered mechanisms such as a steam engine, steam train, and steam car. The exhibit will depict how technology has evolved over the years.

While You're There!

Joy's Country Skillet is a different kind of step into the past. During a time when the greasy spoon has been supplanted by gastro pubs and trendy hotspots with industrial chic interiors, in decor, Joy's in Norwich is the antithesis of that, but their food hits a home run. The interior does not look as if it has changed since at least the '60s. When the guest opens the menu expecting only traditional diner fare, he or she may be pleasantly surprised! Although coffee, omelets, and pancakes are on the menu, so is an entire selection of Mexican entrees. When I come to Joy's, I go for the Mexican food. Be it a breakfast burrito in the morning or a tostada in the afternoon, to me Mexican is their specialty. Joy's is at 671 West Thames Street in Norwich.

Muhammad Ali Museum

Bethany

Talk about an out-of-the-way museum, this home-based collection of all memorabilia related to "The Champ" is truly a hidden gem. Located in the home of Richard Kaletsky in Bethany, it displays everything and anything "Ali."

Although many small Connecticut-based museums are written about in various guidebooks and most certainly on the Internet, it is hard to find anything about this museum in print. I happened upon it by watching a documentary film about the museum's proprietor, Kaletsky, directed by Steve Depolito. Even richer than Kaletsky's collection of Ali artifacts are his stories. His recollections cannot be, for the most part, tangibly seen at the museum, but a guided tour by Richard will fill in the blanks with his larger-than-life personality and storytelling.

The museum itself is a personal collection of a Muhammad Ali fan who has accrued Ali mementos for the better part of his life. It consists of many posters, photographs, fifteen different items signed by Ali, stamps, over fifty books, art, and toys all related to the famed boxer. He has memorabilia from all over the world, including Zaire and Turkey. He also has various punching bags on display. This collection could be deemed heaven for the Ali enthusiast.

Kaletsky authored a self-published book called *Ali and Me: Through the Ropes*, a recollection of Ali's life told by one of his biggest fans. Ali is quoted as calling the book "the greatest book about me in the world." Quite an accolade for someone who could have a library dedicated to the works solely written about him. At age fifteen, Kaletsky called the pugilist, then known as Cassius Clay, on the phone and spoke with him. After he read Kaletsky's book, Clay, by then known as Ali, called Richard almost twenty years after their first phone conversation to express his gratitude for the book. Kaletsky grew up alongside Ali in a way. He was able to meet "The Champ" several times and was able to watch him fight in person five times, including Ali versus Frasier fights one and two. Kaletsky's passion for all things Ali has led him to amass quite a collection. While in Bethany, make sure to look into seeing the Ali Museum, it is a real TKO.

While You're There!

During the Halloween season, visit the Amity Road Horror, also in Bethany, for a knock-your-socks-off scare-tacular haunted house. Lauded as one of the most frightening, if not the most, the back story tells the tale of a diabolical mine owner whose property was located on the site of an old burial ground. Expect the unexpected around every turn on this walk-through attraction. In addition to the accompanying story and spectacularly designed October diversion, the building itself has its own reputation. According to residents of Bethany, this former bank is supposed to be actually haunted!

Philip Johnson Glass House

New Canaan

My first thought when I heard about noted modernist architect Philip Johnson's Glass House, was that he must be passionate about proverbs (those who live in glass houses should not throw stones) or a diehard Little Anthony and the Imperials fanatic whose favorite song is "I'm on the Outside Looking In," which can easily be done at this house.

Although in my research of Johnson neither proverbs nor Little Anthony were ever mentioned; Johnson had a fascinating life. Philip Cortelyou Johnson was born in Cleveland in 1906. He worked as director of architecture at the Museum of Modern Art and designed such modernist masterpieces as the *Gate of Europe* in Madrid and the *Crystal Cathedral* in California. He was openly gay and was a Nazi sympathizer (which later in life he recanted, harboring enormous guilt).

Johnson's residence was a literally see-through (except a small area in the center of the home that contained the bathroom) rectangular box-shaped glass house. Anyone outside the structure would be able to see almost the entire interior. It is the kind of place that would be anathema to a hoarder. Johnson and longtime partner David Whitney must have truly abided by the "when in doubt, throw it out" mantra, since in looking at their bedroom, only a bed without any ornamentation, a nightstand, and a single lamp adorn the room. Johnson's fascination with glass can also be seen at the previously mentioned Crystal Cathedral, whose façade is completely glass (not of the see-through kind though). Through the years that Johnson lived in the Glass House, he accumulated more and more property (forty-seven acres!) and created a modernist approach to an estate.

The house and environs can be visited today via guided tour, which is available for different lengths of time starting with an hour and whose price climbs with the tour duration. It is not a place where the visitor can simply park in a lot and wander the grounds; reservations are best made ahead of time.

Johnson originally bought five acres in New Canaan in 1945 on the site of a former farmhouse. After his design, the Brick and Glass houses were fully realized in 1949. The idea of his house was that its residents and visitors would be able to see the natural canvas displayed before them. Its farm location, with meandering stone walls, creates quite a juxtaposition with the modern design forms. Unlike interiors of most homes, whose color scheme or room arrangement may change only once every few years, Johnson's Glass House was constantly changing along with the seasons. The Glass House overlooks a nearby pond. The house was also important regarding how seamlessly it is camouflaged by its surroundings. When most architects' grandiose visions are made of brick and mortar, Johnson's was viewing nature's palette from his living room and his kitchen and his dining room. Each piece of furniture was impeccably placed and has meaning within the context of the house. Much of it came from his New York City apartment. (Johnson did not simply run out to Caldor to buy a recliner). For instance, the chaise lounge was designed by fellow famed architect and Johnson friend, Mies Van Der Rohe. (The Glass House was in part designed based on Van Der Rohe's Farnsworth House in Illinois).

The Brick House (and no he was not a Commodores fan that I know of) complements the Glass House as the ying to its yang. Whereas the Glass House is translucent, the Brick House is impermeable to light. Only a few tiny windows bring any natural light to this structure, which housed guest rooms. Both structures are fifty-six feet in length, although the Glass House is wider than the Brick House.

As the years passed, Johnson's creative mind brought to light an array of other structures. Dating from 1962, Johnson created a columned pavilion, which is set on the backyard pond. Since Johnson was a lover of art, he needed to create a gallery space to hold his large modern art paintings, which include pieces by Andy Warhol and Frank Stella. Not simply a typical gallery, this looks more like an underground war bunker. It resembles a tunnel cutting through a hillside. All of the pieces in his architectural collection have inspiration from historical designs. For instance, the Painting Gallery is designed after a Mycenean Tomb.

Since Johnson had a Painting Gallery, he then needed a Sculpture Gallery. The focal point of the interior of this gallery, which dates from 1970, is its staircases, which are seemingly everywhere giving it an Escher-esque feel, although the

inspiration for this creation came from villages of the Greek Isles. The visitor will not find traditional sculpture forms though, except what looks like a large, upside down V and a bed. The building presents itself on all different levels, where each piece is emphasized by its relation to the ambling staircases.

Johnson's library and study are housed in a single room that contains a work space and a library full of books on architecture. The actual building containing this room is angled on a sloped hillside. His gatehouse of sorts, named Da Monsta (from "the monster") pays homage to Frank Gehry (architect of notable buildings including the Guggenheim in Bilbao and the Experience Music Project in Seattle). Johnson thought of this building as being personified. Also on the property is the intriguing Ghost House, although no haunted tales are associated with it. The house is completely see through and blends into the background (hence "ghost"). This small structure is built in a traditional "home" style. Also on his property is the thirty-foot Lincoln Kirstein Tower that is named after a friend. The best way I can describe it is that it looks like a slew of Tetris pieces stacked on one another without symmetry. Johnson used to enjoy climbing it.

All in all on the property there are fourteen structures scattered on forty-seven acres designed by a genius of modern architecture. The contrast between the buildings and the landscape with its stone walls, barn foundations, and trees is extraordinary. Walking through the Glass House, you can only imagine the tranquility of nature as viewed by Johnson and Whitney in all four seasons, a constantly changing masterpiece. From the autumn's glorious foliage to a bright snow-filled sky to the buzz of a summer afternoon, the Glass House and environs highlight the surroundings' natural beauty.

When a "home" is represented by four walls, privacy, and shelter, the Glass House challenges these ideals of what a typical home is. What happens inside these walls is on view for all, although the house being transparent simply disappears in its surroundings. The house represents purity—a purity in its natural beauty of the scenery, purity that is represented by the fact that nothing can be hidden within the house, and purity in the design, a minimalist approach to this residence. The visitor is able to marvel at the Glass House and its environs as an architectural wonder and to some degree a novelty, but also as a view into the splendor of nature.

Make sure to call ahead for tickets, as previously stated. The property also holds rotating gallery installations.

Witch's Dungeon Classic Movie Museum

Bristol

The present location of the Witch's Dungeon Classic Movie Museum at the Bristol Historical Society is appropriate. Although the building does not have any actual ties to witches, dungeons, or classic horror movies, the ornate, mid-nineteenth century flair is undeniable and makes a perfect backdrop to house such a museum. My visit happened to be on a gloomy Saturday in October. Not knowing which entrance was correct, the Creature from the Black Lagoon staring down at me from an upstairs window clued me in that I was in generally the correct area.

The museum pays homage to the classic monster movies of yore, showcasing spooky cinematic favorites like *Frankenstein*, *Phantom of the Opera*, and *Planet of the Apes*. For a nominal fee, the visitor can view this small museum. On view are characters portrayed by genre legends such as Bela Lugosi, Vincent Price, Lon Chaney, and Boris Karloff, who haunt the halls of the historical society, although only on weekend evenings in October. One room includes an Egyptian tomb with Karnak from *The Mummy* appearing out of his sarcophagus. Another display shows Dr. Van Helsing impaling Dracula. The museum's curator, Cortlandt Hull, founded the museum when he was only thirteen years old. At an early age he was intrigued by the makeup used in films. After visiting many wax museums, he felt let down by the lack of monster movie characters housed in them and thought this injustice should be remedied.

He came up with the idea of Zenobia the Gypsy Witch who became the hostess and unofficial mascot of the museum. (Zenobia's mug adorns an advertisement for the museum.) Famous voice actress June Foray eventually lent her pipes to Zenobia. Foray is well known for voicing characters such as Cindy Lou Who from Dr. Suess's *How the Grinch Stole Christmas* as well as characters on Hanna-Barbera cartoons like *Scooby Doo, Where Are You?* and is most well known for playing the voices of Rocky and Natasha on the *Rocky and Bullwinkle Show.* Zenobia was Cortlandt's childhood creation as he first imagined her in 1965. Her unusual first name was in homage to a classmate's mother.

The museum has existed in one way, shape, or form since 1966. Cortlandt's father built him a small house in which Cortlandt could display his creations and called it The Witch's Dungeon. More recently it has moved to the historical society on Summer Street. Although the museum's admission is a suggested donation of five dollars today, this not-for-profit museum's entry fee asking price started out as a free admission in the 1960s. The price was a quarter in the '70s, and was raised twenty-five cents by decade through the 1990s. In 1992, Universal Studios allowed their characters to be used by the museum.

Although this museum showcases the unusual monsters of the silver screen, Bristol also has a reputedly true haunted location. The Church of Eternal Light, at 1199 Hill Street, is said to have permanent guests of the spirit kind. One speculation is that a former member of the congregation, who was struck by lightning near the church, has never left. Faces have also been spotted peering out of the windows and in the small church's tower.

While You're There!

After being scared out of your mind at the museum, or just looking for an excuse to have a quality beer, I suggest walking or driving down the hill from the museum to Firefly Hollow Brewing Company. A microbrewery housed in a former factory building, the industrial exterior contrasts beautifully with the taproom inside. Beers include Cone Flakes IPA, Toadstool Oat Stout, and Photon Imperial Crimson. Have a few inside or take them out in either a growler (2 liter jug) or a squealer (1 liter jug).

Connecticut Beer Scene

Throughout Connecticut and Part of Rhode Island

Just like the plethora of wineries that have ripened in Connecticut to a "drink local" movement, its beer producers have followed suit. From the northeast to the southwest, breweries dot what was a barren landscape in terms of craft beer. The state has its stalwarts like Cottrell, Thomas

Hooker, and Southport Brewing Company, but in the last few years many of Connecticut's 169 towns include a brewery, brew pub, or great beer bar. Similar to the wine trail, I have unfortunately not been able to try libations from each company nor have been able to visit each brewing facility. I can say though, from those I have, Connecticut is making a strong impact on the craft beer scene. The state has taken a while to catch up to other mightier beer-heavy New England states, like Vermont and Maine, but its industry is beginning to grow. Even though this idea of "craft beer" may seem new, once upon a time in every tavern and ale house in colonial New England, proprietors brewed their own pints.

One of my favorite beer-tasting journeys occurs in Stonington with three stops over the border in neighboring Westerly, Rhode Island. Beer'd is a unique nano-brewery which is located in Stonington's Velvet Mill. Here you can get a growler with the brewery's logo, the bearded mug of its owner, filled. Some of their best include the Dogs and Boats Double IPA, Frank and Berry Double IPA, and Devil's Pitchfork American Pale Ale. What is on tap is constantly rotating, but expect high quality from this little brewery. The authentic industrial interior of the mill makes a trip to this brewery unforgettable. Their beer can be found in local restaurants like the Engine Room and Pizzetta in Mystic.

The next stop is Cottrell. Cottrell is best known for their Mystic Bridge IPA. Cottrell opened in 1997 and was on the forefront of the Connecticut craft beer movement. The brewery is located in the Pawcatuck section of Stonington. It is a bit difficult to find since their taproom is all the way at the back of the building. Safe Harbor, a brewery out of New London, also brews here. Cottrell can be found in local restaurants, such as Mystic Pizza. They also contract brew for other brands. I enjoy Cottrell's Oktoberfest and their

Take home a growler from Beer'd featuring the bearded face of its owner.

Mystic Bridge as well as Safe Harbor's American Blonde Ale on my trips to their factory.

Over the border in Westerly, Rhode Island, are three other fantastic beer-related places. Grey Sail, is a superb brewery that features tasty selections such as Captain's Daughter Double IPA, the Flagship of which is a cream ale, and the Flying Jenny, an extra pale ale. Nearby are two fantastic beer bars: Malted Barley, which has an incredibly extensive draft list (sampler flights are available) and features fabulous pretzels; and Perks and Corks, a coffee shop by day and a bar by night.

The New England Brewing Company out of Woodbridge is well known for its recently renamed double IPA, G-bot, and their Sea Hag IPA. If these two beers are indicators of the rest of their craft, then I would certainly like to try more! Two Roads Brewing Company has quickly become the hottest beer out of Connecticut. Its factory in Stratford is huge! Be aware: the place gets packed! Well worth it though, they churn out tasty libations, (many which name check local area sites) like

the Road 2 Ruin Double IPA, Honeyspot Road White IPA, and the Rye 95 Tripel. Their beer can be found in practically every package store in the state if you wish to sample from the comfort of your own home. The factory offers tours, food trucks outside, and tasting flights in the taproom. Black Pond Brews fills growlers on site at their brewery in Danielson. Although I have yet to venture there, I have enjoyed the Israel Putnam Brown Ale and the Razor Blades IPA. The Norwich Nano Brewers have interesting beers which all contain the word "face" in the name. My favorite so far has been Cactus Face lager. They do not have a brick and mortar facility. Back East Brewery, out of Bloomfield, has a delectable IPA, their Misty Mountain IPA. One of my favorite beers to order at the Griswold Inn in Essex is the Ten Penny Ale, made by the Olde Burnside Brewing Company from East Hartford. Many of the breweries are open to the public. Others like City Steam in Hartford can be found in stores, but are also brewpubs. City Steam in Hartford is housed in an architecturally ornate building, inside and out, and is a truly phenomenal dining experience. Tables are set all over the former Cheney Building, which was built by Henry Hobson Richardson. Diners eat and drink in a variety of areas from the first floor, on platforms on the grand staircase, and even on the balcony. The now classic Naughty Nurse is their flagship beer. Other restaurants, even without brewing their own, are known for their extensive beer lists like 2 Brothers Pizza in Salem, Eli Cannon's Tap Room in Middletown, and Strange Brew in Norwich.

Many other of the state's breweries are mentioned in the "While You're There" sections of other chapters in this book or the first. These include Thomas Hooker Brewing Company (which recently opened a test kitchen at the Mohegan Sun Racebook as well), DuVig, Thimble Islands,

Overshores, Stony Brook, Willimantic Brewing Company, and Firefly Hollow. There are many others I am excited to try, but have not been able to yet including, but not limited to Outer Lights from Groton, These Guys in Norwich, Steady Habit Brewing Company in East Haddam, and OEC in Oxford.

Connecticut's Beer Trail keeps getting longer and longer, which is certainly not a bad thing for the craft beer connoisseur. The next time you head for a cold one, make it a brew crafted here in the Nutmeg State!

The Connecticut Wine Trail

Statewide

California? Definitely. Washington? Sure. France, Italy? Uh-huh. What about Connecticut? For many, wineries and vineyards are not thought of in the same sentence as Connecticut, but that is only if they have not heard of the Connecticut Wine Trail! The trail, which first began in 1992, meanders throughout the state stopping (at the time of writing) at twenty-five separate destinations. Although I love to cross things off lists, I have not yet been able to reach every destination, but have been to an admirable twelve of them (especially for someone who lives most of the time out of state). Unlike many of the chapters in this collection, which dive into history, with dates, facts, and figures, this chapter is truly amateur hour on the wine trail. I enjoy wine, but truthfully am much more of a beer buff. I do enjoy the process of sampling, which many of the locations offer, and I like supporting homegrown businesses as well as the adventure that the wine trail presents. To boot, many of these wineries offer pristine

views and many are in rural corners of the state that are typically off the beaten path. Without further ado, here is a rundown of the twelve wineries in which I have imbibed. A passport is offered yearly in which the visitor receives a stamp at each wine destination. By submitting a fully stamped passport, the visitor is in the running for a dream vacation.

Bishop's Orchards in Guilford

This tasting area is inside a large supermarket-style store that is Bishop's Orchards. Although pies and treats are available, this is much more than a farm market. The idea threw me off a bit when first visiting. We decided to visit after a book reading at the Milford Library, since this was a convenient stop along the way (right off exit 57 on Interstate 95) back home. We sampled their different offerings, including Happily Impeared, Sachem's Twilight, and my favorite, the blueberry Leete's Island Blues, at their tasting area counter. Bishop's is also known for their fall activities as well as a pumpkin patch. Their hard cider is also worth a taste.

Chamard Vineyards in Clinton

This wooden building with stone foundation not only has a tasting room, but also a bistro. On my visit, I bought a bottle of their Riesling, which I enjoyed very much. It was crowded inside, and unfortunately I did not have time for a full tasting. The view from the building is glorious in any season, but the rural Clinton landscape pops with color in the autumn.

Haight-Brown Winery in Litchfield

One of Connecticut's most venerable wineries, it has been producing wines since the mid-1970s. This winery also has a restaurant on site on the first floor. My visit occurred on a glorious day in late September, which of course led to a very crowded tasting room. My wife and I were lucky though, as we were able to scoot into two empty seats at the tasting room bar. I enjoyed many of their wines, including the Chardonnay and Picnic Red, but my favorite was certainly the Honey Nut Apple—the flavor notes resembled liquid apple pie. Cheeses and other food platters are available.

Holmberg Orchard in Gales Ferry (Ledyard)

Holmberg's had been a destination of mine long before they were producing wine. In the fall my family would often take trips to Holmberg's to pick up pies, apples, and other seasonal goodies. Since moving out of Connecticut, I had not been to Holmberg's in years when my mother asked if I would like to accompany her there one day in October. I obliged and was surprised to see their line of wines and hard ciders available. Although I did not imbibe in a tasting, I did buy a few bottles of their hard cider. I tried three varieties, the MacIntosh, Cortland, and Russett, and enjoyed all three, but the Russett was my favorite. It had a bit more of a tartness to it. Of course I had to also pick up a pie, a bag of apples, and white chocolate pops in the shape of a ghost. (See this chapter does have a paranormal reference!).

Jonathan Edwards Winery in North Stonington

As part of my "research," friends and I took a beer-tasting trip in November of 2013 in New London County. In April of the following year, we reconvened with a wine adventure in the same region. Jonathan Edwards was the first of our three destinations of the day. A gorgeous spring day, we enjoyed our tastings outside at the tasting area. Good timing too, as a large group of ladies from a bachelorette party had just left and the place was pretty empty. The landscape is superb, with the deck overlooking the farm and growing grapes. Since it was such a nice day, we stayed outside so did not experience the

interior, but the large white barn-like building did look impressive from the exterior. Their wines are made with grapes both grown in state and some in California. I enjoyed their Estate Connecticut Pinot Gris and Chardonnay the best. My palate tends towards the white wines, although their California-grown reds were good as well. The winery plays host to concerts, including Ben Taylor, who has played there often, and Martin Sexton.

Maugle Sierra Vineyards in Ledyard

Located inside a stately barn building, this vineyard offers beautiful views of the surrounding landscape, but due to the cold winter day that we were there, we stayed inside. My favorite selections here included the St. Croix, Ledyard Sunset, and 1740 Ledyard House White. I particularly enjoyed sitting around the barrel tables.

Miranda Vineyards in Goshen

Driving by nearby Sunset Meadow Winery and seeing it too packed to venture into, we were skeptical about how crowded this vineyard would be. Upon arrival, the parking lot was not overwhelmingly busy. Boy were we happy that we did go in, since both my wife and I enjoyed the wines produced here very much. Our favorite wines included the Rose, Cayuga White, and Woodbridge White. The tasting room's space was open with plenty of area to walk between samples.

Preston Ridge Vineyard in Preston

A newcomer on the wine trail, the tasting room opened in 2012, and the vino did not disappoint. This was also our last stop on our mini wine tour in spring 2014. Located in a barn with patio overlooking the Preston countryside, this winery had a jovial, unpretentious feel to it. It was especially scenic at sundown. The server (whom I knew from high school) tended our table instead of our being situated at a bar or counter. My favorites here included the Riesling, Zundell Farm Rose, and the Rock Ridge Red.

Priam Vineyard in Colchester

Priam is in yet another barn-like building, but situated at the bottom of a hill, affording the taster with a view up the hill of the growing grapes. I particularly enjoyed the Salmon River White (look for tales of the Salmon River in another chapter!), the Riesling, and the Gewurztraminer the best. Wine can be enjoyed inside the tasting room or on the patio.

Saltwater Farm Vineyard in Stonington

In my mind, Saltwater Farm wins for best view of all of the wineries I have visited on the trail. The dimly lit building offers tastings on the second floor with a patio looking out over the growing grapes with an ocean inlet just beyond. It combines the rural beauty of many of the wineries with coastal accents of the nearby water. Unbelievably this building, which inside has similarities to many of the other winery buildings, was a former airplane hangar! The grounds, which were previously used as an airfield, were converted into the gorgeous tidal vineyard only in the 2000s. My favorite wines here were the Estate Chardonnay, Sauvignon Blanc, and Cabernet Franc/Merlot Blend. My most memorable experience in trying to view the beautiful scenery was walking directly into the glass sliding door, which caused my slightly tipsy wife to break out into hysterics, causing enough of a scene that our party was clearly followed out to the car by winery employees.

Sharpe Hill Vineyards in Pomfret

To me, this vineyard is the Ace of Spades in the deck of Connecticut wineries. Long before ever venturing to this section of Pomfret, I had enjoyed their "Ballet of Angels" white wine for years. Denoted by

its painting of a child from a bygone era on the label, it had always been a favorite of mine. Pomfret has long since been an ultimate autumn destination for me. Traveling up Route 169 from Norwich and meandering through the perfect mix of apple orchards, country boutiques, and outstanding natural beauty, this part of the Quiet Corner is a sight to behold. For all my ventures up that way, I had never crossed to the Hampton side of Pomfret to check out Sharpe Hill. Down a breathtaking country road, Sharpe Hill's scenery is quintessentially bucolic New England. Located in what looks like a classic country estate, this colonial red building is the perfect setting. Also on site is an award-winning restaurant and garden where the produce is grown. My first venture to Sharpe Hill is still my favorite. It was my first Connecticut winery visit. I was lucky enough to be there on a perfect autumn day, with crisp air and a slight breeze, but comfortable enough to be tasting on the outside patio, especially with the warmth of the sun shining down. I thoroughly enjoyed many of their wines, recalling that the Red Seraph and the St. Croix were among my favorites, but in the end, the Ballet of Angels still reigned as number one. The unrushed feeling of sampling these wines on the patio was an incredible experience. Couple that with the fact it was my first visit to a winery and had no expectations going into it that it led to an unforgettable experience. I have been back twice more, enjoyed myself each time, but nothing has topped my initial visit. Although my first trip was on a perfect day in the fall, it was not crowded, so it seemed as if it were my hidden jewel. On my next two trips I realized that the treasure of Sharpe Hill had certainly been discovered, as large groups pushed their way through, angling their way towards the tasting area.

Stonington Vineyards in Stonington

Stonington Vineyards I liken to an old reliable friend. The winery has been in existence since the late 1980s. The wines are all solid, their most popular with good reason being their Seaport White. Their building overlooks the growing grapes. It has never been an ordeal to taste here; simply show up, pay the tasting fee, and walk to one of the tasting areas. They have a very good Riesling and Chardonnay, but my favorite is the classic Seaport White. Come to Connecticut's "Old Faithful" and you will not be disappointed.

Seems like a lot of wineries? I have not even been to half of them (although I would like to)! The other wineries on the wine trail (at the time of this writing) include: Connecticut Valley Winery, DiGrazia, Gouveia, Hopkins, Jerram, Jones, Land of Nod, McLaughlin, Paradise Hills, Rosedale Farms, Sunset Meadow, Taylor Brooke, and White Silo. I tried to go to both Land of Nod and Hopkins, but unfortunately, I was there too early in the morning for it to be open. What, wine shouldn't be served with breakfast? The wine industry in Connecticut, just like the vines, keeps growing. We are lucky to have such delicious wines at our fingertips. They also lead to fun stop-offs while traveling. Let's say the family is planning a trip to Mystic Seaport, drop by one of the local wineries such as Stonington Vineyards, Saltwater Farm, or Maugle Sierra "while you're there."

Connecticut Barns Trail

Statewide

Connecticut certainly has its share of trails. After the success of the state's wine trail, others have followed suit. Visitors can hop along the chocolate trail, the women's heritage trail, freedom trail, antiques trail, and even an authors' trail. Just like the wine trail, which provides maps of the locations of the wineries and vineyards throughout the state, the barn trail does the same. The seven routes separate Connecticut into seven distinct regions and outline the path from one barn to the next.

The barn in autumn is often the focus of a quintessentially New England scene. On a crisp, clear fall afternoon, absolutely nothing beats meandering down routes like 169 or 87 to simply take in the view. Along with maples in midst of a color change with white steeples peeking through the branches, the barn exemplifies rural Connecticut. Whether painted red and equipped with a silo, dilapidated and in disrepair, or acting as a carriage house, barns bring the state's agrarian past and present into the limelight.

The Connecticut Trust for Historic Preservation has created a fantastic brochure highlighting the seven routes and barns of note to see along the way. Many of them are part of historic sites or working farms that can be visited. They also offer an app for the smartphone if you prefer mapping your barns electronically. For a more detailed cross section of Connecticut barns, log on to connecticutbarns.org. They have an interactive map feature that allows the browser to click on a town of choice and then to scroll based on the town's geography to show what barns are in the town, their function, and picture. I had quite a surprise when I tried this feature on the website. I naturally clicked on Norwich first, the town where I was raised. I immediately honed in on the Norwichtown section and noticed a few barns on my family's street. Lo and behold there was my house on the barn tracker! What I had always merely thought of as a garage and storage location for such childhood items as bicycles, beach chairs, and water guns is actually a historic carriage house. There was the front of my home in the picture, with part of the garage/carriage house peeking out from the end of the driveway. The listings include the address, a historic name, and the barn's historic as well as present use. The present use and historic name were left as "unknown" on the website, although I wanted to update it with "Samuel Abbot House—present use: hiding place for Dad's Mazda Miata, yard equipment, and old theater sets and props."

Although I thought of its current use in somewhat of an amusing fashion, it actually brought to light a greater point. Whereas many structures have changed in function and architecture, the barn truly has not. Maybe in the eighteenth and nineteenth century this carriage house was not housing a red Miata, but it was serving the same function, protecting the family's vehicle, hypothetically some kind of carriage. It did not contain an electric lawnmower in those days, but I would conjecture that it did store more primitive yard equipment. Although certain buildings are created due to need, for instance a gas station or a mall, which go hand-in-hand with modern amenities or technology, barns stay the same. A barn built in 1700 or in 2015 has generally the same function.

After scrolling through the barns of Norwichtown, I came to a section of town not far from there called Bean Hill. Plain Hill Road, the major thoroughfare, is predominantly active farmland. Each barn

on the road was included on the website. I then clicked on two nearby towns, which are almost completely agrarian in nature, Bozrah and Franklin, and scrolled through a smattering of the respective towns' barns. Similar to the carriage house, no matter the year of construction, in these rural communities the barn serves the same function as its original intended use: shelter for cattle, storage for grain and farm equipment.

Despite the fact that my house did not make the "Thames Valley and New London County" driving route on the barn trail, many of the nearby rural towns justly did. In addition to Thames Valley and New London County, the other six sections include: Northwest Hills, Connecticut River Valley North, Quiet Corner/Northeast, Connecticut River Valley South, New Haven and the Shoreline, and Fairfield County and the Western Shore. The Connecticut Trust for Historic Preservation estimates around 10,000 historic barns dot the state's landscape.

In addition to the act of protecting these structures for history's sake, many are architecturally beautiful. In an era when sprawl is encroaching on every inch of green space, preserving these gems of the state's agrarian identity is increasingly important. Stop and take a moment to think of the breadth of styles and uses that Connecticut's barn buildings encompass. The app and brochure identify not only the location of the barns, but their intended use. Tobacco sheds, which are popular in the northern Connecticut River Valley region, the onion storage sheds of Fairfield County, and the statewide dairy barns, are among the identifiable categories. Others include the chicken coop, corn crib, potato/mushroom barn, carriage house or barn, and the gentleman's barn. It also categorizes them by style; for instance, gambrel, round, English, New England or Bank. The types range from one far corner of the state to the opposite. Each location's address and vital information, as well as a description of its historic and/or present use, is given. The routes are presented in a drivable, or sometimes even, bike-able manner.

An example would be the Bellamy-Ferriday House in Bethlehem. The entry gives important information for visiting, such as hours, seasonal details, and the type of barn. A description of the property is also included. For instance, the brochure describes this home as a Georgian property built in 1754 by Reverend Joseph Bellamy, who was a leader of the Great Awakening. The property is noted for its Colonial Revival garden. Additionally, on site are sheep, carriage, horse, and cow barns. Even many properties that are featured in this collection of Connecticut Lore or the last are highlighted: Zagray Farm in Colchester, Blue Slope Country Museum in Franklin, the horse barns of UCONN, and the carriage house at Roseland Cottage are featured, to name a few. Similar to this book's "While You're There" sections, the app and brochure list places that include stops for ice cream or snacks. For a destination like Buell's Orchards, come for the barn building but stay for the pick your own apples.

Unless someone has a job tied directly to farming or a related industry, many of us take the presence of barns for granted. The Connecticut Trust for Historic Preservation wants to make sure that the barn is preserved for posterity to enjoy. The Trust saw Connecticut's barn buildings as endangered species and wanted to try as hard as they could to take steps to guarantee their future. They have worked to submit the top 200 barns in the state for inclusion on the National Register of Historic Places. With the country's continual trend towards organic produce and farm to table restaurants that go hand in hand with work done by preservationist groups, the future of the barn looks brighter than it did in the not so distant past.

Thimble Islands
Branford

Although Connecticut is not typically synonymous with the word "island," one band of them off the coast of Branford in Stony Creek Harbor totals 365! Well, some argue that there are 365 Thimble Islands while others figure that only twenty-five of them can technically be called islands since they are inhabited, whereas the others are considered only rocks. Names like "Potato Island," "Davis Island," and "Mother-in-Law Island" are only a few of the many thimbles in the sewing kit that is this archipelago (although its moniker stems from the thimbleberry, not the sewing tool). Although not far from New Haven and thus the sprawling New York metropolis, the Thimble Islands are most certainly a world away.

Many of the islands have quite a story to tell, especially from outposts of the rich and famous, such as Davis Island housing the "Summer White House" of President Taft; Doonesbury cartoonist Gary Trudeau and his wife newswoman Jane Pauley, who have a home on Governor Island; and Tom Thumb's abode on East Cut In Two Island. One former hotel, the Thimble Island House, is now a private 6,300-square-foot home that is available for rent (for $1,700 a night!) The eleven bedroom former hotel witnessed steamboats that used to shuffle visitors over from New Haven for a night of dinner and dancing. For those who can't stand their neighbors, a private island could do the trick, as some small thimbles only contain one house, albeit typically a large one. As of the time of this writing Jepson, Belden, and Potato Island are all available to purchase. If you are not quite ready for the purchase of your own island, you can always enjoy a tour of the Thimble Islands by boat. Captain Mike and his Sea Mist ship takes passengers on a forty-five-minute tour of the island chain, which was originally discovered by Adrien Block (who also found, hence the name, Block Island off the coast of Rhode Island).

The smallest island is Exton's Reef, which at high tide is only as big as a tennis court. It is one of the outermost islands. The raised one-room lofted house is a far cry from the lavish grounds of the Thimble Island House. Grand estates have their own private tennis courts, while others that are more like huts do not even have running water or electricity. Cedar Island is also for sale. It only has a gazebo, fire pit, and patio and has a price tag $285,000 for any prospective buyers at this time. The islands need to be at least one acre in size for a home to be built on it.

Any place with such intrigue and curiosity as the Thimbles surely has adventure to tell. Notorious Captain William Kidd, the sailor accused of piracy and eventually executed, is said to have buried his famed treasure on Pot Island, named for the potholes left by a moving glacier. Kidd's legend tells that he buried his riches en route from New York to Boston. Visible evidence of digging for Kidd's treasure can be seen.

For the visitor, Outer Island is open to the public. Horse Island, owned by Yale University's Peabody Museum of Natural History, is the largest. Another is Governor's Island, which has fourteen residences. Money Island, which is the most populous island, once housed a small bowling alley, church, hotel, store, and post office. Money Island is also known for its "book booth," a former phone booth which acts as a library. Belden Island was the location for *Love Prison*, a short-lived reality television show on the A&E Network featuring couples who met via online dating. A few of the islands are owned by a reclusive heiress.

To reach the Thimbles, take exit 56 off Route 95 for Leetes Island Road. The Stony Creek Museum offers a great beginning to your Thimble Island trip. The museum, which was once a church and community center, showcases artifacts having to do with the Stony Creek section of Branford and the Thimble Islands. The museum opened in 2012. The collection includes a display of the pink granite that was quarried nearby in Stony Creek. This granite is used in such buildings as the Brockton, Massachusetts, City Plaza, and South Station in Boston, as well as the Statue of Liberty and the Brooklyn Bridge. Stony Creek Quarry is the last active quarry in an area that was once littered with seventeen granite quarries.

While You're There!

A great place to stay to witness the Thimble Islands up close is the Thimble Islands Bed and Breakfast, although the name includes the Thimbles, it is on the mainland in Stony Creek. Its prime location has an amazing view of Long Island Sound and is a perfect getaway.

For a good brew after a day of exploring the Thimbles, visit the Thimble Island Brewing Company in Branford for a pint, a flight, or a growler fill. I recommend the flagship American Ale. Thimble Island offerings are available at local establishments like the tasty seafood hotspot, Lenny and Joe's, which has a handful of coastal locations in the towns of Westbrook, Branford, New Haven, and Madison. Other libation creations like their Coffee Stout, Pumpkin Porter, and IPA are available as well. Want more local beer? Branford also has its own Stony Creek Brewery with offerings that include Dock Time American Lager, Big Cranky Double IPA, and Sun Juice, their Belgian Summer Ale. Take home your favorite flavor in a growler or belly up to the bar at the tasting room with a flight or a pint. The DuVig Brewery is also in town and features lower alcohol session style beers, which contrasts with nearby Overshores Brewing in East Haven, whose beers are produced in the Belgian style, full bodied and typically higher ABV (alcohol by volume). There are enough breweries in the Branford area to make a full day of it!

On another odd note, nearby, scientist Jonathan Rothberg created a Stonehenge-esque celestial calendar in the Sachem's Head area of Guilford.

Seaside Mansions of Glory
Waterford and Groton

Branford House

Branford House, on the campus of University of Connecticut's Avery Point branch in Groton, and Eolia, the mansion at Harkness State Park in Waterford, are stately timeless testaments to the wealth of their previous owners. The word "impressive" is an understatement in describing these two mansions, both of which would seem at home along Newport's Ocean Avenue. The splendid palaces look if as they had been kept up meticulously since their use as private summer homes. This is not the case, for both were left in various states of disuse for years, with the Branford House eventually in need of serious repair. Luckily, both architectural gems escaped from the shadow of the wrecking ball. Today, they are used for venues such as weddings and other receptions and what venues they are, with a glimpse of the high life, at least for one evening. The story of Branford House and Eolia involve two families, unfathomably wealthy through industry during the late nineteenth and early twentieth centuries, but whose legacy lives on in the philanthropic work that the families endowed, as well as their grand summer abodes that can now be enjoyed by the public.

Harkness State Park

Harkness State Park is named for Edward and Mary Harkness, the couple whose summer retreat they called Eolia, named for Aeolus, the Greek god of the winds' island home, Aeolia. Harkness is truly a 230-acre paradise by the sea. Being a part of the Connecticut State Park system, access to the grounds is granted for a nominal fee during summer. Harkness is a park that can be explored for hours. Although the mansion was the center of the Harknesses' lives, it is not the focal point of the state park. After parking the car, a wide expanse of lawn greets the visitor. Perfect for kite flying and family picnics, this area can be loud and full of revelers. Long Island Sound was literally in the Harkness family's front yard. From the lawn, watch the ferries, sailboats, and other watercraft coming and going out of the New London harbor. Past the wide swath of green lawn, dirt roads lead to entryways. The one on the right hand side is a boardwalk that crosses over sand dunes leading to the beach. This beach, although small compared to nearby Westerly, Rhode Island beaches, is a perfect place to dip your feet in the water. Swimming is not permitted, but wading in for a quick cool-down is more than allowed. The left side of the beach is noted for its large boulders and on the right is an inlet. Notice when looking on the right a spire rising above the horizon; this is the tower of the former Seaside Sanitarium. Harkness has many nooks and crannies to explore. Although I had been going there ever since I can remember, as the years rolled on, I discovered more and more facets of the property of which I was previously unaware. On the eastern edge of the property is an amphitheater, hidden behind shrubbery and with a direct view over the marsh to Long Island Sound. Close to this spot is a path that traverses the marshland of Harkness. Even when the parking lot is full of cars and the smell of barbecues are overwhelming, certain spots in the park, like the marsh path, will be deserted. It is truly an explorer's delight. Closer to the mansion, shaded behind tall trees is a former water tower that used to have a windmill attached to the top. Also on the grounds are acres of former farmland, with roads and paths that wind around, toward the western end of the property. Due west though is Camp Harkness, which, through Mary Harkness's philanthropic legacy, is a camp for children with special needs that has its own facilities, including a beach with ramps that make it wheelchair accessible. In addition to the impressive gardens that flank the mansion itself, other gardens pop up in unexpected places, close to greenhouses, which are tucked away on the property. The four-bay carriage house contains a small gift shop that is open seasonally; in most places, this building would be the centerpiece! I even discovered in the shade of an ancient-looking tree with twisted branches, a small burial plot, seemingly for family pets. Speaking of pets, dogs are most certainly allowed at Harkness!

The area of land where the mansion was built is called Goshen Point. In my early years going to Harkness, I remember vividly the gardens on the grounds being in full bloom. Equipped with Asian-themed and gnome statuary, they were stunning. Unfortunately, for many years they were not tended to, and the mansion itself was looking a bit forlorn. Thankfully, those days are long gone. The mansion and gardens are kept up meticulously today. The gardens, designed by famed landscape architect Beatrix Jones Farrand, ever changing with the season, are lined with paths. Some paths are geometrically traceable, and others meander here and there. Highlights are an Alpine rock garden and an Oriental garden featuring a statue

of Buddha. It is simply a taste of Europe, as the visitor is allowed to linger on the stone benches in the pergola supported by stunning columns with vines snaking above and alongside the trellis. Just like the park's grounds, the gardens harbor splendid little corners that veer off the beaten path.

Eolia Mansion, built in 1906, designed by the firm of Lord and Hewlett, and bought a year later by the Harknesses, is simply stunning. Eolia was built in second Renaissance revival style, equipped with a Spanish hip roof. Looking north at the mansion from Long Island Sound, the Italian inspired palazzo is flanked on one side by the breakfast room. With large glass windows, the room is adorned with stenciled flowers and leaves, climbing and snaking alongside its cathedral style archways. On the other side is another pergola that is utilized as a porch. Inside the mansion, a grand staircase gracefully descends from the second floor to the first, directly to the glass doors facing the ocean. Sparsely decorated, although years ago the walls were adorned with prints of birds, the rooms spring to life during events as personal accoutrements are on display. Nighttime festivities are lavishly bathed in candlelight, which suits the mansion perfectly. The interior is colonial revival and other features of the house include balustrades, Palladian windows, and chimneys. During its heyday, the grounds included a squash court, a billiard room, and a bowling alley. Even the current restroom facility and the guard booth were once part of the estate. Sixty-one buildings encompass the entire property (including Camp Harkness to which the public is not granted access).

Edward and Mary Harkness were originally from Ohio, and Edward was the heir to his father's fortune. His father had been a silent partner of John D. Rockefeller, investing in Standard Oil. In a poll in 1918, Edward was ranked the sixth richest man in the United States.

A lighthouse adorns the campus of UConn Avery Point.

Incredibly philanthropically driven, the Harkness name appears on buildings throughout the country including the Harkness Tower at Yale and the Harkness Chapel at Connecticut College. Generous donations have been made to other colleges, including Harvard, Brown, and Columbia.

The Harknesses' year-round home was another fine mansion on New York City's Fifth Avenue. Another remarkable Harkness gift is the Temple of Perneb to the Metropolitan Museum of Art. This is the immense Egyptian temple that one can actually walk into as part of the museum's extensive Egyptian collection. In total, the Harkness family, which included Edward's philanthropic mother, Anna, contributed upwards of one to two hundred million dollars to worthy causes. The final gift that Edward and Mary left was their estate to the state of Connecticut to be enjoyed by all for posterity.

Camp Harkness was created by Mary Harkness as a summer camp for children who were stricken with polio. In 1920,

she welcomed thirty children from New York City to spend the summer on their estate and created the basis for what would become Camp Harkness. This lasted for years, and eventually, when the state attained the land in 1952, Camp Harkness itself was founded as a state park accessed by individuals with special needs. Facilities include a dining hall, a beach, cottages, tent sites, and horseback riding. Also on site was a working farm, where the family raised its prized Guernsey cows, grew their own vegetables, and produced their own milk and eggs. The food would be utilized at the summer home, but also eaten year round in the New York estate.

Harkness State Park is located on Great Neck Road in Waterford, just down the street from the Eugene O'Neill Theater Center. In the summer, the lawn plays host to music, much of it classical in nature, but national names like James Taylor and Spyro Gyra have graced its stage.

If Harkness is close to the western border where the Thames River meets

The grandiose Branford House is the site of many functions and is located at Avery Point.

Long Island Sound, then another phenomenal estate, the Branford House, serves as a guardhouse to the eastern shore. This manor, today also used for functions, is on the campus of UCONN Avery Point. Although it has a similar backstory to Harkness (wealthy businessman, or heir to one, buys elaborate summer home on the shores of Long Island Sound), its popularity has only blossomed since complete renovation of the site in 2006. The Branford House, summer retreat of Morton Freeman Plant, a railroad and steamboat magnate, was named after Plant's hometown of Branford, Connecticut. This is an imposing seaside estate designed in the Tudor style that no longer has the accompanying lavish gardens that it once had, as Harkness does, but similarly has an unspoiled view of the sound. The estate was built by craftsmen and artisans employed from Italy and Germany. If Eolia resembles a grand Italian villa, the Branford House's reference point would be a castle or grand English countryside estate. Just like Harkness, the estate held the family's cow barn and gardens in which they grew their own produce. Although Avery Point lacks a beach like Harkness, it does have a wide expansive lawn and its rocky coast is popular with fishermen. Mr. Plant was also a generous benefactor of many institutions including a hospital in Clearwater, Florida, which bears his name.

Although the estate was given over to the state of Connecticut, it spent years as an outpost for the United States Coast Guard. The Coast Guard built barracks and other unsightly buildings on campus and unfortunately left the gorgeous Branford House in a state of decay. When UCONN Avery Point opened its doors in the late 1960s, the school was confounded as to what to do with the former glorious mansion. After being hit by Hurricane Gloria, and after years of continuous neglect, its fate was uncertain. Luckily, the beautiful building has been refurbished and now is a very popular wedding venue.

Other former estate buildings are now utilized by the campus, case in point, the police station. The stone cottage containing the police department is as ornate and stunning as its larger counterpart, albeit on a much smaller scale. One highlight of the estate's time under Coast Guard control is the lighthouse that was completed in 1943. Its concrete block design is accentuated by an octagonal lantern. It served as a beacon to the New London harbor for twenty-five years and is now listed (along with the house, and Eolia for that matter) on the National Register of Historic Places.

The public is encouraged to enjoy today's Avery Point. Its pathway is a favorite of dog walkers and is unparalleled at sundown. Both of these estates are hidden jewels of Connecticut. They are uber-popular wedding venues, with good reason. (Given my affinity for Harkness, this is where my wife and I were married, and it simply was the perfect venue.) Often overlooked in favor of the weirder (Gillette Castle), the celebrity occupied (Mark Twain House), or those located near the New York metropolitan area (Lockwood-Matthews House), these two most certainly are worth investigating. Harkness is perfect for an afternoon of exploration, the beach, a picnic, and of course a dog walk, but just in time for sunset, drive two towns farther east and enjoy the view at Groton's Avery Point.

While You're There!

Literally, you will be there if you visit the Branford House, since Project Oceanology is also located on the campus of Avery Point. This environmental study group was founded to educate area children about the seascape around them. Although they often take out groups of school children or campers on ocean study trips, they do offer public outings as well. Their tours include a marine biolo-gy-oriented oceanographic cruise, a lighthouse cruise (Ledge Light is just offshore), and a seal-watching cruise. The trips are fun and educational! Visit www.oceanology.org for more information.

Lourdes of Litchfield

Litchfield

Just off the picturesque Litchfield town green is a shrine to the Virgin Mary, created as a replica of the shrine in Lourdes, France, where fourteen-year-old Bernadette Soubirous saw visions of the Immaculate Conception in 1858. Her story was popularized in the novel and film *The Song of Bernadette*. For those pilgrims who cannot travel over the Atlantic to France, the Litchfield version will suffice. Suffice it has, since during the peak season, May to October, the shrine attracts as many as 600 visitors per day, although it does not compare to the daily hordes that the French shrine witnesses.

Pilgrims venture to Litchfield looking for redemption, prayer, and solace. My visit happened on a glorious autumn day. After parking, I walked through a stone archway that was flanked by statues. Autumn leaves dazzled in a spectacular display that day, with vibrant reds and oranges overhanging the grotto. The stone grotto, based entirely on its French counterpart, is highlighted by a statue of the Virgin. Mass is said here during the warmer months. All parts of the grounds can be explored, even near the altar, save for when mass is being said. The place exudes a sense of calm. Although busy at the time of my visit, the area was completely quiet, except for the sounds of nature reverberating around us. Leading up a

161

For a moment of quiet introspection visit the Lourdes in Litchfield Shrine.

hill and winding around are statuary depictions of the stations of the cross, eventually culminating with a cross representing Jesus's crucifixion at the precipice of the hill. In addition to the grotto, the property includes a chapel, cafe, and gift shop.

The shrine was built in 1958, on the 100-year anniversary of the future St. Bernadette's visions. Lourdes is on Montfort Street along with the impressive stone Montfort House (built circa 1927 as a summer home) that sits at the foot of the lane. This is a seminary and a retreat house operated by the Montfort Missionaries, who also run the shrine.

Although to today's secular traveler, the site of a religious shrine may seem out of place, it seems to fit perfectly in the Litchfield Hills, more specifically in the shadow of Litchfield's town green. This area of the state is a perfect getaway. Drive on the rolling hills to simply take in the view. The next time you are visiting the Litchfield Hills and stopping at farm stands, walking in state parks, or exploring museums, make sure to pull off Route 118 at the sign for the shrine.

Roaring Brook Nature Center

Canton

Roaring Brook Nature Center in Canton is an ideal place to learn about the natural surroundings of central Connecticut. With its motto "In harmony with nature," harmony is the key word, since the nature center also plays host to folk music concerts throughout the year. On location, the visitor will find a menagerie of mostly local, coupled with a few exotic, animals. Indigenous frogs, toads, turtles, squirrels, hawks, and turkey vultures can be viewed

alongside organisms from other areas of the country, like the California King Snake and the Boa. Roaring Brook also rehabilitates hurt animals. The center showcases exhibits like "Ancient Forest and Native Americans," "From Farms to Forest to Lawns," and "Wild and Scenic Farmington River." A highlight of the museum portion is the walk-through longhouse that showcases the way local Native Americans lived. Other views are stuffed animals presented in a diorama type setting. The beaver wetland provides information on the fascinating rodents while providing depictions of dams.

The nature center provides plenty of walking trails for the visitor to enjoy and offers many seasonal activities, demonstrations, and presentations, such as the Hobgoblin Fair, All About Owls, and Native Americans of the Eastern Woodlands. Many of the exhibits and special events cater to children, but are also informative for adults. Special events that coincide with certain holidays often offer treats such as cider in the fall and hot chocolate during the winter.

Some evenings the Roaring Brook Nature Center transforms itself into a folk music venue. A small stage is surrounded by folding chairs in the nature center itself. It has been host to many national folk music acts, including the legendary Dave Van Ronk, Geoff Muldaur, and the Five Chinese Brothers. Look at their website for details and schedule.

Something Fishy

Plainfield, Burlington, and Norwich

Did you know that Connecticut's state fish is the American shad? Shad are anadromous fish, which means they spend most of their lives in the ocean, but swim up freshwater rivers to spawn. Other varieties of fish, such as salmon, herring, and eels, are also anadromous. American shad, consumed by colonial settlers, was a dietary staple of Native Americans living in present-day Connecticut. During the era before the Industrial Revolution, these fish were plentiful. Connecticut's fish conservation efforts are trying to turn back some of the unfortunate practices that caused turmoil to the state's ecological systems. By putting in fishways to subvert the effect of dams and by breeding fish at hatcheries, the state is putting forth profound conservation efforts.

Quinebaug Valley Trout Hatchery

Let's start in the northeast part of the state. The town of Plainfield is home to the Quinebaug Valley Trout Hatchery. Off a residential street of the village of Central Falls is Trout Hatchery Road that will lead you to your destination. From the parking lot, the hatchery looks like a nondescript utilitarian building. A visit to the hatchery is self-guided, where the visitor can look at a few informative bits of information about trout, the process at the hatchery, and a history of the hatchery itself. One fact I thought was especially neat was that they hatch about 380,000 pounds of trout per year, or 600,000 fish for stocking. Behind glass windows, you can see many yellow circular pools with the smallest trout in them This room resembles a specialized warehouse. Along the wood-paneled wall are tanks with the different types of fish bred at the hatchery, including rainbow, brown, and brook trout. Doors lead outside where the visitor can look into a series of pools where the older, larger trout are kept. The full-grown fish are quite large! Only a certain section of the outside is accessible to the public, but the rest of the facility can be seen from afar. The inaccessible part is basically circular fish pools upon circular fish pools.

Burlington Trout Hatchery

The Burlington Trout Hatchery has quite a different feel from Quinebaug Valley. Where the Quinebaug Valley's building is nondescript with no-frills architecture, the Burlington building looks homey and is nestled in the woods of Nassaheagan State Forest on Belden Road. The hatchery was founded in 1923 and includes trout pools, trout ponds, the hatchery house, and nature trails. There is also a raceway with baby fish on site. There is less to see at this hatchery, but it is more picturesque. There are 130,000 various kinds of trout bred here per year, as well as the 200,000 additional salmon fry. This hatchery tour is also self-guided. Both of these hatcheries raise fish to be stocked in the state's rivers and ponds. Fishing is prohibited at both hatcheries. "Dam it all!"

In 1828, the first dam in Norwich was erected on the Shetucket River in Greeneville. This was followed by others upstream in places like Ponemah Mill in Taftville and in the smaller mill village of Occum. Dams were built to utilize water to power places like factories. Along with harnessing electricity, which provided many benefits for a new, forward-moving society, dams created negative environmental effects. Anadromous fish like shad were blocked when they tried swimming upstream to spawn.

In later years, towns have begun to implement ways for fish to get around the dams, other than knocking them down completely. Fish ladders or fishways and fish elevators, or fish lifts, are some of the more popular ways that successfully allow fish upstream. Shad and other upstream swimming fish are not able to jump over a gigantic dam, but they are able to make small jumps of about a foot. Often located on the side of the dam, fish are able to jump a step into a small pool. This process is repeated as fish scale the height of the dam. The fish elevator literally transports fish up from one level to the next. By means of fish ladders, they can swim upstream as far as Willimantic and Putnam. Fish reclaiming their natural swimming grounds help out more than just the fish and the fishermen. This process brings further balance to the ecosystem, with natural predators like eagles, herons, and osprey becoming more abundant. Visit the Greeneville fish lift from April to late June to see the Shad run and the fish lift in action. Roughly 2,300 fish use the lift yearly. The dam is made of wood. This part of the river is a prime spot for fishermen, eagles, and small tent cities of homeless people. The Shetucket River's water quality has vastly improved in recent years. In the past the nearby paper factory had a profound effect on the natural environment, such that, depending on what color paper the factory was churning out, the river would turn that hue.

Tours are available from May 1 to June 30. The Greeneville Dam is off Roosevelt Avenue in the Greeneville section of Norwich.

So if you want to see fish, but do not feel like shelling out the cash to visit an aquarium, try one of these. All are free and open to the public, but make sure to plan other activities in the area since neither visit will take up much of your precious time. The Rainbow Dam Fishway on the Farmington River in Windsor is another prime example of a fish ladder and includes a viewing area.

Conclusion

From the Gold Coast to the Quiet Corner, thank you for accompanying me on this journey through Connecticut. Although it is the third smallest state, it is chock full of out-of-the-way locales, interesting history, ghosts, and forgotten places. I hope you had as much fun on this trip as I did!

Bibliography

Battista, Carolyn. "Teacher's Tales are a Ghostly Lot." *New York Times*. (October 30, 1988).

Bayles, Richard M. "Alexander's Lake." History of Windham County, Connecticut. (New York: W.W. Preston & Co., 1899).

Benson, Judy. "Explore Bailey's Ravine's Rocks, Ridges and Rarities." *New London Day*. (October 8, 2011).

Benson, Judy. "Shad Run Effort Appear to have Leveled Off." *New London Day*. (July 12, 2010).

"B.F. Clyde's Cider Mill." American Society of Mechanical Engineers. (October 29, 1994).

Braccidiferro, Gail. "If You Lead a Fish to a Ladder..." *New York Times*. (July 3, 2005).

Burgeson, John. "Three Historic Lighthouses Up for Grabs, Penfield Included." *Connecticut Post*. (July 14, 2013).

Campbell, Susan. "Architectural Gems." *Hartford Courant*. (July 6, 2007).

Campbell, Susan and Bill Heald. *Connecticut Curiosities*. (Guilford, CT: Globe Pequot Press, 2002).

Caulkins, Francis Manwaring. *History of Norwich, Connecticut: From Its Possession by the Indians to the Year 1866*. (Published by the Author, 1866).

Childress, Lillian and David Kurkovskiy. "Author Discusses Elm City's Dark History." *Yale Daily News*. (October 2, 2013).

Cho, Jenna. "Lantern Hill." *New London Day*. (August 10, 2011).

Chronicle Show. "Thimble Islands." (September 23, 2014).

Connecticut Trust for Historic Preservation. Connecticut Barns Trail brochure. (Hamden, CT: 2014).

Connecticut Trust for Historic Preservation. "The Last of the Puritans: Long Society Meeting House, Preston." *Connecticut Preservation News Volume XXXVII Number 6*. (Hamden, CT: November/December 2014).

Cothren, William. *History of Ancient Woodbury, Connecticut*. (Waterbury, CT: Bronson Brothers, 1854).

Deluca, Dan W, and Dionne Longley. *The Old Leather Man: Historical Accounts of a Connecticut and New York Legend*. (Middletown, CT: Wesleyan University Press, 2008).

D'Entremon, Jeremy. "Connecticut's Penfield Reef Light: No Longer Ghostly." *Lighthouse Digest*. (October 2002).

D'Entremon, Jeremy. The Lighthouse Handbook: New England. (Kennebunkport, ME: Cider Mill Press, 2008).

DePold, Hans, "Ghosts of Bolton Past and Present." *Bolton Community News*. (February and June 2003).

Dugas, Rene. *Taftville, Connecticut and the Industrial Revolution*. (Published by the author, 2001).

"Eric Sloane Museum." *Connecticut Cultural Treasures*. Connecticut Public Broadcasting.

Fair, John D. "The Search For Elmer Bitgood: The Paul Bunyan of New England." *Iron Game History: The Journal of Physical Culture Volume 5*. (October 1998).

Federal Writers Project of the Works Progress Administration. *Connecticut: A Guide to Its Roads, Lore and People*. (Boston, MA: Houghton Mifflin Company, 1938).

Fellman, Bruce. "Leading the Libraries." *Yale Alumni Magazine*. (February 2002).

Fillo, MaryEllen. "Yankee Names Cedar Hill One of 'Most Beautiful' Cemeteries in New England." *Hartford Courant*. (September 30, 2014).

Gendreau, LeAnne. "Some See Jesus in a Wallingford Tree," NBC-CT News. (June 15, 2010).

Gibson, John. Weekend Walks Along the New England Coast: Exploring the Coast from Connecticut to Maine. (Woodstock, VT: Countryman Press, 2003).

Ghost Hunters. "New London Ledge Light." Sci-fi Network. (Season 12, Episode 5).

Golfin, Jenny. "Ghost Hunters Coming to Yankee Pedlar in Torrington for Overnight Experience." *Litchfield County Times*. (January 31, 2013).

Gordon, Robert B. *A Landscape Transformed: The Ironmaking District of Salisbury, Connecticut*. (Oxford, UK: Oxford University Press, 2000).

Grant, Steve. "Barns of Connecticut Document a Nutmeg Treasure." *Hartford Courant*. (November 12, 2013).

Green, Penelope. "The Monoliths Next Door." *New York Times*. (October 13, 2005).

Haar, Dan. "Historic Buildings Offer Windows to East Hartford's Past." *Hartford Courant*. (August 1, 2014).

Harte, Charles Rufus. "Connecticut's Iron and Copper." 60th Annual Report of the Connecticut Society of Civil Engineers. (1944).

Hauk, Dennis. *Haunted Places: The National Directory*. (London: Penguin Books, 2002).

Hayward, John. *Hayward's New England Gazetteer of 1839*. (Concord, NH: Israel S. Boyd and William White, 1839).

Hazlett, Alexandra. "Secret AIG Golf Course? Not Quite." *Danbury News–Times*. (August 17, 2009).

Hamilton, Jesse. "Coast Guard Center Moving," *Hartford Courant*. (August 3, 2007).

Hermann, Richard A. "Lisbon Town Historian Annual Report," (1996-1997).

Hesselberg, Erik. "Portland Hires Consultant To Find Ways to Rescue Elmcrest Manor," *Hartford Courant*. (January 18, 2015).

Hesselberg, Erik. "Elmcrest Manor Property In Portland Gets Historic Preservation Grant," *Hartford Courant*. (August 29, 2014).

Hladky, Gregory B. "Coltsville National Historical Park Wins Final Approval." *Hartford Courant*. (December 13, 2014).

Holzer, Hans. *Ghosts: True Encounters With the World Beyond*. (New York, NY: Black Dog & Leventhal Publishers, 2004).

Horsman, Reginald. *Frontier Doctor: William Beaumont, America's First Great Medical Scientist*. (Columbia, MO: University of Missouri Press, 1996).

Hosley, Bill. "Hartford Can Take Pride: In Coltsville." *Hartford Courant*. (December 4, 1999).

International Television Association, and Connecticut Humanities Council. *The Road Between Heaven and Hell the Last Circuits of the Leatherman*. (Hartford, CT: ITVA/CT, 1984).

Ives, J. Moss. "A Connecticut Battlefield in the American Revolution." *The Connecticut Magazine*. Volume 7, Number 5. (1901).

Kilbourn, Dwight Canfield. *The Bench and Bar of Litchfield County, Connecticut 1709-1909*. (Published by the author, 1909).

Kimball, Carol W. "The Mystery of Waterford's Princess Nellie." *Hartford Courant*. (January 4, 2010).

Langlois, Mark. "Doctor Turned Author Tells of Danbury Upbringing." *Danbury News-Times*. (March 29, 2004).

Laschever, Barnett D. and Andi Marie Cantele. *Connecticut: An Explorer's Guide*. (Woodstock, VT: Countryman Press, 2006).

(The) Last Green Valley. "Bara-Hack, Ayer Mountain, Woodstock Cemetery and Ponemah Mill Walks." Walktober 2012-2014.

(The) Last Green Valley. Walktober Brochure, 2012.

Lefkowitz, Arthur S. *George Washington's Indispensable Men: The 32 Aides-de-Camp Who Helped Win the Revolution*. (Mechanicsburg, PA: Stackpole Books, 2003).

Lemoult, Craig. "Search for Clues Only Deepens 'Leatherman' Mystery." WSHU-National Public Radio. (May, 26, 2011).

Lincoln, Allen B. *A Modern History of Windham County, Connecticut: A Windham County Treasure Book Volume 1*. (Salem, MA: Higginson Book Company, 1994).

Lodi, Edward. *The Haunted Violin: True New England Ghost Stories*. (Marlborough, MA: Rock Village Publishing, 2005).

Mandell, Nina. "Meet UConn's New Mascot, Jonathan XIV, Who is an Adorable Puppy." *USA Today*. (January 30, 2014).

Marshall, Benjamin Tinkham. *A Modern History of New London County, Connecticut*. (New York: Lewis Historical Publishing Company, 1922).

Marteka, Peter. "Bolton Notch State Park Contains A State Rarity: A Cave." *Hartford Courant*. (August 16, 2009).

Marteka, Peter. "Faulkner's Island Light-Lonely Outpost Full of History Off Guilford Shore." *Hartford Courant*. (September 12, 2014).

Marteka, Peter. "History of Haley Farm State Park in Groton Stretches Back to 1648." *Hartford Courant*. (May 21, 2010).

Marteka, Peter. "Mill History Lives Along Nipmuck Trail, Fenton River." *Hartford Courant*. (February 9, 2012).

Marteka, Peter. "Nature: From Mine to Mountain Top." *Hartford Courant*. (January 19, 2012).

Martin, John H. "Saints, Sinners and Reformers: The Burned-Over District Re-Visited." Crooked Lake Review. (Fall 2005).

McElveen, Akaya. "Ghosts in the Halls: Many Believe ECSU Dorm is Home to the Paranormal." Willimantic Chronicle. (October 31, 2014).

McGirr, Sarah. "Branford House: Two Views-Private Capital." New London Day. (October 20, 1985).

Megan, Kathleen. "Islands of the Sound." *Hartford Courant*. (August 14, 2008).

Miller, Julie. "The View From Taftville; Life Returns to a 19th-Century Textile Mill." *New York Times*. (March 26, 1995).

Munkittrick, Alain via the Portland Historical Society. "Elmcrest's Historic Buildings." Elmcrest Campus Advisory Committee. Available (Online) www.elmcrestportlandct.com.

Myers, Kendra. "Two Partners In Success: Doctors Complete Purchase of Elmcrest Hospital." *Hartford Courant.* (October 17, 1994).

Newman, Rich. *Ghost Hunter's Field Guide: Over 1000 Haunted Places You Can Experience.* (Woodbury, MN: LLewellyan Publications, 2011).

Nixon, Amy Ash. "Ailing Faulkner's Island Needs Rescuing." *Hartford Courant.* (March 27, 1996).

Nolan, John D. "History of Taftville, Connecticut." www.historic-structures.com/ct/taftville/ponemah_mills.php

Orlomoski, Linda. "Town Spotlight: Ledyard-Historical and a Little Hip." *Norwich Magazine.* (March 2015).

Pancoast, Chalmers. "Profile of Sachem Uncas on Chimney of Norwich House; Carved After Long Research." *New London Day.* (September 5, 1935).

Parsons, Greg B. and Kate B. Watson. *New England Waterfalls.* (Woodstock, VT: Countryman Press, 2010).

Pawloski, John A. *Connecticut Mining.* (Mount Pleasant, SC: Arcadia Publishing, 2006).

Phillips, David E. *Legendary Connecticut: Traditional Tales From the Nutmeg State.* (Willimantic, CT: Curbstone Press, 1992).

Poro, Joan. "Carriage House Razed at Haley Farm." *New London Day.* (June 1, 1973).

Preiss, Amy Beth. "Pachaug Forest Home to Ghostly Sightings." *Norwich Bulletin.* (February 26, 2003).

Pressler, Jessica. "How AIG's Private Golf Course Got Its Name." *New York Magazine.* (August 2009).

Ragali, Andrew. "Newly Available UFO Files Detail Two Sightings in Meriden." *Meriden Record-Journal.* (January 23, 2015).

Reitz, Stephanie. "A Light With A Future." *Hartford Courant.* (September 7, 1997).

Revai, Cheri. *Haunted Connecticut.* (Mechanicsburg, PA: Stackpole Books, 2006).

Reynolds, James. *Ghosts in American Houses: A Collection of Ghostly Folktales.* (New York City: Bonanza Books, 1982).

Rhinelander, David. "History of Wells Woods Shady at Best Without Documentation." *Hartford Courant.* (November 20, 1998).

Richards, T. Addison. "The Norwich Arms." *Harper's New Monthly Magazine.* (1864)

Ritchie, David and Deborah. *Connecticut: Off the Beaten Path.* (Guilford, CT: Globe Pequot Press, 2000).

Robinson, Kenton. "Nooks and Crannies: Gravity Hill." *New London Day.* (March 29, 2008).

Salzer, Dick. "The Norwich Gun Industry." American Society of Arms Collectors Bulletin. Available (Online) www.norwichhistoricalsociety.org/resources/pdfs/90_salzer_norwich.pdf.

Seay, Gregory. "Former Elmcrest Hospital Moving Patients." *Hartford Courant.* (August, 2, 2003).

Shelton, Jim. "New Haven's Lincoln Oak Bones Date to the 1790s, Researchers Say." *New Haven Register.* (October 31, 2013).

Shelton, Sandi Kahn. "Sleeping Giant Has a Name: Hobbomock and Guilford Author Has New Illustrated Book About Him." *New Haven Register.* (November 21, 2011).

Starr, Markham. *Barns of Connecticut.* (Middletown, CT: Wesleyan University Press, 2013).

Strap, Chris. "'Gertie' Lives on in Burr Hall Legend." *Campus Lantern.* (November 29, 1984).

Trimel, Suzanne. "Columbia Sells its Former Engineering Summer Camp in Northwestern Connecticut for Open Space." *Columbia University News.* (April 5, 2000).

von Zielbauer, Paul. "Paddling Hartford's Scenic Sewer, An Abused Underground River, Up Close and Noxious." *New York Times.* (July 31, 2003).

Wisbey, Herbert A. *Pioneer Prophetess: Jemima Wilkinson, the Publick Universal Friend.* (Ithica, NY: Fall Creek Books, 2009).

Wood, Alan. *New England Lighthouses.* (Atglen, PA: Schiffer Publications, 2012).

Woodside, Maureen and Ron Kole. *A Ghost a Day: 365 True Tales of the Spectral, Supernatural and... Just Plain Scary!* (Avon, MA: Adams Media, 2010).

Zoe, Vivian F. "The Mysterious "Colonel" Charles Augustus Converse." *The Muse-Newsletter of the Slater Memorial Museum.* (Summer 2007).

Visitor Information

(In order of appearance)

Note: places inaccessible to the public are not included in this listing

Beckley Furnace
140 Lower Road
East Canaan, CT 06024
Beckleyfurnace.org

Sloane-Stanley Museum and Kent Iron Furnace
31 Kent Cornwall Road
Kent, CT 06757
www.ericsloane.com/museum.htm

The Connecticut Antique Machinery Association
31 Kent Cornwall Road
Kent, CT 06757
www.ctmachinery.com

Old Newgate Prison and Copper Mine
101 Newgate Road
East Granby, CT 06026
* Closed at the time of publication

House of Books
10 North Main Street
Kent, CT 06757
www.hobooks.com

Hop River State Park Trail
Hop River Road
Columbia, CT 06237

Beaumont Park
Village Hill Road
Lebanon, CT 06249

Hartford Union Station
1 Union Place
Hartford, CT 06103
www.hartfordtransit.org/unionstation.
html

Senator Thomas J. Dodd Memorial Stadium
(Home of the Connecticut Tigers baseball club)
14 Stott Avenue
Norwich, CT 06360
Cttigers.com

Alexander Lake
Upper Maple Street
Killingly, CT 06241

Camp Columbia State Park
West Street
Morris, CT 06763

Pachaug State Forest
219 Ekonk Hill Road
Voluntown, CT 06384

Salmon River State Forest/ Comstock Bridge
34 Comstock Bridge Road
Colchester, CT 06415

Day Pond State Park
Day Pond Road
Colchester, CT 06415

NuNu's Bistro
45 Hayward Avenue
Colchester, CT 06415
Nunusbistro.com

Captain Grant's 1754
109 Route 2A
Poquetanuck Village (Preston), CT 06365
www.captaingrants.com

Maple Lane Farms
57 NW Corner Road
Preston, CT 06365
www.maplelane.com

Curtis House Inn
506 Main Street South
Woodbury, CT 06798
www.curtishouseinn.com

Litchfield Inn
432 Bantam Road
Litchfield, CT 06759
www.litchfieldinnct.com

G.W. Tavern
20 Bee Brook Road
Washington Depot, CT 06794
www.gwtavern.com

The Yankee Pedlar Inn
93 Main Street
Torrington, CT 06790
www.pedlarinn.com

Norwichtown Green
Corner of Town and East Town Streets
Norwich, CT 06360

171

Book Club Bookstore and More
100 Main Street
Broad Brook, CT 06016
www.bookclubct.com

Makens Bemont House
307 Burnside Avenue
East Hartford, CT 06108

Abigail's Grille and Wine Bar
4 Hartford Road
Weatogue, CT 06089
www.abigailsgrill.com

Eastern Connecticut State University
83 Windham Street
Willimantic, CT 06226
www1.easternct.edu

Yale University, Woolsley Hall
500 College Street
New Haven, CT 06511
http://music.yale.edu/concerts/venues/
woolsey/

Ledge Light Foundation
New London, CT 06320
www.ledgelighthouse.org

Stonington Harbor Light
7 Water Street
Stonington, CT 06378
www.stoningtonhistory.org

WCNI—90.9 FM
Connecticut College
New London, CT 06320
www.wcniradio.org

The Telegraph
19 Golden Street
New London, CT 06320
Telegraphnl.com

Glebe House Museum and Garden
49 Hollow Road
Woodbury, CT 06798
www.glebehousemuseum.org

St. Paul's Episcopal Church
294 Main Street South
Woodbury, CT 06798
www.stpaulswoodbury.org

Woodbury Pewter
860 Main Street South
Woodbury, CT 06798
www.woodburypewter.com

Thomaston Opera House
158 Main Street
Thomaston, CT 06787
www.landmarkcommunitytheatre.org

Railroad Museum of New England
242 East Main Street
Thomaston, CT 06787
www.rmne.org

Warren's Occult Museum
Monroe, CT 06468
www.warrens.net/Occult-Museum-Tours.
html

Former site of "Jesus Tree"
Joes Hill Road
Danbury, CT 06811

Wooster Square
New Haven, CT 06533

New Haven Green
165 Church Street
New Haven, CT 06511

Keeler Tavern Museum
132 Main Street
Ridgefield, CT 06877
Keelertavernmuseum.org

Bozrah Farmers Market
45 Bozrah Street
Bozrah, CT 06334
www.bozrahfarmersmarket.org
Market open from late April to mid
October on late afternoon/evening on
Fridays

Great Hill Cemetery
Cemetery Road
Seymour, CT 06483

Devil's Den Nature Preserve
33 Pent Road
Weston, CT 06883

Gravity Hill
Main Street
Sterling, CT 06377

Colt Armory
140 Huyshope Avenue
Hartford, CT 06106

Prudence Crandall Museum
1 South Canterbury Road
Canterbury, CT 06331
Friendsofprudencecrandallmuseum.org

Canterbury Cones
57 North Canterbury Road
Canterbury, CT 06331

The Brooklyn Fair
15 Fairgrounds Road
Brooklyn, CT 06234
www.brooklynfair.org

The Golden Lamb Buttery
499 Wolf Den Road
Brooklyn, CT 06234
www.thegoldenlamb.com

The Vanilla Bean Café
450 West Road
Pomfret, CT 06258
www.thevanillabean.com

Lapsley Orchard
403 Orchard Hill Road
Pomfret, CT 06259
www.lapsleyorchard.com

Woodstock Fair
281 Route 169
Woodstock, CT 06281
www.woodstockfair.com

Primitive Crow
290 Route 169
Woodstock, CT 06281

Mrs. Bridge's Pantry
292 Route 169
Woodstock, CT 06281

Scranton's Shops
300 Route 169
Woodstock, CT 06267
www.scrantonshops.com

Woodstock Orchards
494 Route 169
Woodstock, CT 06281
www.woodstockorchardsllc.com

Roseland Cottage
556 Route 169
Woodstock, CT 06281

Sweet Evalina's Stand
688 Route 169
Woodstock, CT 06281

Christmas Barn
832 Route 169
Woodstock, CT 06281

Still River
Off of Route 198
Eastford, CT 06242

Chamberlin Mill
Old Turnpike Road
Woodstock, CT 06282
www.chamberlinmill.org

Sawmill Park
172 Iron Street
Ledyard, CT 06339
www.ledyardsawmill.org

Fort Trumbull State Park
90 Walbach Street
New London, CT 06320

Fort Griswold Battlefield State Park
Park Avenue
Groton, CT 06340

Fort Nathan Hale
36 Woodward Avenue
New Haven, CT 06512

Fort Saybrook Monument Park
College Street
Old Saybrook, CT 06475

Captain Scott's Lobster Dock
80 Hamilton Street
New London, CT 06320
www.captscotts.com

Lebanon Town Pound
Exeter Road
Lebanon, CT 06249

Lantern Hill
Trailhead behind Two Trees Inn
240 Indiantown Road
Ledyard, CT 06339

The Mashantucket Pequot Museum and Research Center
110 Pequot Trail
Mashantucket, CT 06338
www.pequotmuseum.org

Cedar Hill Cemetery
453 Fairfield Avenue
Hartford, CT 06114
www.cedarhillcemetery.org

Holiday Lights Fantasia at Goodwin Park
1130 Maple Avenue
Hartford, CT 06114
www.holidaylightfantasia.org

Long Society Meetinghouse
Long Society Road
Preston, CT 06365

Gurleyville Gristmill
Stonemill Road
Storss, CT 06268
http://joshuastrust.org/gurleyville-gristmill-and-house

Mansfield Hollow Dam
Mansfield Hollow Road
Mansfield, CT 06268

Hosmer Mountain Soda
217 Mountain Road
Willimantic, CT 06226
Hosmersoda.com

Lebanon Green Historic District
West Town Street
Lebanon, CT 06249

Mark Twain House
351 Farmington Avenue
Hartford, CT 06105
www.marktwainhouse.org

Harriet Beecher Stowe House
77 Forest Street
Hartford, CT 06105
www.harrietbeecherstowecenter.org

Samuel Huntington Home
34 East Town Street
Norwich, CT 06360
* Now part of United Community and
Family Services
Visitors are allowed to walk around the
grounds as well as the adjacent meadow
and cemetery

Denison Homestead/Pequotsepos Manor
120 Pequotsepos Road
Mystic, CT 06355
www.denisonhomestead.org

Roseledge Country Inn and Farm Shoppe
418 Route 164
Preston, CT 06365
www.roseledge.com

Ward Pound Ridge Reservation
(Home of the Leatherman Cave)
6 Reservation Road
Pound Ridge, NY 10576

Ayer Mountain
Ayer Road
North Franklin, CT 06254

Meiklem Kiln Works/Centerspace Wellness Studio
46 Norwich-Lebanon Road
Bozrah, CT 06334
Mkwcenter.com

Aicher Preserve
Freedley Road
Pomfret, CT 06259

Haley Farm State Park
Haley Farm Lane
Groton, CT 06340

Ford's Lobsters
15 Riverview Avenue
Groton, CT 06340

Elizabeth Park
1561 Asylum Avenue
West Hartford, CT 06117
Elizabethparkct.org

Bartaco
971 Farmington Avenue
West Hartford, CT 06107
www.bartaco.com

Sleeping Giant State Park
200 Mt. Carmel Avenue
Hamden, CT 06518

Beinecke Rare Book and Manuscript Library
121 Wall Street
New Haven, CT 06511
http://beinecke.library.yale.edu/

Lipstick (Ascending) on Caterpillar Tracks
Tower Parkway
New Haven, CT 06511

Time Machine Hobby Shop
71 Hilliard Street
Manchester, CT 06042
Timemachinehobby.com

Shady Glen
360 Middle Turnpike West
Manchester, CT 06042

Garde Arts Center
325 State Street
New London, CT 06320
www.gardearts.org

Tony D's Restaurant
92 Huntington Street
New London, CT 06320
www.tonydsrestaurant.com

Keystone Bridge
Lower Blissville Road
Lisbon, CT 06351

Bolton Notch State Park (Squaw Cave)
Off of I-384 and Route 44
Bolton, CT 06043

Sprague Historical Society Museum
76 Main Street
Baltic, CT 06330

TJ's Café
191 Main Street
Baltic, CT 06330

174

Clyde's Cider Mill
129 North Stonington Road
129 Pawcatuck, CT 06379
www.bfclydescidermill.com

Olde Mistick Village
27 Coogan Boulevard
Mystic, CT 06355
www.oldemistickvillage.com
* Cabin Fever Chowderfest held on the
last Saturday of February

Flanders Nature Center (Buz Russell Museum)
596 Flanders Road
Woodbury, CT 06798
www.flandersnaturecenter.org

Zagray Farm Museum
544 Amston Road
Colchester, CT 06415
www.qvea.org

Hidden Valley Bed and Breakfast
226 Bee Brook Road
Washington Depot, CT 06793
www.hiddenvalleyct.com

Lock Museum of America
230 Main Street
Terryville, CT 06786
www.lockmuseumofamerica.org

New England Air Museum
36 Perimeter Road
Windsor Locks, CT 06096
www.neam.org

Trash Museum
211 Murphy Road
Hartford, CT 06114
www.crra.org/pages/Trash_Museum.htm

Thomas Hooker Brewery
16 Tobey Road
Bloomfield, CT 06002
Hookerbeer.com

PAST Antiques Marketplace at Nature's Art Village
1650 Hartford-New London Turnpike
Montville, CT 06370
Naturesartvillage.com

Joy's Country Skillet
671 West Thames Street
Norwich, CT 06360

Amity Road Horror
667 Amity Road
Bethany, CT 06524
www.amityroadhorror.com

The Glass House
199 Elm Street
New Canaan, CT 06840
Theglasshouse.org

Witch's Dungeon Classic Movie Museum
90 Battle Street
Bristol, CT 06010
www.preservehollywood.org

Firefly Hollow Brewing
139 Center Street
Bristol, CT 06010
Fireflyhollowbrewing.com

The Beer'd Brewing Company
22 Bayview Avenue #15
Stonington, CT 06378
Beerdbrewing.com

Cottrell Brewing Company
100 Mechanic Street #22
Pawcatuck, CT 06379
www.cottrellbrewing.com

Grey Sail Brewing
63 Canal Street
Westerly, RI 02891
Greysailbrewing.com

Malted Barley
42 High Street
Westerly, RI 02891
www.themaltedbarley.com

Perks and Corks
62 High Street
Westerly, RI 02891
www.perksandcorks.com

New England Brewing Company
175 Amity Road
Woodbridge, CT 06525
www.newenglandbrewing.com

Two Roads Brewing Company
1700 Stratford Avenue
Stratford, CT 06615
Tworoadsbrewing.com

Black Pond Brews
21 Furnace Street
Danielson, CT 06239
www.blackpondbrews.com

Back East Brewing Company
1296 Blue Hills Avenue
Bloomfield, CT 06002
www.backeastbrewing.com

Olde Burnside Brewing
776 Tolland Street
East Hartford, CT 06108
Oldeburnsidebrewing.com

City Steam Brewery
942 Main Street
Hartford, CT 06103
www.citysteam.biz

Bishop's Orchards Winery
1355 Boston Post Road
Guilford, CT 06437
Bishopsorchards.com

Chamard Vineyards
115 Cow Hill Road
Clinton, CT 06413
Chamard.com

Haight-Brown Vineyards
29 Chestnut Hill Road
Litchfield, CT 06759
www.haightvineyards.com

Holmberg Orchards
12 Orchard Lane
Gales Ferry, CT 06335
www.holmbergorchards.com

Jonathan Edwards Winery
74 Chester Main Road
North Stonington, CT 06539
www.jedwardswinery.com

Maugle Sierra Vineyards
825 Colonel Ledyard Highway
Ledyard, CT 06339
www.mauglesierravineyards.com

Miranda Vineyard
42 Ives Road
Goshen, CT 06756
www.mirandavineyard.com

Preston Ridge Vineyard
100 Miller Road
Preston, CT 06465
www.prestonridgevineyard.com

Priam Vineyards
11 Shailor Hill Road
Colchester, CT 06415
www.priamvineyards.com

Saltwater Farm Vineyard
349 Elm Street
Stonington, CT 06378
Saltwaterfarmvineyard.com

Sharpe Hill Vineyard
108 Wade Road
Pomfret, CT 06258
Sharpehill.com

Stonington Vineyards
523 Taugwonk Road
Stonington, CT 06378
www.stoningtonvineyards.com

Thimble Island Brewing Company
16 Business Park Drive
Branford, CT 06405
www.thimbleislandsbrewery.com

DuVig Brewing Company
59 School Ground Road
Branford, CT 06045
www.duvig.com

Stony Creek Brewery
5 Indian Neck Avenue
Branford, CT 06045
www.stonycreekbeer.com

Overshores Brewing Company
250 Bradley Street
East Haven, CT 06512
www.overshores.com

University of Connecticut—Avery Point
1084 Shennecossett Road
Groton, CT 06340
Averypoint.uconn.edu

Harkness Memorial State Park
275 Great Neck Road
Waterford, CT 06385

Project Oceanology
1084 Shennecossett Road
Groton, CT 06340
www.oceanology.org

Our Lady of Lourdes' Shrine
83 Montfort Road
Litchfield, CT 06759
www.shrineinct.org

Roaring Brook Nature Center
70 Gracey Road
Canton, CT 06019
www.roaringbrook.org

Quinebaug Valley Hatchery
141 Trout Hatchery Road
Central Village, CT 06332

Burlington State Fish Hatchery
34 Belden Road
Burlington, CT 06013

Greeneville Dam Fish Lift
Roosevelt Avenue
Norwich, CT 06360